Published by Ockley Books Limited,
Huddersfield, England

First published May 2019

ISBN - 978-1-910906-187

Layout & design by Michael Kinlan,
edited by David Hartrick

Printed & bound by:
Biddles Printing, King's Lynn

Mensch
BEYOND THE CONES

JONATHAN HARDING

WHAT SETS GERMAN COACHING APART

OCKLEY BOOKS
.com

For both of my families.

About The Author

Jonathan Harding is a freelance sports journalist who specialises in German football. He writes predominantly for Deutsche Welle, but has also contributed to the likes of FourFourTwo, Rabona Magazine and 11 Freunde. Jonathan has lived in Germany since 2012.

Acknowledgements

The goal of this project, one that lasted over two years and left me with a new perspective on the words patience and angst, was to share stories. But I also wanted to start a conversation about human values in a field that I think is losing touch with its humanity. To even attempt this I needed the help of lots of people. My thanks to them all is endless.

Firstly, I'm grateful to all the people I spoke to for this book, especially Sascha Ochsendorf, Frank Wormuth, Stefan Reinartz, Uwe Hünemeier, Lily Agg, Verena Hagedorn, Helmut Groß, Lars Kornetka, Daniel Niedzkowski, Ismail Atalan, Eckhard Krautzun, Rainer Willfeld, Hannes Wolf and many others. Special thanks go to Frank and Lars who went above and beyond to help me make this book possible. A big thank you also goes to Marcus Dippel at the BDFL for being so helpful and making the ITK so accessible. I'm also very grateful to Matthias Lochmann, who was open, friendly and helpful in providing even more insight into his youth-coaching revolution. The book would not exist were it not for you all.

Holger Tromp and Paul Camillin were accommodating and helpful in organising some of the interviews I requested early on in the project – and I appreciate that because it's not always the case.

I'd like to send special thanks to Ben Lyttleton, Raphael Honigstein and Uli Hesse for their support, encouragement and advice. You have all been such great trailblazers. Thanks must also go to Michael Calvin, because it was his fantastic book *Living on the Volcano* that planted the first seeds of inspiration in my mind. All of you helped make this possible.

Thanks must also go to Michael Yokhin and David Luxton for their help. Understanding the lower league system in Germany was tricky, and without the help of Lars Pollmann and FVM's Ellen Bertke I would still be lost – thank you. I'd also like to thank Mr. Bellars, who helped keep my German going all those years ago.

Thank you to everyone on social media and online that has been supportive over the years. Many of whom I don't know or haven't met, but your input, feedback, constructive criticism and encouragement never went unnoticed and regularly made me pause for thought, so thank you. I hope I have been worth reading.

I couldn't have managed some of the writing sessions without a whole host of musical artists but special mentions must go to Bonobo, London Grammar, The 1975, The National, and Janelle Monáe – your music helped.

To my editor at Ockley Books, Dave Hartrick I can only say thank you for giving me this chance and for helping me every single step of the way. I'm also indebted to Richard, Roger and Sam for their tireless help editing the book and getting the best out of it. Thanks also to Mick for the brilliant cover design.

I must also thank all of those who I know and work with in the same field, because they too have inspired parts of this project. Archie, thank you for the trips to Bochum and Dresden. They made a big difference to the shape of this book. Ali, thank you for all your help and encouragement. Going through the editing process at a similar time was really beneficial. Sophie, you are fantastic. I am always learning from you. Ross, you've taught me a great deal since we've met and your encouragement with this project always helped - thank you. James, thank you for helping me take the first big steps in the Bundesliga world. I am delighted and grateful we have become such good friends since those early days. Jose, thank you for every single *abrazo*. Lewis, thank you for your enriching friendship. To the team I work with at DW, thank you for your encouragement and education – I've learned a great deal working with you. Lara, thank you for believing in me. You supported me right at the start and your words will stay with me. Always.

Musa, there are not enough words. You are one of the best people this world has – and someone we will need more than ever in the years to come. Your friendship has been a blessing on my life. Jenn and Dana, your support and wisdom when I needed it helped me out of the shadows. The world isn't ready for your brilliance, but it should be because it's coming. Nina, look how far we've come. Thank you for always encouraging me and for the effort you always make for me.

Chris, Maz, and the little one (now two) – thank you for keeping me young and reminding of the joy in the world. You mean so much to me.

Beth, there isn't enough space to say thank you. You helped me make this the best version it could be. Your input and support have been incredible. You're a superstar.

Dan and Family B, words cannot express the magic you have brought and continue to bring to my life. You have made this possible by making me a part of the family and giving me even more stability and love when I needed it all those years ago. Big Kober DB.

Dad, all the words and support you've sent helped me get the inches I needed. Mum, every card you sent (I've kept them all) made it better just when it needed to be. Matt, everyone conversation we've ever had about sport over the years helped me get here. All I've ever wanted is to make you all proud. I love you all very much.

And thank you for reading *Mensch*. It brings me more joy than you can imagine to have been able to share these stories with you. Remember, there is always a person behind the player. There is always a *Mensch*.

Prologue

When Jürgen Klopp became Liverpool head coach, Germany's coaching blueprint appeared complete. One of the most charismatic and motivational coaches in the game had been given the job at one of the biggest and proudest clubs in the world in the world's most popular league. But Klopp wasn't alone. David Wagner made history at Huddersfield Town, while Daniel Farke hopes to do the same at Norwich City. Later, Daniel Stendel joined Barnsley, keen to prove Hannover made a mistake in removing him for a more experienced head coach. It wasn't just individuals who were desired, it was the concept of German coaching that appeared intriguing.

Over two years, I travelled around Germany to find out more about what it is to be a coach in that country and what the traits are that make a good one. I spoke to coaches who missed out on the top jobs but never lost their love for the game, players who experienced the very best of German coaching, international assistant coaches, the men who coach the coaches, and one of Sir Alex Ferguson's best friends.

I wanted to hear about life as a talented coach in a country that has become a recruitment source for top coaches. What makes Julian Nagelsmann a resounding success? How does Ralf Rangnick keep nurturing talented players? How important a figure is Matthias Sammer for German coaching? How does it feel to be a head coach without a job?

In the end I kept coming back to two central questions: what makes a good head coach? And what is it that German coaches contribute to that ideal? More often than not, the answer was about people. I learnt that, just like many parts of work and society, it's about being a *Menschenfänger*. This is a brilliant German word that highlights the beautiful logic of the language. Literally translated it means 'people catcher', and while also a word for a pole weapon, the modern meaning is far less sinister. It means you have to be someone that people believe in. Someone whose belief and drive and understanding are so strong that others are caught up in them and want to follow.

Suddenly, questions about the world, collective thinking, space to reflect and core values became part of the conversations I was having. It became clear just how much there was to learn from the people working in the world's most popular sport, particularly those working behind the scenes.

Popularity does have its price though, and that's part of the reason that comparisons with English football are important. For all the stars on the pitch and in the dugout in the Premier League, there are concerns about the development of and opportunity available to young English players and coaches. Germany isn't perfect, but what it has done in terms of coaching and player development is in many ways exemplary. There is value in not being at the top of football's food chain.

Mario Götze, Thomas Müller and Christian Pulisic are some of the most talented players in Germany, but they wouldn't be part of Germany's football history were it not for the people who developed them. Michael Calvin wrote a fantastic book about how head coaches in England are *Living on the Volcano*. In Germany, head coaches are growing in the rich soil just below the mountain. This is just part of their story.

1

Leidenschaft
(Passion)

---

*'Amateur football is like a circus on the streets,
the Bundesliga is the Cirque du Soleil.'*

– Sascha Ochsendorf

A week after making my debut for Bonner SC II, I made my second appearance, coming on after an hour with the score at 3–2. Admittedly, this is perhaps the worst time for a centre back to come into a game, but even if my tactical understanding wasn't as sharp as some of the other lads, I had played in two teams before this one, my German was top and I was fitter than I had ever been. What could possibly go wrong?

We lost 7–4. I was overrun. My first touch under pressure remained wobbly and I was desperate not to lose the ball rather than to use it sensibly (i.e. not hopefully send a long pass in the direction of our strikers). In a very short space of time, my head coach – who arrived new to the team at the same time as I did – helped me panic less and play more. The goalkeeper became an option I actually remembered about in games. I started to notice when the pass through the midfield to the strikers worked and I grew the courage to try it.

I felt what it was to be coached well, and while this is not a revelation, anyone who has benefited from strong coaching, be it on the football pitch, in the workplace or in life generally, will vouch for the immensely satisfying feeling of learning. It was and always will be a wonderful moment.

Once I had woken up from childish dreams of how good I would have been had I sought out this level of coaching when I was much younger, I began to enjoy the basic human process of improving. The grind of cold Tuesday night training sessions became an addiction.

My head coach, Sascha Ochsendorf, was the most obsessed, though. He was always there, even when it seemed there was no way he could be. Despite juggling parental responsibilities, working nights at a postal company at the airport and studying, he was there, demanding the most from us. He tested us in new ways, thought up new drills and was as honest as they come. I liked him straightaway, and not just because of his soft spot for the English.

Sixteen games and twelve points later, Sascha was sacked. His emotional approach didn't always sit well with everyone in the changing room, but it was the results that saw him go. As the 37-year-old later told me, 'If you're successful, no one cares.'

The decision proved fruitless because at the end of the season we were relegated anyway, but it reminded me that even at the start, life is difficult for a coach.

So the stories begin with Sascha, because his is the first step of every coach's career, whether more steps follow or not. I went back to meet Sascha before one of his evening shifts at the airport where he still works. We sat down to talk about where and how life starts for a coach in Germany.

'It's an industry, the UPS idea. You're a number. When you're not there anymore, the next one comes,' Sascha tells me.

Much like Karl Marx's belief that everything centres on economics, and how that leads to humans being treated as commodities by their employers, coaches and players suffer the same fate at the hands of management structures. How is it that in the world's greatest game, remarkable commodification of humans takes place?

Even though I stopped playing – a broken metatarsal and more work at the weekends (unavoidable as a sports journalist) led to my demise – Sascha didn't stop coaching. Almost a year later, he joined SC Liessem 1990 in the *Kreisliga C* (see Table 1) and guided them – a relegated side – to a respectable fifth place. After a poor pre-season the following campaign, Sascha was once again without a job.

During his time as my head coach at Bonner SC's reserve team in the lowly *Kreisliga B* of North Rhine-Westphalia, I saw first hand in Sascha what I spent week in, week out trying to understand as a journalist covering the Bundesliga, but rarely (if ever) got to see close up. The effort, the desperation, even the pressure – because while amateur football remains a world away from the professional game, that base drug remains: winning.

That's the reason Sascha was sacked as head coach of Bonner SC's reserve team. The team just wasn't winning enough. Four levels lower than the Bonner SC first team, the board, so I heard, were keen for the second team to play at a higher level so as to be of greater benefit to the main eleven.

Bonner SC were in the second division (north) in the 1976–7 season, but financial issues and their location (for talent pinching) have since seen them struggle to return to such heights. The first team recently earned promotion to the *Regionalliga West* – one of five fourth divisions. In 2017, they made the first round of the German Cup and gave a spirited display against Hannover before eventually succumbing to defeat. Now the first team is aiming for promotion to Germany's third division, one of the most complicated processes in German football. The table below shows the league system for the Middle Rhine region, and the *Kreisliga* set-up (in blue) for the Bonn district. The term *Mittelrheinliga* is the name of the region's *Verbandsliga*, the fifth division. The number of leagues in a division is shown in brackets.

When I played for Bonner SC's reserve team in the 2014–15 season, I played in the:

MIDDLE RHINE REGION, BONN DISTRICT, KREISLIGA B DIVISION, LEAGUE ONE.	3. Liga (Third division)
	Regionalliga West
	Mittelrheinliga
There are nine local districts in the Middle Rhine region.	Landesliga (2 divisions)
	Bezirksliga (4)
Each one has a Kreisliga A–C set-up with a varying number of leagues in each district (some might have more Kreisliga C leagues than others for example).	*Relegation to local district divisions*
	Kreisliga A (1)
	Kreisliga B (2)
	Kreisliga C (3)
Only six of the districts have Kreisliga D leagues.	Kreisliga D (3)

'I never wanted to be a coach,' says Sascha, whose playing career was curtailed by bad luck and injury. 'I could influence things as a player, but not as a coach ... But I learnt quickly that everyone could learn. I didn't want to consume, I wanted to create. Fortunately, the first club I was at gave me the support I needed. My first doubt was: "Who says I will be a success?" It's always a case of doubt, questioning yourself and your techniques, feeling tense ahead of training.'

Sascha started coaching at FC Blau-Weiß Friesdorf's third team in *Kreisliga C*. Training on grass by the riverside, often with depleted numbers, he led the team to back-to-back promotions – the success that eventually led to our paths crossing in Bonn.

'The easiest is when you get something to work with. So for example, you have someone who is crazy about being a centre back but has no idea what it means to be one, what kind of commitment they have to make to the team. For example, so many centre backs want to dribble. They see space and want to bring the ball forwards, but they don't understand what they're breaking by doing so. They only see what they're doing well, moving the ball from A to B, 20 metres away from goal. Really, they just have to put the machine in motion,' he says, almost taking me back to our time together on the training ground when he helped me get better. And although he uses the words 'put the machine in motion', he never forgot that the cogs were human.

'But if you have a central defender who understands that but can't put it into practice, but still tries in a game, then you recognise that and work from there if you're a good coach. You have to know. You can have some officials telling you what to pass on, of course, but you still need a basic level of quality in the individual. That's why Bundesliga coaching is so much easier than amateur football. You have a basis of quality. You only have to tighten the screws and if your left back doesn't work, the next one comes in. The difference is that the opposition try to do the same and then it's difficult again. Here, we focus on the player, what qualities have they got, what can I work with and how can I help people make the right decision at the right time?'

While Sascha's claim that Bundesliga coaching is 'so much easier' than the amateur game is perhaps a little too bold, anyone who has worked in the latter will know what he means by that statement. At that level, it is a hobby not a job, although those lines often blur (more on that later).

Sascha tells me that if football was forgotten tomorrow, he would create it and the world would be able to play the day after. Without knowing him, his unwavering confidence appears to be raw arrogance, but it's coming from a good place. He cares, and that's what helped us form a connection. I wanted to play for him because I knew he cared, even if sometimes he cared too much.

'There's nothing worse in life than when you're taught something wrong. Parents can spoil their children and head coaches can spoil their players, both the player and the person. You have to throw out the right people. You have to ask, is it them or their values? You can't bend your values just for him,' Sascha tells me.

Across the top sports there have been numerous examples of players being thrown out because their attitude didn't match the group. At that level, headlines are written and tournaments are decided on such decisions, but on the amateur stage such a move is a move against someone's hobby (i.e. an activity done for someone's enjoyment). And that can prove tough.

'I used to flip out as a player, and then as a head coach I learnt that just can't happen. As a player, you're one of 11 and if things go badly, it's on the head coach, but if you're the coach and you're behaving badly, that can't be. I was always afraid of that.'

Sascha's comments throw up two aspects. One, 'if things go badly, it's on the head coach', is a further reminder of how aware players are about the pressure on the head coach even when they play badly. Two, the attention on the head coach, is, whatever the level, immense.

'If I throw the bottle of water onto the ground and it breaks, how does that look? Is that seen the same way as a foul? Emotionally, the same feeling is behind both. But one has the opportunity to foul and the other doesn't. It's always difficult to find the balance between the two,' Sascha says.

It's fair to say Sascha didn't always get that balance right, but he's not alone. When Borussia Mönchengladbach equalised against TSG 1899 Hoffenheim in October of the 2017–18 Bundesliga season, Hoffenheim head coach Julian Nagelsmann threw a water bottle in frustration, accidentally hitting a fan in the crowd. He later apologised and was issued a warning by the German FA (*Deutscher Fußball-Bund*, or DFB). We are all human.

Hearing Sascha speak so passionately about the job made me see the other side of it, the side I couldn't see as one of his players or on a Saturday when I was working as a journalist. It's the side so often forgotten.

'There's a Mats Hummels on the pitch and a Mats Hummels in private, just like there's a Sascha Ochsendorf on the pitch and one in private. On the pitch, he's pushed into structures. If you fall out of those roles, then there are consequences – a red card and goodbye. You get annoyed for 10 seconds. I can't believe some professionals. They get a red card but then they turn to the referee. You've already seen red. Then it takes 10 seconds. And then you leave the pitch.

'You don't have that as a head coach. The ref will come over sometimes. He'll say "be quiet", but sometimes you can be unlucky and you can say something you don't want to and you get sent behind the fence. It's the same in amateur football as it is in the Bundesliga. I was sent off in my first game. I was too loud. The ref had no tolerance for it.'

There's a fine line between passion and disrespect, and coaches at all levels tread it all the time. Former Bayer Leverkusen head coach Roger Schmidt was sent to the stands by the referee during a home defeat to Hoffenheim, after he told Nagelsmann to shut up and called him a *Spinner* (German for 'weirdo' or 'nutjob', although the word is more insulting than its English equivalent). Freiburg head coach Christian Streich came out in support of Schmidt, saying that coaches felt 'monitored', that everything was collated and Schmidt was, 'driven through the village like a sow' (in other words a big fuss was made). While there are no microphones or multiple television cameras at amateur level, escape is no easier to come by in the smartphone era.

Sascha, who was back coaching in *Kreisliga C* with Godesberger Fußballverein 2006 when we met, is a motivator, and that can work for some more than others, particularly at amateur level when comfort is key and change is always questioned. 'I know I can connect with my players by communicating during the game, regardless of how, and so long as it's not an insult, then it can change things,' he says.

'If it doesn't, you lose the game. Over time, I got to know refs and it became more acceptable. After all, there are no rules against noise level,' he adds with a grin.

I remember Sascha shouting at me once in a friendly we lost when the opposing defender kept doing all the things I should have been doing: 'That's how a centre back plays, Jon!' He roasted me at halftime in the changing room. It was tough, but it also motivated me.

'If my team could play well and I could say nothing, I would do it. But it won't happen. It's football. You need to perform at the highest level. It doesn't matter which team, it's part of it. Carlo Ancelotti might well be a quiet coach, but someone near him goes berserk,' Sascha says.

It's easy to dismiss the amateur game as unimportant, but it's where it all starts for everyone. Good teaching in the early stages of any development makes a huge difference to the end outcome. Often, actors recall their first teachers, musicians their first experiences with other musicians, writers the first books they read and felt empowered by. Football is no different. The difficulty at the beginning though, is balance. Either people don't care or they care too much.

'The problem with the amateur game is this balance between success and relaxation. There's no in between. If the lads just want to meet up and have a kick around, then that's fine. But it's not for me,' Sascha says without a hint of a joke.

'If I'm a high jumper and I can jump 1 metre 80, I don't just keep jumping 1 metre 40, do I? What does that do for me as a sportsperson? As a head coach, it's your job to give the players the chance to push the boundaries, in my eyes.

'I remember a striker I used to coach who shot us to promotion. He was young, really fast, but his technique was a bit wild. He struggled in one-on-one situations, but I recognised his passing game was great so I told him, "Why don't you focus on playing a pass to the far post? Don't even look at the goalkeeper." He exploded. He did it in training and that was it. He really enjoyed playing football and started to feel like a star because he kept scoring goals. It was great to see and I thought, anyone can do that, anyone can see that, anyone can teach him how to develop. But apparently, not many can,' Sascha says.

Although my technical deficiencies would have been clear for any coach to see, Sascha was able to take his knowledge and transmit it in a way that allowed me to develop. The more people I spoke to, the more I was reminded of how having the knowledge is only half the task – the real art lies in transmitting it.

The amateur game can never escape one issue. For some, it's a chance to stay fit and hang out with friends, but for others it's a chance to get better, improve and be successful. For a head coach in the amateur game, particularly an ambitious one like Sascha, handling a squad with a mix of the two is one of the hardest things.

'Everyone starts a game the same way, whether it's the *Kreisliga* or the Champions League final: the same number of players, a ball, a pitch. The one difference is that one group gets millions for it, while the others only get a good feeling. And at some point, the good feeling isn't enough anymore, especially when you aren't winning.'

Sascha says he would be keen to know how head coaches work with fun, because the base level of quality is there. 'So the question is, why isn't Mario Gomez playing at the moment, or why isn't he scoring?'

The reason why could possibly be personal, an issue some within the media often want to be the first to post about rather than the first to understand. That personal aspect, at amateur or professional level, remains a part of success or failure whether it is acknowledged or not.

'In amateur football, you've still got your mates, in the next game, training, whether you push the boundaries or not. The coach has to keep the mood high. Many at the amateur level do the job just to do it, without the intention of teaching. Some do it because someone has to, not because they want to train the players.

'All the time, you have to remember you're an influence on people's lives. This is not *Football Manager*. It's real. If you get them to run and they pick up an injury then it doesn't just affect your choices, it affects them. Even if my players don't believe me, their injuries are just the same as in the Bundesliga, so why should you put in less?

'If you go diving, and you know that at 10, 20 metres the pressure is so great that without help you can't get there, you take the help. Why don't you do that in sport? You need conditioning, desire. You can't just rock up 10 minutes before the game having not trained all week and expect to play.'

For me, that's what made Sascha a good coach. He never treated it like a Sunday run around after a big Saturday night out. He cared about the result, the training, the performance, us. His way of showing that didn't always work for everyone, but he never wavered from who he was, and I respected that. Given his relationship with the game, it's no surprise either.

At the age of 13, he was scouted by Bayer Leverkusen. He had a trial with 50 other players to join the youth team. Week by week, the numbers grew smaller until three were left; Sascha was one of them. Following approval from his school, Sascha played in an international tournament in Nantes, France, where he impressed further. On the bus back the head coach asked if anyone in the team would object to Sascha joining.

'It was a cool moment. I had proof that it wasn't just a football decision, but also a personal one,' Sascha says, his face struggling to resist the joy the memory still gives him.

Ahead of the new season, Leverkusen's youth coach changed and Sascha had to impress all over again. This time, it didn't work. There was no academy accommodation, and the moment attending all three training sessions became difficult, the Leverkusen chapter of his life was over.

His reputation at youth level was still outstanding though, and soon he had a trial at 1. FC Köln. As a fan of the club, he thought it was fate that delivered him that chance. The pressure was on when he went to train with the team, but trialists played in a 25 vs. 25 game and, naturally, no one was able to shine.

Brief chats with Borussia Mönchengladbach soon after ended in nothing, and despite his talent, Sascha was left unattached. A frustrating year at Bonner SC followed and despite impressing, he was released. Sascha believes he was released then for the same reason he was later dismissed as head coach of the club's second team – his emotional approach.

Years spent playing at lower levels followed and then Sascha received a serious injury to his knee and eventually his chance slipped away. Then came the question from local team Friesdorf: a coach was needed for their third team – was Sascha interested?

'You have to know what you're doing, understand the game and the solutions. Players often lack this, an overview,' he says. 'More than that, you have to have social understanding. As a pro coach, it's a big advantage if you're a people person, if people can follow you. In amateur football, it's indispensable. You have to get people to work hard every day, and that's really tough.

'Having an assistant coach in amateur football is a luxury. Not everyone can love you and you can't love everyone either. Amateur football is like a circus on the streets, the Bundesliga is the Cirque du Soleil.'

It's clear that Sascha never stopped believing he was good enough for the top. Even though, as he recalls his story, there's a hint of frustration that he wasn't a young teenager in today's world.

'I scored goals in my life, if they were on YouTube I would have a billion clicks. There was one in the U19s. A goal kick bounced into the opposition half. I had the defender behind me. I looked into the middle of the pitch, where I wanted to play the ball, but it was tight. I was 50-odd metres away from the goal. No one was in the middle of the pitch, but I had already made the move so I took the shot anyway, and it went straight into the top corner. I couldn't believe it. Had that been today, it would have been on YouTube, straight in focus, and then a few stepovers later and you're the next Messi.

'Today, they're in academies, like in [RB] Leipzig, where if you do things wrong, you're out. That's the right way to select. Not, "You can't afford it so you can't do it." You don't do that in school. Everyone in Germany has the right to A-levels, but not everyone had the chance to be a Bundesliga footballer. Whoever fit into the system worked. With 50 players brought in, there were just too many. There was not enough inspection. There were a few good players there, but even if there hadn't been, 50 were picked again next year. After winning the World Cup in 1990, the feeling was that everything was working. But we saw my generation wasn't any good. They all came afterwards,' Sascha says.

A man whose life is made up of a patchwork of brilliant stories, Sascha recalls another, about the former Bundesliga player Marcel Ndjeng, to highlight how fine the line is between HD Sundays on Sky Sports and cold Sundays down the park with a crowd of three people and an uninterested dog.

'He and his brother used to play against me in the district game. Whoever played better out of us won the game. One time it was them, the next it was us. He went on to play international football for Cameroon and found a head coach, Jos Luhukay, who liked him. And I coached Friesdorf in *Kreisliga D*,' Sascha says, matter-of-factly.

'Ndjeng drove past in Friesdorf in his big open-top car once, and chatted. I wrote to him that it would be great if he could come to training, and how much the lads would love it. I never heard from him. Back then he was a top guy, but what gives him the right when others have invested just as much, if not more? It's a game of luck.'

I joked with Sascha that had he made it we would never have met. His reply summed him up perfectly. 'We would have, just in the mixed zone after the game,' he said with a grin, before adding, his smile disappearing almost as quickly as it had appeared, 'But then I wouldn't have had my daughter either, so ...'

Sascha doesn't have a coaching badge. I only found out when we spoke. Never once did I doubt his coaching ability or think it was lacking the necessary quality. 'Let's put it like this,' he said, 'if you have a driving licence then you can drive a car, but the licence doesn't just allow you to drive; it also teaches you how to. I never had that with football. Football is me. I don't need someone telling me it's that way.'

I asked about getting the UEFA B Licence. Sascha said he was interested, but that he felt his personality hinders him from being given a chance.

'If you're with someone who drives like a madman, but you know they have a licence, what can you do? Everything's kosher. If he didn't have one, you'd ask them to drive slower, or say, "Did you see that sign?" It's exactly the same in football. If someone doesn't like you, then they don't want to spend time with you three times a week. From *Kreisliga A* onwards, you don't have that anymore. It's about success and performance.

'If you go with your gut, then you're vulnerable. It's not easy, and that's why I often have problems. How do you answer people who say, "Why did you do it that way?" They don't believe you because you don't have a badge. Criticism arises from the team more quickly.'

Sascha would likely be presented with some of those answers if he were to take his badges. I hope he will one day. Germany offers one of the best coaching educations in the world, and after all he did for me, I think about the coach he could become if his mind was filled with even more football.

Key Lesson

Even at the lowest level of the game, Sascha was able to make a difference as a head coach because he was passionate about it. While caring deeply is not a uniquely German trait, passion is a necessary ingredient for any teacher or coach. If people care about their work, they will always be more productive than those who care about the reward – and tend to get the reward as a result of their passion. Sascha was willing to reschedule his life, work and family so that he could make us better footballers, perhaps in the hope we might learn something as humans as a result.

Half of the German word for passion – *Leidenschaft* – means to suffer *(leiden)*. Half of doing what you love is suffering, hurting for it. Sascha did that for us in the hope we'd do the same for him. At the amateur level or not, a good feeling isn't enough at some point, especially when you aren't winning. Growth becomes paramount.

Kompetenz
(Competence)

'We don't learn for tests, but for life.'

- Frank Wormuth

Welcoming from the start, Frank Wormuth is like an old friend you haven't seen in months, but when you do, it's like you've never been away. For the majority of the past nine years, he has been the chief coaching instructor of Germany's coaching academy in Hennef. Without Frank, this would be just another sleepy town tucked away in a forest in Germany, but instead it's the understated birthplace of Germany's finest coaches.

Past the corridor along which tactical outlines of Germany's greatest goals hang on glass lies a cluster of modest classrooms that would be at home at any primary school. Beyond that lies an office split in two. There's something humble about the place, simple but quietly full of a special power. Its charm doesn't lie in its appearance, it lies in the people.

'It's not the world,' Frank tells me.

'But you've moved worlds with it?' I reply.

'Yes! I like that. It's not the world, but we've moved worlds with it. Trademark it,' he replies, with a huge grin that I get used to seeing over the course of the day.

I wanted to talk to Frank about the highest level of coaching education in Germany, to find out about the details of the course, how personal the approach was, and how coaches like Julian Nagelsmann or Domenico Tedesco developed into the talents they are today. I wanted to go to the source of the country's coaching talent and ask the man in charge all about the process.

Everyone I meet over lunch with Frank is friendly and welcoming. There's an external lecturer from Borussia Mönchengladbach discussing structural issues related to youth players getting enough face-to-face coaching time. The academy's leading psychologist is sitting a couple of seats further down. The conversation is fascinating, and it all revolves around Frank. A player with Joachim Löw at Freiburg, later his assistant at Fenerbahçe, the former defender went on to be a head coach, mostly in Germany's regional leagues but also with Germany's U20s, before he became the coaching academy's chief instructor in 2008. His focus at the time of our meeting was on the optimisation and reformation of the current coaching system. During our time together, there's a hint that Wormuth misses the dugout, and almost a year later, I smiled when I read the news that he would be taking charge of Eredivisie side Heracles Almelo for the 2018–19 season. The allure of the dugout is as great as the withdrawal that comes with prolonged time away from it.

While no longer in charge of the academy (Daniel Niedzkowski took over as chief coaching instructor at the end of March 2018, but more on that in chapter eight), the majority of the information Frank told me stands today. Changes will inevitably be made, as is customary to keep up with football's unrelenting evolution, but the core focus of what Frank told me when I visited him remains.

To coach in the top three divisions in Germany, you need to have the elite licence, called the *Fußball-Lehrer*. The German language has a reputation for being harsh and unattractive, but it is prone to moments of literal beauty. *Fußball-Lehrer* translates into 'football teacher', and the more I spoke to Frank the more I realised that is exactly what the academy creates. 'Our main goal is to make conductors who don't have to be able to do everything, but should be aware of everything,' Frank tells me.

Only the B and C licences are handled at regional levels. Above that is the Elite Youth Licence, the A Licence, and finally the *Fußball-Lehrer*. The Elite Youth Licence is a step up from the usual B licence, and is the first step into elite coaching in the eyes of the DFB, part of the reason the qualification is a must in Germany (unlike in other countries).

There are subtle differences between the *Fußball-Lehrer* and the UEFA Pro Licence in England, and they start with the name. In England, 'The FA Level 5' is the somewhat formulaic title given to the UEFA Pro Licence coaching badge, whereas in Germany the course name is far more literal.

In England, according to the FA website, coaches require 245 hours of 'guided learning' to complete the course. In Germany, you need nearly 800 hours. Why is there such a drastic difference?

'They are minimum requirements set by UEFA,' says Frank. 'There are countries where this isn't as important, and they can't demand 800 hours because of finance or mentality. They're looking for a foundation.'

'Here in Germany, typical German, if we want to do something, we'll do it right,' Frank tells me. The thing about doing it right is that it forces quality to rise. 'The door is open to everyone, but you have to get in, and once you're in, you have to be good,' says Frank.

According to the English FA, the course takes 18 months to complete but most are done in 12. In Germany, the course takes 10 months. To do the *Fußball-Lehrer,* it costs approximately €11,000 (travel not included). In England, FA coaching members can do the course for €10,165, non-members for €11,140. Statistics do not depict the entire outline, but it is intriguing to see that while things are perhaps slightly cheaper in England, there's an alarming gap in terms of learning hours.

Every year in January, the closing date for applications, many coaches realise they are not good enough. The rigorous application process leaves no room for anything other than the highest quality. On average, 66 coaches apply for the *Fußball-Lehrer* every year. Half of that group attends a three-day assessment centre from Monday to Wednesday, the other half from Wednesday to Friday. The evaluation includes written, oral and practical tests. Eventually, a final list of 24 is selected for the course.

'Our task is not to say you can't do it. We can't do that,' says Frank. 'We can't make them a personality if they don't have one. If you want that, go out and pay someone 200 euros an hour for five years and maybe in three years you'll have changed. Perhaps your attitude will be positive. Negative-thinking people always see the glass half empty.

"Yes, that's true," they say. "OK, then look at the glass half full." Their reply is "OK, but how?" Reframe it. If you've lost and you're aggressive towards your team, you can lose them. Try reframing it and take something positive from it. And if you can internalise that then maybe you'll come across differently.

'We give them tools. We don't know if it'll work, but at least they have a plan. We ask how can they control this emotion? That's the role of our psychologist, or me as coach. We can show them what they're like, but we can't change them.

'We are all personalities. Whether they fit outside in that role is another question. But someone who is quiet and shy also has a personality. And they know that. We don't tell someone who doesn't talk to talk. We just ask them how they are going to connect with the team. Find your way,' Frank tells me.

Frank says he has seen coaches be successful in the top flight when that might not have looked likely at the start. Effective networking and the right words at the right time can make all the difference. Sometimes coaches don't have to be great to be successful.

The system is complex – it has to be to deal with such a variety of personalities – but it is also fair to each candidate. And that is seen in the balanced weight of the marking. The aforementioned entry-assessment tests are weighted as follows: 15 per cent written, 25 per cent oral and 40 per cent practical. The remaining 20 per cent is based on your experience. If you weren't a pro, but had 10 years of experience in the fifth division of German football, that helps, but if you had no experience as a coach and used to be a pro, then that helps too. Previous coaching experience clearly has an edge though. 'You get points. If you were a player and a head coach, you get more points. If you work with professionals later, then it's always an advantage to have been one before ... We're fair,' Frank tells me.

Former England midfielder Jermaine Jenas wrote an exclusive piece for *Yahoo! Sports* on how the out-dated FA coaching system is to blame for the lack of English coaches. His argument read as follows:

I'm not saying coaching has never crossed my mind. But it's worth pointing out that if I decided tomorrow that I wanted to be a manager and I started getting my badges through the FA, it would take me four and a half years to complete my training. While I have no doubt I'd get a great education, it's a long time. Too long. The question is, should an ex-footballer have to go through the same four-year course as the man on the street?

There's an argument that people shouldn't get 'special treatment' just because they're an ex-pro. But in comparison to someone who has never played the game professionally, I think there is a difference. You can't underestimate the value of experience. Of playing in major tournaments and the Champions League. Of knowing what it's really like in the dressing room in those incredibly high-pressure situations. Not to mention working with some of the world's top managers.

Former Bayern Munich and Germany international Mehmet Scholl made similar comments in Germany, releasing a tirade against the so-called 'laptop coaches' in an interview with *Spiegel:*

They have never played at the top level and have no idea how a pro at the highest level works. They think about top-level football, but have never experienced it ... It starts on the Fußball-Lehrer course. I've experienced it. The more I observe the candidates who qualify with the best scores, have the typical faces of those who are the best on the course and have absorbed all the information, the more my hair stands on end. For them, tactics are the prime directive, they're laptop coaches.

As a former player, Jenas has strong reasons to believe there is a defining difference between former players and those who have never played the professional game. And he is right to suggest that the FA should address the way it approaches the opportunities afforded to talented young coaches in England.

However, while certain aspects of having already experienced that world can be advantageous, being a former player doesn't guarantee you'll be a good coach, and so it shouldn't guarantee you a better chance either. All experience is of value, but to prefer one over another would be a mistake, and that's why Frank's points system makes sense.

After all, not all good journalists make good editors; not all good politicians make good prime ministers or presidents. If there was one thing the last few years have shown quite drastically, it's that leadership and aspects of character associated with leading are more often assumed than developed. So why should former footballers get preferential treatment when it comes to coaching?

'We used to have that, but since I've been here we've treated everyone the same,' says Frank. 'And we've got good head coaches out of that. Julian Nagelsmann was not a professional. We've had good head coaches that have come out of education, psychology, and they know football really well. They might have played, which is always an advantage, but were never pros. They still know how the pro game works. This move away from former pros, and former internationals, we've opened the door to people who are now in the Bundesliga. Stefan Effenberg has the pedigree, but was never a head coach and then just became one. The Paderborn situation was unlucky,' Frank says, referring to Effenberg's brief stint in charge of the then second-division club where he managed only two wins in 15 games and saw his side beaten 7–1 by Borussia Dortmund in the second round of the German Cup.

'It didn't work, but the question is does he have another chance now? Well, the chances look good. He has pedigree, can manage games, but has not much experience as a head coach – and you see that. Unlike Christian Wörns, who has Bochum youth, Dortmund youth, Augsburg youth experience. When he breaks through at the top one day, he won't have any problems. He learnt the job from scratch.'

Julian Nagelsmann is clearly the example the academy aspires to. At 30, he has quickly made a name for himself at Hoffenheim. He saved the club from relegation and then led them into Europe for the start of the 2017–18 season, where they lost out in Champions League qualifying to eventual finalists Liverpool. The extent of Nagelsmann's talent was questioned when Hoffenheim's European debut ended with a whimper, but he secured qualification for Europe again with another strong second half to the league season. Impressively, this came after a poor start and having lost Sebastian Rudy and Niklas Süle to Bayern Munich the previous summer. During the summer of 2018, it was announced that Nagelsmann would become RB Leipzig head coach for the 2019–20 season. And all this coming from the man who said on a *Bild* podcast that the Bundesliga was a players' game not a coaches game.

Frank has long had the feeling that Nagelsmann could become a top *Trainer*. Once again the German language reveals its hidden magic. The word *Trainer* can be translated into coach, trainer or football manager, but in Germany a manager is something different. A *Trainer* trains teams and coaches players. Management is part of his job, but the focus clearly lies on development. Looking at a coach like Nagelsmann, it is clear why Germany uses the word *Trainer* for their head coaches.

'He was assistant head coach under Markus Gisdol and also won the league with the U19s, so he has experience in youth football,' Frank tells me. 'The reformation in 2000 when the DFB made youth academies a must meant more and more head coaches started appearing in youth football. And really, the head coach of an U19 Bundesliga team doesn't do anything differently to a Bundesliga head coach. It's just not as much in the public eye, with a different income, and the quality of the players isn't as good. But he does the same training, six, seven times a week, and pre-season. The big advantage is that the club can see their own talent developing. Nagelsmann was good, and presented himself well to those upstairs. Why get an external candidate when you know he's it, even if he's 29 years old? You send him away and then three years later, he isn't any better. He's already good.'

The move to internally promoting candidates prompted a new movement that started thanks to the success of Jürgen Klopp and then Thomas Tuchel. Both showed that not only was it possible to break away from the norm and give the reins to an internal candidate, but that it could also be a successful move. The appointment of Julian Nagelsmann made just as much sense — and his quality was clear to see long before.

'We were outside and I knowingly stepped in – I'm sure Nagelsmann will remember this – and confronted him with something,' says Frank. 'I provoked him because at the end of it, I don't want 24 friends but 24 fully educated coaches. I'm sure he does the same in Hoffenheim but with a different type of confidence and language. He told a player: "You have to attack the ball so the man behind you can't have the ball played to him." I said, "Jule, how can he see? He hasn't got eyes in the back of his head. If he moves out of the shadows, how am I supposed to know?" That's when he realised the theory is correct, but in practice it didn't work … There wasn't much I could give him, but there were a few moments. "Be careful, you're working with grown pros." In

Hoffenheim, things are probably calm with the lads, young lads who play nice football and will give their all for him, but what if he goes to another club, say Dortmund? Then you're working with different types of players. Then a Mats Hummels, who isn't there anymore, would say, "What are you doing here?" It's working at Hoffenheim. Taking the right job at the right time is important.'

Nagelsmann's relatively fast rise has made him a wanted man, but Wormuth's words about future jobs seem pertinent considering the number of factors that play a role in a coach's success. It's exactly why Nagelsmann's move to RB Leipzig – another team with a group of hungry young players – makes a lot of sense for the young head coach.

To get into a position to take the right opportunities when they arrive, you have to make the *Fußball-Lehrer* course. In the end only 24 coaches are accepted onto the programme, each with a mix of knowledge backgrounds. Not all stem from performance bases, not all are former pros. Applications are always balanced to make sure one group doesn't outweigh another.

Before the assumption creeps in that those coaching the coaches are free from criticism, Frank tells me the academy had a two-and-a-half year study done on the course to make sure what they were coaching the coaches was relevant and nothing was missing. 'The profile of the job is only as good as the profile of the education on offer,' he says.

On the *Fußball-Lehrer* course, two psychologists, a Doctor of sports medicine, the top fitness coach in the country (who is also Germany's U21 fitness coach and the coach of all other fitness coaches in youth DFB teams), a nutritional coach, and the chief instructor make sure of the group's progress.

The 10-month (40-week) long course is broken down as follows. The candidates spend three days a week (Mondays to Wednesdays) for 22 weeks at the academy. Twelve weeks are then spent on work experience and six weeks are spent studying from home. Of the 22 weeks at the academy, 19 are spent on coaching the coaches, three are spent testing them. For the 2016 class, the 12 weeks of work experience were split, with one week at the European Under-19 Championship, one week of voice training, eight weeks at a Bundesliga club and two weeks at an association. Foreign internships in countries such as the Netherlands, Switzerland and Austria are also becoming a feature of the course. Wherever the coaches go, it adds up to 10 months of intense learning and development.

That all starts in June, when candidates are welcomed and the course subjects are introduced. This isn't all smiles and photographs, though. It is often at this stage that Frank and his team can get the best feel for what kind of raw characteristics lie inside their coaches.

'We have to have them raw at the start,' says Frank. 'Before Markus Gisdol even had time to change, we had him presenting. Five minutes in an eight-man group. We filmed all of it as we always do. We've had a former player stand up and say nothing. They're used to having to answer questions, not saying something themselves. We might say, "Tell us what you thought of the Bundesliga season last year and what would you bear in mind?" I can recognise whether they have structure. You'll notice that some make loads of notes and then just talk, without structure. You need an introduction, a core argument and a finish. The first sentence is the most important.'

Frank then went on to outline how the course starts with analysis of top-level football. 'We and the English were always at these events, but they were there to film for their team, not for their coaching students. We were the first that filmed for our coaching course. In the Czech Republic recently, there were 12 different countries observing for their pro licence. Word got around what we do here,' Frank said.

The work being done at the academy has been the subject of many an article. The ever-innovative AZ Alkmaar visited after a Dutch journalist wrote a piece on the academy. While the rest of the world was obsessed with scouting their opposition or cultivating their own talent, they forgot to coach the coaches. That has all changed now.

'Analysis work is done in groups of three,' said Frank. 'You cut the film, put it into a PowerPoint and then present and get feedback. It's all about their knowledge. Everything is learnt from scratch so that when you're a head coach, you know what problems the video analyst has. We don't tell them what to do, we just remind them of a few things. It's important not to judge straight away. Everything in football is right – you just have to justify it.'

One of the tasks coaches face is to write what football is on an A4 page. 'They don't believe it is possible. They arrive with huge knowledge, but leave with it structured.'

Work is also done on communication for television or print media, which Frank interestingly says he wants to increase during the reforms (notably the two opening modules for the class of June 2018 were public relations and presenting). Head coaches practice press conferences, playing different roles (such as their first team talk to a new team) and answering difficult questions. 'We've had a few sweating in those seats,' Frank says with a smile.

By August, the preparation for pre-season begins, parallel to the current season. Then in September, the foundation of knowledge is taught. This includes the technical and tactical part of the game, as well as the method and rules. At the same time comes the psychology, which includes educational and communication psychology, in other words 'how do I present?' Then the physiology of football – training, sports medicine, nutrition. In the end, the weekly plan can look something like this (FL = *Fußball-Lehrer* classes):

Monday
Psychology (5 classes), FL (6 classes, 2 practical evenings
with a demo group) – 11 exercises (8 a.m.–8 p.m.)

Tuesday
FL (7 classes, 4 practical, morning together,
evenings with a demo group, U19s of the local team),
Physiology (5 classes) – 11 exercises (8 a.m.–8 p.m.)

Wednesday
FL (5 classes), Rules/Nutrition,
Physiology – 11 exercises (8 a.m.–6:30 p.m.)

'We rarely have frontal classes. We progress through the knowledge of the group. We give them tasks in groups of three, they do it and then present their ideas and all I do is fill in the gaps as the lecturer. They always ask because of my experience of over 20 years and coaching at U20 international level, but I say, "Tell me your thoughts first." Then I fill in the gaps and say how I would do it,' Frank tells me.

Outside of the classroom, each coach gets a theme and 30 minutes with a demo group / local team (three coaches per team). One coach records for content, one for behaviour, and the rest of the coaches watch. The next day, the coach is put on the hot seat and questioned about the session. Every coach on the course is on the hot seat seven times (a number Frank wishes was higher) and each coach can observe and ask questions of all the other coaches during the 161 hot seats. The learning is constant.

'It's not just about the offside line, but how it affects the game. Making the space bigger means we don't get to make the tackles. There are different learning situations and different ways for them to show how their task influences the game,' Frank tells me.

After that, a full 90-minute session follows, with further opportunity for self-reflection and feedback. Then other groups present what you worked on, forcing coaches to know their subject matter inside out. Then Frank shadows coaches during exercises that cover all topics of football, from defensive behaviour to counterattacking. Every coach gets the chance to reflect on his work and give feedback on the work of other coaches.

'I talk to him during the exercise,' says Frank. 'I might say, "The player isn't doing what you just asked him." He replies, "I know. He wasn't listening." "He wasn't listening, or you didn't explain it to him properly?" I ask. "Should I bring the group together then?" "Well, then you lose the rhythm. So maybe later?"' It's this kind of interaction that Frank wants more of at lower levels of the coaching pyramid.

'If you do the *Fußball-Lehrer*, then you've got a fantastic education but up until the A Licence, it's still a bit thin. Here we are working with them for 10 months and they come in and say, "Frank, you mentioned something last week, could we chat about it?" I have the time. For the A Licence you're only around for three weeks. That's what I'm changing now. I want to keep improving the teaching. There's a discrepancy between what I have and what I imagined. The course is only improved through the teachers.'

'*Viel Masse, wenig Klasse*,' Frank says, playing on the rhyme between the German words *Masse* (mass) and *klasse* (class). It translates to 'lots of coaches, not much class'. 'I have to make more *Klasse* from the *Masse*,' he adds with a grin.

'There are 24 coaches and we have a group coaching approach, but we only ever see the individual coach. The education is individual,

even in groups, because a head coach is alone at the end of it all,'
Frank tells me.

One of the tasks that intrigued me most was the concept of 'taking
over a team in October'. Frank and his team stage a scenario in which
four Bundesliga teams in the top flight and the second division have a
problem and have called to prepare the head coach for the interview.
Each club gets six head coaches preparing as if they were about to get
the chance to take over the reins.

'Parallel to their normal work, three weeks long, they get games
of their respective teams, Opta data, and can use the internet. At the
end of the three weeks, they have an imaginary job interview. The
process starts in October. They watch games for three weeks, and
at the start of November they begin their preparation. In February,
they have five lessons to show their preparation, how they would
have done the interview and how they would have trained the team
up until Christmas. We just had Schalke. The day after tomorrow
we have Karlsruhe SC. They then take these experiences forward for
preparation of real jobs.

'Valérien Ismaël later told me 1. FC Nürnberg were impressed with
him because they recognised he had done his homework. It was more
than just his knowledge. It was how he had learnt to give the feeling
he was the perfect man for the job. His preparation had been spot on.'

Frank then joked that half a year later the students would be thrown
out of their coaching jobs because others had no idea about football.
While some of this is Frank's humour, it was also a firm reminder of
the striking reality these coaches were being prepared for. Ismaël only
lasted 14 games at Nürnberg before being dismissed.

In December, the focus on the individual coach is intensified. Work
is done in pairs to figure out where any gaps might be. By this stage, the
coaches are pretty much a *Fußball-Lehrer*. In the new year, repetition
is key to retaining the knowledge originally taught at the beginning
of the course. The presence of guest speakers plays a key role at this
time of the course.

'We work through our opinion first and then have an external speaker
come in and give us their thoughts, not the other way around. Then
everyone knows what we're doing and then we can bring in someone
from outside,' Frank tells me.

Volker Finke, the former head coach of Cameroon and Freiburg (where he holds a record for 16 years in charge) was due to arrive the day after I met Frank to talk about international coaching. Former course members, such as ex-Hamburg head coach Markus Gisdol, call in on Skype to give 20-minute sessions. Even former Arsenal head coach Arsene Wenger made the trip out once. 'After an hour, I said, "You told me you only had half an hour." He could have talked for three hours. He was in his element,' Frank said with a smile.

There's a combination of deductive and inductive learning – both of which are paramount to the role of any head coach. Sometimes, coaches need to tell a player what to do, other times they need to ask to see how far the player has come. The inductive aspect is focused on the participants. 'We want their knowledge,' Frank tells me. 'The task is set, for example: what makes good pressing? The group works together and then presents it.' The presentation in the first week is to test their methods, and Frank focuses on content and behaviour. 'You're talking to the team about playing calmly but your hands are everywhere. How is that supposed to work? Your body language and your words don't match, and then they don't feel right. That's what we explain. We let them work. Whoever teaches, learns. If you explain something, you realise whether you've understood it or not. Consistently presenting helps that and the course lives off exchanges.'

Frank's favourite part of the course is the mirroring – 'to show them what they actually are, not what they see. Who am I? Where am I going? We constantly ask these questions. The point of the mirror is to get them out of a loop. You were a player and heard what a head coach said. Then you're a head coach and you do exactly what your coach did. Breaking that circle is what we focus on here. We had a head coach say, "I coached wrong for 15 years." I say "No, you trained differently." So you can either carry on coaching as before, or take something from here, from the entire group. He took that on board and changed.'

From the middle of February until the middle of March, it's exam time. 'We don't learn for tests, but for life,' says Frank with a grin. There are three module tests in all subjects but each test only counts 5.5 per cent towards the final grade. These are in the standard question-and-answer style, and are done to make students learn during the course.

Julian Nagelsmann was asked when he was made head coach how he managed to balance his coaching course while managing a Bundesliga team. Frank said he had no problem because he had done the modules. He already had the knowledge.

The final tests at the end are where students have to apply their knowledge. There is a three-hour written test, a one-hour oral, one 10-minute presentation of their football philosophy and then there are 45 minutes of questions from lecturers, doctors, other coaches and the psychologist. Then they are handed a topic to work with and have to complete a 30-minute practical with their demo group. 'Their coursework is their football philosophy, training philosophy, leadership, and organisation in 12 to 15 pages,' Frank tells me. 'It's a workbook and it remains a reference point. What I have in my head is now in book form.' This is how coaches can go from just making players better to making players realise why they're better.

By the end of it, the coaches have gone through an eight-level structure of competence development. It starts with subject competence, but they also have to be able to transmit this knowledge, which takes them to the second level: imparting competence. None of that makes any difference if they can't speak properly, so speech competence is also there. When speaking, social competence is pivotal so empathy, authority, identity and character are studied. Logically, leadership competence is also included, as well as media competence. There's also an 'I' competence: who are you? And network competence: what happens if you're out of the loop and you need to make some calls? You need that network. That gives the 24 coaches on the course a start.

As phenomenal a first step as this is, it is often not enough for a coach to survive. In the first half of the 2016–17 Bundesliga season, a record seven head coaches lost their jobs. In the 2017–18 season, five of the nine coaching changes were made before January. Was this due to increased attention and expectation on the Bundesliga and its head coaches, or just part of football?

'It's not the pressure, but what I, as the recipient of that pressure, do,' Frank says. 'It appears that many in leading positions at clubs don't have the patience or the strength for that, to stand next to someone. They seek the easiest way and that's change, but it doesn't guarantee you anything - but you can say afterwards that you tried everything. I always find it amusing when sporting directors say this was our ideal candidate on the first day and then half a year later say, "We're sorry it didn't work out." Then you also have to question the person who brought him in.

'Sporting directors should be in place to retain that philosophy for the club and then they should hire a head coach that fits the club,' Frank tells me. Stuart Webber is a strong example of a sporting director in England helping mould philosophies at clubs either short of one or unsure how to develop an already existing one. As director of football operations at Huddersfield Town, Webber played a huge role in bringing David Wagner to the club at a time when Webber believed the club was in need of cultural change. Webber then moved to Norwich City, where he was responsible in bringing over Daniel Farke, another Borussia Dortmund youth coach. In both cases, Webber identified a need for philosophical change at club level and then made the appointment that gave the club the best chance to succeed in doing so. Both Wagner and Farke have changed the culture at their respective clubs, which is pivotal at a time when player transfers have become a much harder science.

'You can't just buy players,' Frank continues. 'You have to develop them. Using this short lifecycle you run into the danger of a player arriving, giving him three days, and if he doesn't work you get the next one. They can play football though. They weren't bought for millions for no reason, so I have to approach players in a way that makes them perform. And if he can't perform, then I have to question my scouting team. That's why I say, when a player cannot perform at a club it's 90 per cent the fault of the head coach, because he has to approach him in a way that makes him work. Of course there will be cases where the coach says I don't get on with him and yet he's still bought, then he can't be blamed. Klaus Allofs and Thomas Schaaf worked together for years at Werder Bremen and they only ever bought players if they both agreed. I as head coach have to do something to make sure the player is happy. But then he has to perform and push himself. And if he doesn't do that, then I didn't do my homework beforehand. I have to know if he's someone who can perform under pressure. Lots of people are involved in a player's success,' Frank tells me.

Success for one can make it harder for another and there is a feeling in Germany that with the arrival of Nagelsmann and Schalke's Domenico Tedesco, a new mindset is entering the German game. The phase that began with Klopp has been reignited, as young head coaches continue to get their chance at the top while former heroes watch on. But is the narrative of the day really its reality?

'It isn't harder because of coaches like Nagelsmann, but because of the high number of head coaches who have already worked and built a reputation. A while ago, there were 20 head coaches for 15 spots. The door is bigger now, because of our coaching work here and in youth academies. Before, what you achieved or whether you were a former pro gave you a chance. Valérien Ismaël, Joe Zinnbauer, Nagelsmann, Klopp, Tuchel – there's a new door. There are more applicants because more people can show their experience. It will be harder for everyone to get in now,' Frank tells me.

Of the seven head coaches sacked in the first half of the 2016–17 Bundesliga season, three internal coaches ended up being their replacements, while Torsten Frings jumped clubs to jump roles, moving from the staff at Werder Bremen to head coach at Darmstadt (where he spent almost a year). By January 2017, 12 of the then 18 Bundesliga teams had promoted a head coach internally. Ingolstadt – one of the two sides relegated that season – appointed former second team head coach Stefan Leitl (who was, after 36 matches in charge, relieved of his duties not long after the start of the 2018–19 season), and four more internal appointments were made at the Bundesliga clubs in the 2017–18 season.

In the 2016–17 season, both Craig Shakespeare (Leicester City) and Mike Phelan (Hull City) became head coaches after being appointed internally. Neither lasted more than four months. In the 2014–15 season, caretaker head coach Chris Ramsey signed a three-year deal to become Queens Park Rangers' (QPR) head coach. Six months later he was sacked. The trend is clear. English football has been hesitant towards making such decisions. And when they have made them, they've either been too rash or the coaches haven't been given enough time. Perhaps it's less a case of more head coaches than before, but rather more openness to the idea of members of the coaching staff becoming head coaches. It's about trusting someone to lead a team, not just be part of one.

Such is the pressure in the Premier League that it takes a brave man to make this decision. Sam Allardyce has been a head coach of seven different Premier League clubs over the years. Mark Hughes has coached six Premier League teams, Alan Pardew five and David Moyes four. By the end of the 2017–18 season, those four men had managed nine of 20 teams in the Premier League. At the end of the same season in Germany, eight of the then-employed coaches had managed 13 of the then top-flight teams. Managerial merry-go-rounds are normal in many countries, Germany included, but it seems quite astonishing that nearly half of the Premier League had been shared between just four men.

'I know the fear,' Frank tells me. 'We had it years ago. The person in charge picked a young head coach, it didn't work and then they looked bad in the press and then the club is relegated, or loses sponsorship money. I'm afraid, so I bring in a name, even if the name isn't great, it's a name. He doesn't work, but you tried, you brought in a name, you tried everything. With Thomas Tuchel at 1. FSV Mainz 05, the sporting director Christian Heidel said, "I'm convinced by him." Thankfully, it worked, he was successful, but then others began to realise, we could get a young coach too. So Stuttgart's sporting director says, we'll take Hannes Wolf. He has won three titles at youth football in Germany. He's good. But take Hannes Wolf to Hamburg. He has those upstairs … They would tear him apart. It has to fit.'

Ironically, months later, Hannes Wolf was announced as the new head coach of Hamburg near the end of October 2018. While I didn't doubt the decision by Wolf to get back into the dugout, I was surprised that he chose to do so at Hamburg – for exactly the reason Frank had told me, months before his invented example became reality.

After all, Christian Titz, the coach removed in order to be replaced by Wolf, had restored some sentiment of order to the club and had given young players a chance. After only 11 games of the new season though, and with Hamburg just two points off first, Titz was gone. It was time for a new coach.

'I think young German head coaches are given more of a chance now because of a change in attitude, because of Tuchel and experiments with successful young managers. It started with Klopp.'

Change is what sparks development. In his fantastic book *Legacy*, about the All Blacks, New Zealand's dominant rugby union team, James Kerr uses Will Hogg's four stages for organisational change to emphasise that all levels of change must occur otherwise the likelihood of true change is heavily reduced. Kerr listed them as follows:

A case for change
A compelling picture of the future
A sustained capability to change
A credible plan to execute.

Whether Hamburg had a case for change when they decided to sack Titz and appoint Wolf remains unclear to most, but Germany certainly had one at the start of the millennium when the performance of their national team collapsed. Their plan for the future was to get back to the top of the pile and, after a sustained effort of change, they won the World Cup in 2014. The plan to execute was reflected in Germany's implementation of academies out of which a generation of highly intelligent players (Generation Why — players who ask why they're doing something rather than just doing it) coached by smarter, better-educated coaches was born. After the disappointment at the 2018 World Cup, it will be interesting to see whether Germany can deliver another necessary plan for change and be as successful as before.

Ever since the appointment of Jürgen Klopp at Mainz proved a triumph, other clubs in Germany realised that appointing an internal or slightly younger candidate was possible. Many clubs took a collective stance against external pressure to appoint 'a name' and in doing so changed the cultural approach to coaching appointments. Eddie Howe's success at Bournemouth could have been that moment for English football. Instead, the Premier League kept growing, kept signing bigger talents, and kept appearing on television screens in the most rural bars in Vietnam. There is a price to pay for it all.

What is important about Klopp's appointment was that the 'gamble' paid off. There is certainly a case to be made that had Klopp not been successful at Mainz, Germany's coaching landscape might look a little different now. Two consecutive Bundesliga titles and a German Cup at Borussia Dortmund saw his coaching and identity reach another level. By the time he had guided Liverpool to the Champions League final in 2018, Klopp had become so much more than a man who changed a coaching culture in Germany. He had become one of the best in the game, and partly because he grew along with the players he developed. As Melissa Reddy points out in her marvellously in-depth article for *Joe* titled 'From Hong Kong to Kiev: At the end of the storm, there's a golden sky...', Klopp's story is about 'hugs, fist pumps and rants, but should be about the composed leader, who is able to read the room and never ducks a big call'.

An unremarkable player, but always a remarkable character, Klopp has become the modern symbol for German coaching, and yet in many ways he isn't very German.

'Klopp fits in any team because of his incredible connection to players,' Frank says. 'Although some players came to me when I was Germany U20 coach and said they sometimes find his positivity frustrating. Why? They'd say, "Because he praises me to the heavens but I don't play." Another example of his positivity is when he told me about a player with an amazing left foot. I call him up and then think this must be the brother. He exaggerates sometimes about how much of a special character this player is and then he arrives and he's just another player. I love Klopp's positivity, but in reality it's easy to understand why misunderstandings happen. That helps players though, and I think it's a good quality because it's better to see the positive over the negative. We Germans often see the negatives before we even talk about what was good. 'Kloppo' isn't German in that respect. He's always positive.'

So many great people have been working in English football for years. Some of their stories were brilliantly and poignantly told in Michael Calvin's *Living on the Volcano*. And yet, too many never get the chance to step out of the shadows, and when they do, they are often burdened with unrealistic expectation. There was an interesting discussion on *BT Sport Score* at the start of December 2017 in which Jermaine Jenas, John Hartson, Tim Sherwood, Michael Owen, Chris Sutton and Robbie Savage discussed 'Who is blocking the path for young managers?'

Remarkably, Owen said that 'the last thing' he'd think of doing would be to get his coaching badges because the only job he'd get would be in the National League. Owen added he'd have a better chance of being successful at Premier League level than at non-League level, because he doesn't know the players or the systems at that level. While Owen's point that the FA isn't giving opportunities to English coaches is in some respects understandable, the line of argument is questionable. Doing your badges or being a well-known ex-player shouldn't automatically guarantee you a job at the highest level – and if it does then there's something wrong with the system.

Young English coaches aren't getting opportunities in part because club boards want to appoint 'a name', and that often happens to be a successful foreign coach. This is largely because the Premier League wants to cultivate its status as the 'one with all the stars', and considers head coaches to be part of that. For that to change there needs to be a cultural shift in English coaching, one that starts by focusing on making the right appointment for the club rather than deciding based on the aforementioned reasons.

In many ways, Arsenal's decision to appoint Unai Emery is a perfect example. Emery is undoubtedly a successful and experienced head coach, but is he the right coach for Arsenal? Mikel Arteta appeared to be a more appropriate coach for the Gunners, one with all the right attributes. A former Arsenal player who understands the club and its culture, and a man who has played and worked in the Premier League – most recently as a coach with Pep Guardiola's remarkable title-winning Manchester City side. Of course, this doesn't guarantee success. Emery may well work out as Arsenal head coach, but Arsenal's decision not to make a strong and brave transition into a new era of coaching after Arsene Wenger is an opportunity missed.

West Bromwich Albion, eventually, appointed the 'right' man for the club. After nearly lifting the club clear of what looked like certain relegation at the end of the 2017–18 season, Darren Moore went from being interim coach to the man in charge permanently. Whether the club would have made such a bold decision had they retained their Premier League status is unknown, but Moore's appointment is no less significant. In the end, results elsewhere ensured The Baggies dropped down to the Championship, but Moore picked up 11 points in his six games in charge – a run that saw West Brom beat Manchester United and Tottenham Hotspur and draw with Liverpool.

A former West Brom player, Moore had been working as a youth coach at the club since 2012, gradually working his way up. Brought on as a first-team assistant to Alan Pardew, Moore was then handed the job on an interim basis when Pardew was sacked. Six games, as impressive as they were, shouldn't be the only aspects of an assessment of Moore's suitability. This is a man who knows and has respect for all levels of the club – having won Premier League Manager of the Month for April 2018, Moore shared his success by taking a photo with 118 staff members. This is a man who used to play for the club, and understands the community in which it is based. This is a man who is qualified, capable and perfectly suited to the club in question. His appointment by no means guarantees success, but it shows greater consideration of all the factors that can lead to it.

'By me sitting here in the role I've got it's an inspiration to all young British coaches,' Moore said after his permanent appointment. 'And hopefully the role today inspires them right the way from grassroots football right in the professional game. And if it does do that to individuals, then I'm extremely proud.'

Moore's appointment is a chance for West Brom and English football to start changing coaching culture to include opportunity for young and internal coaches. For that cultural change to take root, Moore will have to be successful. There's no escaping that without proof on the pitch, the decision to choose a younger, lesser-known coach is less likely to become part of the thought process.

The hope is he's given time to do so, but in England time appears a lost commodity. When Leeds United sacked 40-year-old Paul Heckingbottom he had coached just 16 games. Of the club's last eight head coaches, only one has lasted a whole season. They are numbers to support the statement that clubs' approaches to head coaches are often reckless, as well as proof that the recruitment process of head coaches at some English clubs is in need of work.

Moore's appointment offers a unique opportunity though, one far more important than recognition of unknown coaches. It's a chance to change the racial discrimination of black, Asian and minority ethnic (BAME) coaches in England. As Jonathan Liew, *The Independent*'s brilliant chief sports writer, wrote in a frighteningly true article:

'Since 2000, the proportion of black footballers playing for England has risen, but while 25 per cent of white players have been given a managerial job since retirement, that drops to just 10 per cent for black players… Just 7 per cent of the current Premier League and Football League managers are BAME.'

Sol Campbell, who has a UEFA Pro Licence and has gained experience at club and international level, waited a long time before being given a chance. At the start of December 2018, the side bottom of League Two, at that stage the lowest ranked full-time professional team in England, Macclesfield Town, appointed Campbell head coach. While individual beliefs vary, social prejudices continue to be clearly reflected in all manner of workplaces, football included: white head coaches get more chances than BAME head coaches. Like Chris Hughton at Brighton and Hove Albion, Moore's appointment is a step in the right direction, but BAME head coaches remain all-too rare a sight.

In the spring of 2018, what did suddenly become a familiar sight in Britain was white former professionals getting head coaching jobs. In April 2018, Steven Gerrard (38) was announced as the new head coach of Rangers. Not long after, former England teammate Frank Lampard (39) was made head coach of Derby County. That spring also saw Joey Barton (35) announced as Fleetwood Town head coach.

'Imagine Arsene Wenger leaves Arsenal and they give the job to an unknown U19 coach from Manchester City who has done great work,' says Frank. 'Firstly, the mentality of others is: "What's this? We're used to getting the best." The players will say, "What has this young devil got to tell us?" You have to change the mentality.'

Changing the mentality means giving coaches like Gerrard, Lampard or Barton a chance. Admittedly, their appointments aren't free of some troubling considerations when it comes to how qualified they are. Lampard has coached at youth level, albeit part-time, but, as revealed in an interview with *The Guardian* in May 2018, he would only start with the Pro Licence in September 2018. Barton has his UEFA A Licence, but, like Lampard, not his Pro Licence.

Gerrard perhaps has the best experience to qualifications ratio, and stands perhaps the best chance. In an interview with *The Guardian* five months before his appointment, the former Liverpool captain said he had 'aged two years in six months' during his time as head coach of Liverpool's U18s. The former midfielder spoke openly about the benefits of learning the trade away from the cameras and how the time 'will definitely prepare' him for wherever he ends up. For all the benefits of being Steven Gerrard, the former Liverpool midfielder is determined to do it 'the right way,' telling *The Guardian*: 'I'm not sitting here thinking I've done it for five months so bring the job interviews on... In six months or a year or two years' time there might be an opportunity where I think I'm much better prepared than I was five months ago. The MK Dons job, for example, which came up just after I had finished playing, was like a smack in the face. There was no way I was ready to lead a club or a team. Am I closer to that now? Of course, but I am happy where I am right now.'

In an article for *The Times* at the end of May 2018, Oliver Kay, the paper's chief football correspondent, spoke to England's youngest UEFA Pro Licence coach. Kevin Nicholson, 32, told Kay there were something like '335 Pro Licence coaches who had come through the FA scheme.' This number makes the appointments of Gerrard, Lampard and Barton – none of whom had the Pro Licence (England's version of Germany's *Fußball-Lehrer*) at the time of their appointments – all the more difficult to swallow.

'It's not like Germany, where Nagelsmann got the Hoffenheim job at 28 and Tedesco got the Schalke job at 31,' Nicholson told Kay. 'But all we can do, as young coaches, is keep working and hope that our time will come. I hope it does. I think it would benefit our whole game.'

And that's the truth. Whether it's Nicholson, Gerrard or Lampard, every young new head coach has a chance to make a positive impact on the game. Frank believes there are good coaches in England but that the game lacks trust in them. Perhaps Gerrard, now head coach of Rangers in Scotland, will be one to gain enough trust, perhaps Lampard will get enough time at Derby to grow, perhaps Barton will prove the critics wrong, but their potential, and the potential of every young head coach out there, is important for English football to acknowledge. The hope is that if any of the aforementioned coaches are successful, it engenders wider trust in younger coaches, partly made possible by reviewing the experience criteria, and not a rush to appoint former players. For cultural coaching change to work fully, it has to be about the ability of the individual, not the name in the headlines.

There's no denying that Jürgen Klopp's appointment at Mainz changed German coaching, and that when he was made head coach at Borussia Dortmund it was an appointment with a wider effect on German football. The summer after England's youth teams won the U20 and U17 World Cups as well as the U19 UEFA Championship and the Toulon tournament, English coaching also had a chance to make a perfectly timed cultural shift in its approach to managerial appointments, especially after the success Gareth Southgate had with England at the 2018 World Cup. It's time to change the mentality.

'In Germany, through the youth academies, we've got more and more young players,' Frank tells me. 'The Bundesliga has grown younger through these talents and these talents know the type of head coaches who explain football to them, who don't just say "Do that," but talk to them. The coaches fell in with these talents and the players don't expect now for them to be old school and say, "Out we go" or "Run". They expect to be told how to run and if it doesn't work, "Don't worry, we'll talk about it, I have a video analysis we can look at, we'll get you there." It's a question of trust.

'If coaching courses weren't great in England then you can coach internally at your own club. Perhaps that's something England needs to do more of? We do that. I don't think we're better or worse than the French, Dutch, Swiss, or English. We aren't better,' Frank says. 'Everyone has their own way. German head coaches know the system, and through the work they do in youth football they know the system better, they speak the language, they know our philosophy. If I go to England and Italy and get a head coach, I don't know them. They have a language problem. You saw it with Pep Guardiola, and even Carlo Ancelotti. They have a brilliant team, but the language problem is there. I was with Joachim Löw at Fenerbahçe and what we said at the end of it was that we weren't connecting to the players' souls,' Frank tells me.

Discussing the souls of modern footballers is murky water, but is the heart of a good football head coach any easier to understand?

As of May 2017, Frank Wormuth has coached 241 students on the *Fußball-Lehrer* course since he took over. If anyone knows what makes a good coach, he does.

'I am a very structured person. I orientate myself around the eight competences – minus the networking, because that comes later. Then it depends where I am head coach. Sometimes the president of a club calls and says, "I need a new coach," and I always ask, "What is the job description? What does the team look like?" They ask why. I have to know. Do I need a likeable character that connects with people where knowledge is of less importance? Then I would recommend him to Real Madrid. He has to handle people. Whether Zinédine Zidane would be a good coach in Buxtehude (a small town in the north near Hamburg), I don't know. Is he a teaching coach or can he only work with finished products? I have to know that. That's why I can't say, "This is a good head coach." He has to be good in all seven of the competences, but even then it doesn't guarantee he'll fit in the team. A good head coach depends on the job he takes, the team he has. Then I can see if he can work with the team, if he can transfer information, if he has an idea. He might still lose, but he's still a good coach.'

The academy reformations on Frank's mind when we meet will mean changes, especially the addition of the sparkly new performance centre in Frankfurt due to be completed by 2021. With a potential estimated cost of €150m, the new academy will be the most expensive investment in the history of the association. It will heavily incorporate the modern digital aspects of football development. From big data to 360-degree visuals, the 'Silicon Valley' of football, as Germany team manager Oliver Bierhoff has suggested it should be, is a prime example of how Germany are trying to stay ahead. After the team's performance in Russia, one might suggest it's time for Germany to catch up again.

The focal point of the academy will be a think tank. Launched at the beginning of 2018, the project is designed to be a space where innovative ideas surrounding sports science, psychology and fitness can be discussed. In an interview with *Training Ground Guru* in July 2018, Dr Thomas Hauser, the head of the project, revealed a number of intriguing insights into the think tank, a project that had apparently been eight years in the making. From the coaching perspective, the most important message was the integration of the coaches. 'We hope to find answers to support the coaches. They say "we want to coach in an individual way". If you want to do this, you need to understand the biology of an organism. That is not part of the coaching education programme,' Hauser said.

Given the breadth of the programme it's impressive to think the DFB is thinking of even more ways to equip their coaches. One look at Germany's disastrous 2018 World Cup performance (more on that later) suggests that perhaps now is the right time to seek more innovation. England's 2018 World Cup was a success, and that is also down to the work being done at the country's central academy, St George's Park. Hauser said that they had visited England's academy, admitting even though they don't have a think tank the same way the DFB does, that the English were 'much further on with the idea of an academy'.

Creating space to think and discuss in an environment as stubborn and self-confident as football isn't easy, particularly at the highest level, so the DFB's decision to develop and promote the idea of such a project is positive. 'It is like a playground sometimes – we can try things out,' Hauser told *Training Ground Guru*. 'Sometimes we will get results and sometimes we won't.'

However, I heard Hauser speak at the 2018 *Internationaler Trainer-Kongress* (ITK), a congress for head coaches from all over the world, in Dresden, and the positivity of the project was lost somewhere behind another wave of DFB business talk. This was a room full of more than 1,000 head coaches who needed convincing that the think tank was going to benefit them, not a barrage of graphics and neat slogans.

Phrases such as 'The future doesn't just arrive, it's made by us all' and 'The Harvard of football' were used, and an artist's impression of how the new academy would look was displayed. The idea was that the academy would be an environment specifically designed to move you into certain spaces and engage with different people. The way it was depicted mimicked the concept of the movie *Inside Out*, in which personifications of five basic emotions influence the behaviour of a little girl, Riley, from a console within her mind. However, unlike the award-winning animated film, this presentation couldn't keep the attention of the thousand-odd coaches in the congress hall. The startling heat of the summer might have played a role, but quite a few eyes started to close during Hauser's lecture.

The hope is that the concept works out better than the delivery. In a sport as viciously competitive as football, creating space in which to think and sometimes fail is pivotal. After all, the exchange and development of different opinions is at the heart of human growth — as long as it's done correctly. The sentiment of Willy Brandt, the former German Chancellor and Nobel Peace Prize winner, sums it perfectly: 'It often takes more courage to change one's opinion than to keep it.' At the highest level, and on top of an already exchange-rich coaching programme, it seems German football is trying to do just that.

'France started with this type of academy with Clairefontaine,' Frank tells me. 'Spain were always top, and we're always second best when we play them. They work more with game structure, whereas we're a bit Dutch, and focus on passing. Then we look at the Dutch and see they're only focused on positional play, and that's not right. We always compare with outside and are still not happy with our schooling. Typical German, we can never be happy,' Frank says, with a smile.

'We are constantly looking to improve. It's a positive aspect, but life has two lanes and there is also a negative — we have a lot of burnouts. The French don't have as many, or as much success, but they live well. They drink a glass of red, eat white bread and don't get fat. I love that laissez-faire attitude. Ok, so you arrive a little late but life goes on. What we do is somewhat extreme. I think a little bit of French wouldn't go amiss,' Frank tells me. Perhaps that was why France won the 2018 World Cup.

In a remarkable statement on the Bavarian radio station *Bayerischer Rundfunk* in December 2017, Mehmet Scholl said the coaching course was '11 months of brainwashing.' The 47 year old added that 'the Tedescos and Wolfs have sprung up out of nowhere' and that 'German football will have a severe case of the blues' in the future.

Perhaps Scholl's most damning statement regarding the new coaching generation was that they 'weren't really interested in the people or the footballers anymore.' Scholl, who is a qualified coach but hasn't had a coaching job since working with Bayern Munich's youth teams in 2013, feels the players are being coached by robots to be robots. 'The kids have to pass, they can't dribble anymore. They aren't getting the right advice why a pass or tackle didn't work. Instead, they can fart 18 systems.'

The comments caused a stir in the media, and from the coaches at whom the comments were directed. Hannes Wolf, then Stuttgart's head coach, responded by saying, 'I like him a lot, his creativity, his humour, but for him as a former player to question coaches who weren't players is borderline. And I think he knows that.' In an interview with the *Süddeutsche Zeitung*, Schalke head coach Domenico Tedesco dismissed the idea the coaching course brainwashed its students. 'It's not that at all, from my perspective,' he said. 'Everything in football is presented and discussed: possession, long balls, pressing and sitting deep … It's like a buffet with meat, fish, salad, everything. As a head coach I go up and serve myself. Nothing is compulsory there.'

Frank Wormuth told *Bild* he felt Scholl's comments had no basis in fact and that he only saw 'a cry for help from someone who is disenchanted.' But it was Jürgen Klopp's words that resonated the most. Speaking to German TV station *ZDF* in January 2018, Klopp said, 'I don't know what to say really. I like Mehmet Scholl. I don't know him that well, but I liked him a lot as a player and we've met here and there. He really is a nice guy. Obviously, he thinks a lot about football, and somewhere there's always a bit of truth in the things he perhaps says, but it's not *the* truth. All the young head coaches who have come through have enjoyed a top level of education; compared to earlier, a Hannes Wolf has been in charge of a football team for seven years before he got a job in the Bundesliga. Not just anyone, but at the top level – just in youth football. Domenico Tedesco did the same, Julian Nagelsmann did the same. They didn't just get the job overnight. If former pros were willing to go down this road and not coach the big games straight from the start, or say they have to train at a certain level or get a job at a Bundesliga club as their first job … If they were ready to start the job at a healthy level and learn the job – because you have to learn it because the job has nothing to do with being a pro. You have to lead a team, not play in one, and that's a huge difference. So I hope that Hannes, Tedesco, Nagelsmann, all of the names, I've probably forgotten a few, Sandro Schwarz – that they don't think about what Mehmet Scholl said, because it's not important. It's an opinion, he's allowed to hold that point of view, but the lads have all the stuff they need to go their own way in an incredibly difficult environment where everything is judged and controlled every day – so it's no picnic every day.'

From his empathy to his recognition of the value of learning, there's much to support about Klopp's answer. And in truth, the evidence in this chapter explains the efforts being made at the coaching academy to avoid exactly what Scholl feels is happening. Clearly coaches are being taught systems, but also how to handle players, how to develop a wide foundation of competences, how to handle the media, how to manage their own and others' mental strength. They are given tools to survive in an intense working environment and ones that give them the best chance to adapt – a pivotal trait in any profession, but particularly in one as dynamic and evolving as football.

Famous German filmmaker Werner Herzog believes the same. In *Werner Herzog: A Guide for the Perplexed,* Herzog mentions how important handling change is: 'Technical knowledge inevitably becomes dated; the ability to adapt to change will always be more important.' It is hard to suggest that one of these coaching tools is more important than another, but being adaptable certainly gives any coach the best chance. And when the chance comes, you've got to take it. Remember Frank Wormuth's words: 'The door is open to everyone, but you have to get in, and once you're in, you have to be good.'

Key Lesson

The sheer commitment to working hard and achieving excellence is, in my experience, a very German trait. Germans, on the whole, are not afraid to put in the time because they know that time will be recognised. They are not afraid to learn all of the aspects of their work, because there's an understanding of the improvement that brings, both individually and collectively. Frank's words ring true, again: 'If we want to do something, then we do it right.'

This is a cultural understanding across the country. Companies respect employees who work their way up from the intern position. Clubs respect coaches who have worked their way through youth teams. All the time, knowledge is being absorbed and experience is being gained in both the person and the coach. The learning process of life is respected and often rewarded.

Lehrer
(Teachers)

---

*'The head coach is a component of the system,
but they aren't the system.'*

– Matthias Sammer

After Germany's disastrous World Cup in Russia, I was looking for a place where expert analysis would be delivered by the smartest brains in the sport. The ITK, a three-day annual event where top-level coaches met and exchanged ideas, seemed like the perfect place.

The congress is organised and hosted by the BDFL (The Association of German Coaches), a professional organisation for top-qualified football coaches (those with UEFA A Licences or the *Fußball-Lehrer*). It was founded in 1957 by 129 coaches, including the legendary Sepp Herberger. Herberger helped mould the origins of German football and famously led the national team to 'The Miracle of Bern', when they unexpectedly won the 1954 World Cup final, beating a brilliant Hungary team 3–2 despite being 2–0 down after just eight minutes.

The BDFL is a federal association in Germany with eight regional association groups, independent of but partners with the DFB. It's clear that working with the DFB in a capacity that allows them to be critical is a huge positive – one of their mottos is: 'Independence as a key to success'. Perhaps it limits the power the BDFL has to wield, but perhaps the DFB has to do more to make sure that doesn't play a deciding role when it comes to progress.

The congress has hosted more than 1,000 coaches from around 30 countries in the last two years. Membership is voluntary, and according to the association the BDFL currently has 4,900 members, made up of 20 per cent *Fußball-Lehrer* and 80 per cent A Licence holders. Membership is on the rise too, with 300 new members arriving in the last year. About 72 per cent of the top-level coaches (A Licence or *Fußball-Lehrer*) who collected their badges through the DFB are currently members. In short, it is the part of Germany's footballing brain where, across three days of talks, training sessions and exchange between coaching colleagues, synapses fire and neurones bump into one another.

With the main theme of the 2018 congress, held in Dresden, being 'World Cup analysis and future perspectives of German football', I was excited about hearing experts talk about what went wrong for Germany in Russia and why. Sadly, my excitement was short lived.

Joti Chatzialexiou, who is in charge of all of Germany's national teams, informed the attendees that because Germany's World Cup analysis was to be delivered by Joachim Löw at another time, his focus would be on international football generally, using the tournament in Russia as an example. There was time to talk about Germany's future though. What followed was a presentation haunted by the national team's horrible World Cup hashtag (the German word for together (*zusammen*) was abbreviated into a social-media-friendly hashtag #zsmmn). It was slick and full of the right words, but for a different audience (this was not a business congress). Like the absence of vowels from the hashtag, it was short of detail and as a result it left the DFB looking disconnected from the real world.

Phrases and words like 'new impulse', 'smart and simple' and 'new direction' were not going to work on a room full of coaches. This onslaught of business language peaked when Chatzialexiou said: 'It's time "Made in Germany" meant world class again.' Even the 'Made in Germany' part was delivered in English – and it wasn't the only time the English language crept into his speech.

A presentation slide with a road winding off in between distant mountains demonstrating the path built on German values (that would lead them to success) read more like a list of character traits for a superhero than the guidelines for how this team is going to restore themselves to the top of the football tree.

Discipline	Bravery	Determination	
Preparedness	Resilience	Team spirit	
Respect	Optimism	Communication	Passion

That's not to say these values aren't important for a sports team – they absolutely are – but it was as if the DFB thought putting '2.0' at the head of the slide would be enough to distract anyone from the values themselves. Are these traits going to set Germany apart from other international teams, who likely have exactly the same list on their changing room walls? Without many, if not all, of the values above real victory is impossible, and the fact the DFB presented them as the path to the future raises some concerns. Were these values not in place before and if they were, is there an assumption that just working hard on them will be enough?

There were some words on the early exit from the 1998 World Cup in France. 'No one shirked responsibility then, no one will now,' Chatzialexiou said. The comparison doesn't seem to quite fit though, given the drastically different state of German football back then compared to now, and considering that Germany were defending World Cup champions coming into the tournament in Russia (which they were not at the European Championships in 2000).

Chatzialexiou said it would be naïve to think one institution could do it, so he called on all coaches to help get Germany back to the top. That might have held more weight had the word and concept of 'together' not been dragged through the mud throughout the summer. What started with the aforementioned hashtag continued with the team's distance from their fans, and finished with a disjointed squad delivering sub-par performances as Germany spent all summer showing just how far from together they truly were.

Unsurprisingly, hollow talk of 'together' left many feeling somewhat disappointed. Frank Engel, the BDFL's chairman for the north-east, said on the opening day of the congress in Dresden: 'It's a shame that the Germany head coach hasn't shown his face in years at our symposium.' BDFL President Lutz Hangartner added a similar sentiment. Both were met with rapturous applause. Having Löw there instead of another smooth-talking member of the association would have gone a long way to showing that both the DFB and Löw had realised the need for unity — especially among fellow coaches.

This refusal to exchange ideas – in a room full of top-level coaches who would likely have shown more solidarity and understanding than most, considering their profession – leaves the DFB looking further and further adrift from the real world. The words of Dresden-born Matthias Sammer, on the third day, might well have brought the DFB back to earth.

Sammer, currently an advisor to Borussia Dortmund, has experienced almost everything possible in football. Sammer played club football for Dynamo Dresden, VfB Stuttgart, Internazionale and Borussia Dortmund. Internationally, Sammer played for East Germany (GDR) and then the newly united German team after reunification in 1990, winning the European Championships and the Ballon d'Or in 1996. A year later he won the Champions League with Borussia Dortmund. He helped save BVB from relegation as an assistant manager, and in 2002 became the youngest ever coach (aged 34) to win the Bundesliga title, also with BVB. The last time he was a head coach in the Bundesliga was in 2005 with Stuttgart.

'We need football competence,' Sammer said at the ITK. 'We need top people in the positions who understand football, can communicate it and will protect coaches. One can say, "I think Jogi Löw should be here too", but who should tell him? Oliver? I have respect for his work, I see him as more than a manager type ... But where is the competence, the equivalent in the association who says, "Oh, Jogi: go there!"?'

Sammer has a great understanding of that system. He was appointed sporting director at the DFB a few months before Löw became Germany head coach in 2006, a post he held until 2012. His pertinent question about the current structure inside the DFB sheds light on the core issue. Sammer believes more talk needs to be about the football at all levels of the German game, but particularly in leading positions. After all, if the collective is smarter about the topic at hand then when failures do arise collective recovery can be taken rather than singular blame being handed out.

'I think we have to reveal the importance of the head coach, that he's the key, but on the other hand we have to strengthen systems that simultaneously protect coaches in order to understand how coaches work,' Sammer said in Dresden.

Despite Reinhard Grindel being head of the DFB, the hierarchy in German football must be relatively flat if Löw wasn't aware of the importance of his presence at the ITK, or (worse) if no one was in a position to tell him. A flat hierarchy removes layers of management, leaving no separation between executives and staff members. In a best case scenario, this structure should improve communication and speed of decision making because of the reduced number of layers. Germany's reality is somewhat different.

Grindel is a politician posing as a 'modern man' who understands sport, weakening the structure upon which he sits. Löw is the head coach and yet appears far too isolated in his knowledge, reducing his effectiveness. In short, Germany appears to have few if any of the advantages of a flat hierarchy, and too many of the disadvantages. Management — in this case Löw — can easily lose control if there are fewer people providing support and offering alternatives. This isolation of ideas at the top, accentuated if the required knowledge is lacking in potentially supportive roles (such as those held by Oliver Bierhoff and Grindel), can be devastating for any organisation. Germany did not react faster or communicate more effectively, but left Löw isolated and unchallenged. Sammer himself said at the ITK in Bochum in 2017: 'Don't hold this against me, but I can't do anything with flat hierarchies.'

Furthermore, Sammer's point about structure extends to a truth about the head coach. They are a pivotal figure, but if things go wrong they are not the only source of error. 'The head coach, in the key role, is a component of the system, but they aren't the system,' Sammer said in Dresden. In spells of stress or lack of success, the head coach can struggle to protect himself, and it is then that the strength and competence of the structures (at club level the club itself) take on even greater importance.

A new contract for Löw offered prematurely and unnecessarily before the 2018 World Cup, followed by a swift response to Germany's early exit saying he would be carrying on as head coach, has left the DFB looking very much like it revolves around its head coach and not the other way around. Löw does indeed look like the system. As Sammer suggested, the right structure would have likely prevented the current situation.

All of Sammer's comments were an intriguing addition to the current debate on the Germany national team, but they were also an insight into his relationship with Löw. One review of some of the previous quotes from Sammer on Löw reveals the extent of their bond, and adds perhaps further explanation as to why Sammer said what he said in Dresden.

At the 2017 ITK in Bochum, Sammer pointed out the importance of recognising the difference between developmental and top-level coaches – and that Löw was someone who went from one to the other, so much so that he had 'developed himself to the pinnacle' of the sport. Sammer went even further with his praise in a Eurosport interview in the same year in which he said: 'Joachim Löw is the ideal national team head coach, as is his personality. He's present and is clear with his statements. He's also reserved. I can't imagine a better Germany head coach than Joachim Löw. I hope he continues to enjoy it and that he can do the job for a long, long time. It's also important for the connection with the association to have a stable position. That automatically leads to development – and Joachim Löw is a very, very important part of that. It was always wonderful to discuss things with him, and to argue with him. But it was always about the task at hand, the football. He was never resentful and that was wonderful. In all these years, there's been continuous development and with Löw too. Alongside the sporting aspect, he also brought the team forwards. His leadership style, his social intercourse, he is a top, top coach, a World Cup head coach. It's continuation at a very high level. That's impressive.'

This makes Sammer's decision after the tournament to place the blame on the structures around Löw rather than the man himself far more understandable. 'We need football expertise in the top positions,' Sammer said in Dresden, surely hinting at the precarious position of DFB President Grindel. 'We need people who have moulded the identity of football and know how to be successful,' Sammer added. He was perhaps hinting at former sporting director Hans-Dieter 'Hansi' Flick, whose departure from the association Sammer had described as 'regrettable' at the ITK in 2017.

Löw is clearly one of those people, although performances in Russia suggest there's work to be done on updating the 'how to be successful' part. Matthias Sammer is himself obviously the kind of character the DFB could do with. He is a man who speaks with clarity and care, but is also blunt about his desire to win all the time.

His football competence is also beyond doubt. In his 50-odd minutes on stage in Dresden, Sammer talked about how possession football must not be forgotten and said that criticising young players was wrong, suggesting that 'to go in on young people means that old people failed to lead them'. He also argued that France didn't have to apologise for winning the 2018 World Cup in rather ugly fashion because they just did what so many used to accuse Germany of: 'They play ugly, but they win.' Sammer mentioned how important coaches such as Per Mertesacker would be in the future, but also warned: 'the piano player who can play superbly is still not in a position to explain to others how playing the piano works'.

Most intriguingly, and in contrast to how the DFB appears to see it, Sammer sees Germany's current situation as different to the one at the start of the millennium. 'We are not at the end of the 1990s or the start of the 2000s,' Sammer said in Dresden. 'German football, with youth academies, has wonderful organisation but the question is: how strong is the German FA? How is the exchange? How is the exchange in the combination of the association, as the peak, and the youth academies? Is there even communication between the two? We have to set points of focus, without doubt, but where are the guidelines for exchange? Who will deliver this leadership constellation? That's what I'm missing a bit. I don't think the 2018 generation was a worse football generation than 2014. But we have to discuss what the focus will be in the education and development of the future.' In short, as Sammer said about the current state of German football: 'We're not out for the count, but we should be worried.'

That worry starts, hopefully, inside the smartest minds of the DFB. In one of the biggest associations in the world there are plenty of intelligent and capable people who can make the right difference to German football. I was lucky enough to speak to some, but perhaps they just need to be listened to more often so that, as Sammer said, at the top level of management more talk is about football.

At the end of August, Joachim Löw finally did talk football again as the head coach revealed his analysis of what went wrong at the

2018 World Cup. In a near two-hour long press conference, Löw and Oliver Bierhoff revealed why Germany failed so dramatically at the tournament. 'My biggest mistake was to believe that we could get through the group stage with our dominant possession style of play,' said Löw. 'It was almost arrogant of me. I wanted to perfect our possession play. I should have prepared the team the way I did in 2014, when we had more of a balance between offence and defence.'.

With the help of a PowerPoint presentation, Löw even called on statistics, such as the fact Germany sprinted forwards 22 per cent less often than in qualifying, to show concrete evidence as to why Germany exited the tournament earlier than expected. Löw added that he had also failed to 'light the touch paper' in Russia, leaving the team without the right hunger for success, with perhaps too much focus on structure and strategy. Löw said 2014 had been 'a golden centre' for speed and control, where everything came together. Four years later his side had lost that balance.

The 58 year old admitted the controversy around Mesut Özil's decision to meet the Turkish president prior to the tournament 'cost us a lot of power, and nerves, because it was always there. But it was not decisive in our World Cup exit.' On May 14th, Mesut Özil and Manchester City midfielder Ilkay Gündoğan met and posed for photos with Turkish President Recep Tayyip Erdoğan at a hotel in London. Both players brought shirts from their respective clubs. Gündoğan signed his with the words: 'With great respect for my president.' Shortly after the meeting, Erdoğan's party released the photos. At the time, Erdoğan was in the middle of an election campaign, one that he would unsurprisingly win given that he had dismantled many democratic rights in Turkey.

Germany's far-right-wing political party the Alternative for Germany (AfD) and their supporters targeted Özil on social media. Özil's decision not to say anything until more than two months after the photos were taken also didn't play well, especially as Gündoğan had quickly released a statement.

Özil was singled out by DFB President Reinhard Grindel and team manager Oliver Bierhoff, with the latter suggesting in an interview with *Welt* that Germany should have perhaps considered leaving him out of the squad.

Özil, born into a modest family in Gelsenkirchen, released a three-part statement on social media in English, wherein he launched a scathing attack on the DFB and Grindel, criticised the double standards of the German press, spoke about racism and explained his reasoning behind the photo with Erdoğan.

Özil, who wrote he had two hearts, 'one German and one Turkish', stated having the photo 'wasn't about politics or elections' but about 'respecting the highest office' of his family's country. Not to do so would have been 'disrespecting the roots of my ancestors.' The playmaker said he couldn't accept German media blaming his dual-heritage 'and a simple picture for a bad World Cup on behalf of an entire squad'.

When it came to Grindel, Özil wrote: 'In the eyes of Grindel and his supporters, I am German when we win, but I am an immigrant when we lose. This is because despite paying taxes in Germany, donating facilities to German schools and winning the World Cup with Germany in 2014, I am still not accepted into society. I am treated as being "different".'

In 2004, Grindel was a politician and said multiculturalism was 'a myth and a lifelong lie' – something Özil also reminded the DFB president of in his statements. Özil wrote that he knew Grindel wanted him out of the team, but both Joachim Löw and Oliver Bierhoff stuck up for him and backed him. At the end of the statement, Özil stated he would no longer be playing for the national team while he had the feeling of 'racism and disrespect.'

During the presentation of his analysis, Löw said he was disappointed by Özil's decision to retire immediately after the tournament without informing him personally. Instead, Özil's agent called Löw before the third part of the player's statement was released, an admittedly distant move by a player who once appeared to have a very close relationship to Löw.

Bierhoff said the team were complacent, and took fan support as a given. Although admitting he wanted to improve the connection to the fans in the future, Bierhoff rather bizarrely used the fact the players had cycled to training in their pre-tournament training camp in South Tyrol as an example of how close the team were to the fans.

One of the most eagerly anticipated presentations in German football history turned out to be not so much of a revelation. Germany had been too slow with the ball, too dangerous in their defensive approach and too expectant of success. All of this was apparent before Löw presented his analysis, so while he deserves credit for admitting his mistakes and having a desire to salvage the job, there is reason to worry about the future of Germany's national team. Having won the 2014 World Cup, their most costly mistake was to 'believe the processes of development was over.

Löw's desire to perfect his style of play exposed Germany. In pursuing his perfection it appears that Löw forgot to look elsewhere and truly consider what sort of football needed to be played to win a tournament. In his post-tournament analysis, Löw identified a need for more flexibility in tournaments than teams require in a long league season, citing Real Madrid as an example of success. It seems fair to ask though, why this wouldn't have been apparent to one of the world's best teams long before the tournament?

Stating that the lack of hunger was one reason is understandable. It's always harder for champions to maintain the desire to win. Four of the last five World Cup winners have been knocked out at the first-round stage of the following tournament: Germany 2018, Spain 2014, Italy 2010 and France 2002. With that in mind, it seems all the more baffling that Germany allowed such an environment to come to fruition.

A lack of hunger is an obvious issue, but for a team that went through far more ahead of and during the tournament, an explanation of the real atmosphere, even if wishful thinking, was still necessary. Instead, tired phrases such as 'a balance of youth and experience' were trotted out. Löw's way was not the right way, and the DFB's inability to recognise that or to react to it speaks volumes about the current structure.

'Mesut went too far in claiming racism,' Löw said. 'There were never any hints of racism or racist comments inside the team.' This is a baffling statement because Özil had never claimed there had been any racism in the team. Özil's issue lay with the racist abuse he had suffered from certain parts of German society, the DFB's inactivity in protecting him from that, and the racial prejudice he felt existed at higher levels of the DFB. In his statement, Özil wrote: 'people with racially discriminative backgrounds should not be allowed to work in the largest football federation in the world that has many players from dual-heritage families. Attitudes like theirs simply do not reflect the players they supposedly represent.' The DFB's inability to hear what is being said is as concerning as Özil's reason for leaving the national team.

Selecting three new young players for Germany's Nations League game against France in early September 2018, reducing the staff size and removing Assistant Head Coach Thomas Schneider were the first steps of Löw's attempt at resurrecting Germany. The questions remain though, and perhaps none is more pressing than whether Löw will be surrounded by enough football competence to do his job better.

Had he gone to the BDFL's congress in Dresden, Löw would have been in a room full of football competence. At the heart of the organisation is exchange and learning for top-level coaches. And in both 2017 in Bochum and 2018 in Dresden, there were endless examples of why this conference is important for the health of coaching in Germany.

After Chatzialexiou, Stefan Kuntz, head coach of Germany's U21s, and Guido Streichsbier, head coach of Germany's U19s, spoke. While both are employed by the DFB, being coaches made them appear less like company men. They were able to connect with the rest of the room in a different way, the unspoken bond of coaching perhaps making them more engaging. Both made interesting remarks on World Cup trends, revealing what their scouting teams had observed during their time in Russia. One thing stood out, mainly because it's one of the biggest topics in German football at the moment.

'We have to coach them so that if what we've coached doesn't work then they're free to play, and can find other solutions,' Kuntz said, a sentiment Streichsbier shared, saying players need to be flexible to play systems, 'not castrated'. What they said had echoes of the criticisms made by the likes of Mehmet Scholl, as discussed in Chapter Two, that many young players in Germany are so technically and tactically sound that playing outside of the constructs of a game plan appears problematic and sometimes when they do, the system can't handle it. Kuntz and Streichsbier's reminder of freedom inside a game is a timely one, and not just for German football.

Kuntz finished by telling the room that their task was not to be a *Besserwisser* (a know it all, or literally a 'better knower') but a

Bessermacher (someone who makes others better, or literally a 'better maker'). It's not always an easy task, but if you can make others better rather than just know more than others then you're more likely to be a better head coach. The sentiment of *Bessermacher* is applicable to anyone, but is obviously directed at coaches who attend the BDFL's three-day annual congress. This is an opportunity to learn how to be a better coach before putting it into practice.

In both Bochum in 2017 and Dresden a year later, old friends and colleagues caught up and exchanged their thoughts on what was happening in football at that moment, what had been said during the three days and how their own careers were going. Outside the main hall, the latest training equipment and technology was on offer: cameras, technology socks and kit that beeped and shone red and green. Inside, coaches took meticulous notes and endless photos of slides that might hold the key. Lectures were given on stress management, micro nutrition and the importance of cognitive training.

In Bochum, Frank Wormuth, who we met in Chapter Two, talked about chance creation, notably explaining that it is not about getting the ball to a more dangerous phase (closer to the goal) but how you end up there. The implementation of dynamism at the right moment is key, but all of it starts a lot sooner. 'The first touch is a chance,' Frank said.

In the practical sessions, coaches demonstrated drills such as attacking in the red zone, perception and decision making in transition, and how to build up play against a midfield press. Across three intense days, coaches laughed at strangers revealing truths they knew all too well and were reminded that the best form of leadership stems from learning.

In Dresden the focus was primarily on World Cup analysis, with Sammer the star of the show, but there was a great deal more on offer. Former Bundesliga goalkeeper Marc Ziegler evaluated the goalkeeping in Russia, Nigeria's head coach Gernot Rohr and former Cameroon head coach Volker Finke spoke about the tournament from the perspective of the African teams, and renowned German coach Christoph Daum talked about leadership in football. As is customary, Daum had a couple of standout moments. On the media, Daum said they were 'on the same water but not in the same boat' as head coaches, and that 'understanding the person helps us a lot more than data'.

That's not to say that having an overall theme limits the lectures to within that remit. After all, this is a coaching conference and the idea is for people to talk and learn. RB Leipzig's U19 sports psychologist Dr Nils Gatzmaga spoke about the influence of the sports psychologist on the team. His lecture made sound points about how player analysis extends into character reflection but, perhaps somewhat unsurprisingly for the club in question, it all felt a little robotic. Football is obviously a business, but not every human action can – or should – be analysed to see improvement. Gatzmaga explained how one of their methods had been to use the template of a player card from the video game *FIFA*. Along with physical and technical attributes, ratings for their schoolwork, teamwork and personality were also included on the player card. While this has clearly been done to engage with players from different generations, and player personality has become a crucial part of recruitment, rating a player's personality felt too clinical. There are undoubtedly methods used to find out what type of traits someone has and whether those fit the team, but perhaps there's an old-fashioned part of me that believes a lot more can be found out about a person through conversation than testing.

Professor Jan Mayer, sports psychologist at Hoffenheim, gave an intriguing lecture about mental quickness. Mayer has created a brain game room at the club where players come for 20 minutes to train how to think faster by playing games on tablets. All this technology has certainly aided the progress of head coach Julian Nagelsmann, but I asked Mayer afterwards what, from his perspective as a sports psychologist, set Nagelsmann apart? What he told me was remarkable attributes for anyone aged 31, let alone a 31-year-old head coach.

'He does things differently where even as a psychologist you're astounded and you just say, "Wow. Where did that come from?",' Mayer told me. 'He has really great antennae for how to treat his players and it's really important that you develop a feeling in certain situations. "What do I say to them now, and what do I perhaps not say?" I'm not sure if it's talent or a good sense but it's astonishing to observe how he does that.'

There was one lecture, and later demonstration, that absolutely blew me away. Professor Matthias Lochmann from the University of Erlangen-Nuremberg, who also has two PhDs, shook the room awake with strong words on why too few talented young players reach the elite level in Germany. Lochmann outlined, bluntly, how the entire competitive football structure for players aged 6 to 15 in Germany needed reorganising. Lochmann believes the embedding of the game intelligence approach in competitive structures would be a game changer with a disruptive character.

Lochmann feels that too many youngsters in the current system are not being trained properly and not getting enough playing time. They are stuck in fixed positions and have their decision making somewhat stolen from them by head coaches. Too many games are decided by lopsided scorelines, which demotivates the winning team and leaves the losing team feeling like losers.

Mehmet Scholl's comments about young players being able 'to fart 18 systems' rather than dribble were not eloquent, nor were they fully accurate, but one look at Lochmann's evidence raises some intriguing questions about the limitations of youth coaching in Germany and the effect it has had on the production of talent. It is in Lochmann's evidence that Borussia Dortmund's signing of Jadon Sancho makes even more sense. The teenage talent possesses all of the nifty skill and agility that is seen less and less in young German promises in recent years, which is a concern for Germany's youth development.

At one point in his presentation, Lochmann showed a clip of youth football in Germany, with children aged around eight or nine. He let the clip play and then proceed to explain, with genuine dismay, what was wrong. The pitch was too big, the team size was too big, the goals were too big, the games were too long, player positions were fixed, too few players touched the ball, there were lots of clearances. The list was long. Lochmann was passionately enraged by the situation. His words were blunt, but delivered in such a convincing manner that I was left feeling silly for not being part of this movement earlier.

After three years of testing, this approach stands very much on the edge of greatness. Lochmann believes that with continued growth, this system will lead to the world having more Lionel Messis than ever before. One of the ways game intelligence is embedded into the competitive structure is through a format called FUNiño. The original idea came from Horst Wein, who sadly passed away in 2016 aged 75. Wein was a former hockey player and coach who went on to become one of the great football minds and mentors. At the centre of Wein's life and work – he published over 30 books – was the development of game intelligence. And it was in that pursuit that Wein developed the concept of FUNiño (football designed for children), a concept that played a major part in Spanish football development in the early 1990s.

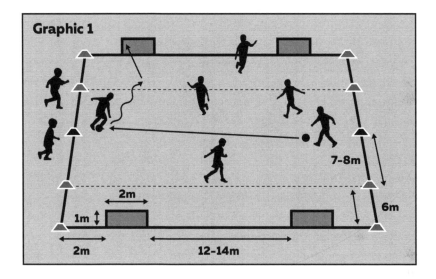

The format sees two teams of three try and attack and defend two 2 m × 1 m goals each, on a 32 m × 25 m pitch (see Graphic 1). Eight games should fit on one full-sized pitch. Each team has one substitute player and there are three balls waiting to be used on the side of the pitch for the restart. Players can only score inside an attacking area, and whenever someone does score the team's sub must replace a teammate. Games are played with a size three or four ball for players under 13 and usually with a standard size five ball for players aged 13 years and above.

With these small changes, the game is revolutionised. It's easier to understand, inclusive, and fun. It gives kids plenty of touches and more exposure to 1v1 or 2v1 situations, and makes them think more. With no offsides, corners or throw-ins, players are forced to decide whether to dribble or pass the ball back into play. It also gives kids at that age a greater chance of doing what they want to do most – score goals. And perhaps the best part is, once the initial explanation is given, the coach is virtually removed from the situation because the game itself becomes the teacher. It effectively hands back the four-phase model of perception, understanding, decision-making and execution to the children. In this model every player gets the chance to experience every phase, so that by the time they're 15 they can enter the 11v11 format with a far wider range of skills.

The game intelligence approach also allows for expansion, with different types of games possible – as Lochmann demonstrated in the training drills outside. The *Fußball-Lehrer* was as direct and provocative as he had been inside, but the game forced the young adults (it can also be adapted for other ages) to figure it out for themselves rather than him just telling them what to do. Even if his approach caused a stir, his passion for making the game more suitable for children was infectious.

Lochmann's key point was that it was time Germany stopped saying: 'We are all world champions.' This sense of unity after winning the 2014 World Cup was an overwhelming positive for the country, but the feeling lingered perhaps a little too long inside the system. Lochmann's approach recognises that. His argument is that it's not about whether Germany will win the World Cup, it's about how many 10 year olds the country can get fully involved and enjoying the game.

The graphic below (Graphic 2) shows how the size of a talent pool is reduced. The base of the pyramid is the potential pool of talent, but the red triangle in the middle is the real pool of talent. The five reasons shown in the graphic as to why the talent pool reduces in size are:

1 – NUMBERS HURDLE
   (In the usual U10s 7v7 format, you regularly need 12–14
   kids in training in order to play 7–10 of them on Saturday.
   If you can't overcome the hurdle of needing 14 kids,
   you can't train properly)
2 – NOT SELECTED (player doesn't play at all)
3 – ON THE BENCH (player gets far less playing time)
4 – FIXED POSITIONS (player is limited to one position)
5 – INSTRUCTION (player hardly ever dribbles with the ball)

Excitingly, if Wein's approach is followed then more youngsters are likely to be equipped with the skills needed to play at the next level, which in turn expands the talent pool and therefore the likelihood of talent arriving at the elite level.

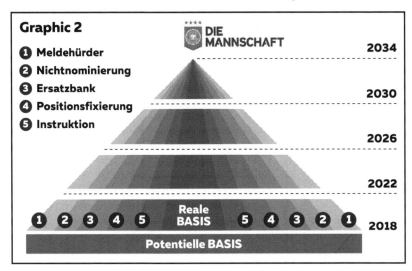

It is a system that is not only fairer to the kids, but also more supportive of the coaches. Lochmann believes coaches for this level of coaching should follow a 12-module matrix that matches games, analytical exercises and coaching ability with the four phases (perception, understanding, decision making and execution), thus making coaches specifically qualified talent developers.

'Every country that systematically implements this plan will have a massive increase in the efficiency of their talent development,' Lochmann wrote in an email to me after the conference as he was about to catch a flight to Guangzhou, China, to spread the word on the game intelligence approach. The revolution has just begun.

While the cloud of Germany's World Cup performance and Joachim Löw's absence hung over the ITK in Dresden, the congress the year before in Bochum was free of frustration and concern. Germany had just won the Confederations Cup and the European Under-21 Championship, and the BDFL were celebrating the sixtieth anniversary of the congress. German football was in a good place and everyone was keen to keep it that way, including Matthias Sammer.

In Bochum, Sammer talked about his 'factors for successful football', and in his opening question was asked about why German football was so strong at the time. His response, in the light of his comments in Dresden a year later, is telling: 'I think it was really important that the coaches could recognise the quality of their players and design the game plan around that. I think in that sense German football has found its identity again, that it has connected its quality with the right idea and mentality, and is perhaps even more unpredictable as a result.'

German football has lost some of its identity – and perhaps Matthias Sammer's absence is part of the reason. After all, Bayern Munich certainly missed him once he left, and some might argue they still do. In 2012, Sammer left the DFB to work as sporting director at Germany's record-title-winning club. Bayern had gone two seasons without a trophy, and had just lost the Champions League final in their own stadium on penalties to Chelsea. The following season – Sammer's first at the club – Bayern won the treble.

'Look at the example of the former Germany internationals Philipp Lahm and Bastian Schweinsteiger,' Sammer explained in Bochum, when asked how he got that last per cent out of players without them knowing. 'They belonged to the loser generation of 2012 because they lost in the semi-finals of a European Championship and lost the home Champions League final. I had the feeling that something was missing, but there wasn't much missing. Philipp, Bastian and Manuel Neuer were the three leaders in the club, and when you spoke to them you noticed they thought a little differently. So it was necessary to create a unity. If we implant a winning mentality into this team and we want to reach that last five per cent, then we first have to create an atmosphere of togetherness. We did that together with Jupp Heynckes. For me, that was two to three per cent that was relatively simple to extract. This unity was important and led us to the treble.'

At the heart of what makes Sammer an excellent coach is his understanding of what individuals and collectives need to be that little bit better than others. And that's why his time with Pep Guardiola at Bayern was so fascinating. Sammer believes the Spaniard enriched football with his use of game plans and organisation of possession football. Guardiola also gave German football the courage to be tactically flexible – either by setting up based on the opposition or by changing approach multiple times during the game. Beforehand, making such changes had been seen as a sign the head coach had got it wrong to begin with, and therefore hadn't done their homework.

There's no doubt football has both benefited from and enjoyed Guardiola's style of play, but the Spaniard's fanatical approach hasn't always made it easy for those on the inside. 'Pep was a perfectionist and unbelievably meticulous,' Sammer said. 'But I sometimes had the feeling I had to tell him that he was just the conductor. The orchestra is playing. And when it's playing, let it play freely. Sometimes he was the conductor and playing in the orchestra at the same time.'

The combination of Sammer's leadership and Guardiola's perfectionism made Bayern a force. Since his departure, Sammer's mentality and approach have been a noticeable absence – particularly at the start of the 2017–18 season when the noise around Bayern grew so loud it recalled the days when the nickname 'FC Hollywood' was commonly associated with the club. It was somewhat ironic that it took Heynckes, the man in charge before the Guardiola years, to restore a degree of calmness. Heynckes replaced Carlo Ancelotti and led Bayern to the Bundesliga title and the Champions League semi-finals. After his departure, it appears Heynckes might have taken some of that calmness with him. With a new head coach in Niko Kovač, and Hasan Salihamidžić in Sammer's old job, Bayern's dugout leadership faces another test.

Intriguingly, Sammer said in Bochum that the role of the sporting director, the one he made his own at both domestic and national level, needs more defining. It's a position that, according to Sammer, is 'not often filled with top people'.

'The clubs have to decide for themselves how they see the role of the sporting director,' said Sammer. 'Perhaps they see him more as a squad planner or maybe as someone responsible for management duties. If he wants to support the head coach and understand the entire system of football then he should have learnt it. In the best case, he too was a head coach, so he can communicate on the same level as the coach. And in the absolutely best case, he also has such strong people skills, which I think is very important, that he can be a mentor for the head coach and the head coach can trust him.'

History shows that the role doesn't have to be filled by a former head coach to be done well. Christian Heidel was the other part of both Jürgen Klopp and Thomas Tuchel's success at Mainz – and played such a large role that Schalke 04 recruited him to rebuild the Gelsenkirchen club. His decision to appoint Klopp in the middle of a relegation battle even though Klopp was still a player at the time and had never coached a team before was more than bold. At Schalke, after paying for Augsburg head coach Markus Weinzierl, Heidel recognised it wasn't working and appointed the inexperienced Domenico Tedesco. That decision looks to be paying off. Schalke finished the 2017–18 season in second place in the Bundesliga, and will return to the Champions League with a number of pairs of eyes on them.

In England, clubs tend to appoint a manager instead of employing the head coach–sporting director model. This means one man is effectively expected to do both jobs. At Arsenal, Arsene Wenger did that, but when Unai Emery was appointed as his successor he was named the head coach. This suggests a change in structure at the club, and is certainly different from normal procedure at most English clubs.

The sporting director is the link between the head coach and the chairman. They are one half of a successful (or unsuccessful) dugout team and they play a big role in the development of a club's philosophy. They are also another point of contact for players. Their role is not to be underestimated, and in his role as an expert on Eurosport, Sammer questioned whether the current structure in German football was the right one. 'I'm not talking about management, marketing or merchandising, or transfers,' he said. 'I'm talking about pure sporting judgement and evaluation ... If I'm responsible for a head coach but have never been one myself, how can I get into the mindset of what they're thinking?'

'They [the sporting director] have to stand by the head coach's side in various situations, in terms of content, but also personally, loyally and as a trustworthy partner. And they also have to offer help in certain moments – not jump into the head coach's role – but act as a stable support, to recognise certain mistakes in practice ... The content of this position of sporting responsibility has to be better defined, and who has the quality for it?'

It's a fair question. Before we even ask whether people in leadership positions have the right amount of quality, we have to look at what the job description is. What are you here to do and is it helping the club get better? In football, as in business, far too many positions are filled because of connections or availability, without true consideration for whether the appointee will benefit the overall performance or output of the collective. Without true understanding of the role, finding the right people becomes impossible.

The sporting director is one of those roles. If they really are there to add support to and form a strong bond with a head coach, then why is it so few leave when a head coach gets sacked? If they aren't a support, then the potential for a rift in the team is enormous, particularly when it comes to transfers or player management.

While not always an easy character, Sammer's fierceness comes from his desire to win. 'I'm fed up when others are more successful than us,' Sammer said in Dresden, and Borussia Dortmund will have been hoping they would benefit from that desire in the 2018–19 season, with Sammer returning to the club in an advisory role.

• • •

Balance is what most people spend their lives pursuing. Often it remains elusive, and the cost of not getting it right can be devastating. Football doesn't appear to have found that balance with its finances. Sir Alex Ferguson said it best when he gave an in-depth interview to the BBC in 2011. 'When you shake hands with the devil you have to pay the price. Television is God at the moment.' The role of money has affected even the assessment of balance in football. For everyone involved in the game, particularly head coaches, the balancing act starts and stops with health.

One of the speakers at Bochum was Prof Dr Michael Kellmann. He talked about burnout in football and how lingering stress and a lack of rest (logically) increased the likelihood of exhaustion. So for all the 'extraordinary' efforts made by sports coaches across the world to get up at four in the morning and come in and study films, the combination of this with managing a large group of different athletes over an extended period of time is a detriment to not only to the quality of the work but also the human mind and body.

Kellmann displayed results from his work measuring stress levels in football. His findings were twofold: February to May is a critical time for coaches to manage their stress levels, and both the winter and summer breaks are pivotal periods for recovery. In the summer, a genuine break that doesn't include pre-season planning is important. Preparation and retention of one's own physical fitness was also a key part of avoiding burnout. Which begs the question: is the amount of pressure and expectation on coaches so great they don't have enough time to look after themselves? In short, it is no bad thing to be an ambitious head coach, but only as long as you know how to recover. If you don't, then not only will your health be in danger, but so will the health of your team.

Creating and maintaining an optimal relationship with your players sounds straightforward, but there were still many coaches making notes and recording during Prof Dr Ralf Lanwehr's lecture on managing team atmosphere. Lanwehr's focus was on taking away the negatives and replacing them with positives. Take away a player's fear of failure and replace it with hope for success. Coaches have a responsibility to question their interactions with their players – assuming authority comes with the role is a mistake. Each player is a different character and requires a different approach: Take the focus off the errors of others and focus on your positives.

Far too often the opposite is the case in the media: 'X made an error', rather than 'Y played well', but the impacts of this are just as severe in coaching. The positives needn't be said too often, but they also mustn't be completely forgotten. The smallest of compliments after a neat piece of play that cost a lot of effort but might not have ended optimally could make all the difference. Squad management is part of the challenge of creating a positive team atmosphere, and players on the bench who have trained well will need to know why they're not playing. Involving them in constructive feedback is one way to give them the feeling they're in control. Don't just tell them what they did wrong, give them the chance to correct themselves.

Lanwehr also talked about the loss of energy from lowering expectations and improving players' understanding of the reality of a situation. If it's clear from the start what you want from them and where they think they are (in terms of quality and squad role) then you don't have to 'waste' energy bringing the player closer to the reality you, as a coach, see.

Perhaps most intriguingly, Lanwehr believes charisma is not something one is born with, a personal brand, but can be developed. Coaches can learn how to take risks, and recognising the importance of not simply presenting themselves in the role of head coach is something they can practice. All of this helps create a positive team atmosphere, and Jürgen Klopp is perhaps the best example of that.

A small part of what makes Klopp such an engaging character for many in England is his command of the English language. Obviously, it isn't perfect, but it is perfect for him. It makes him more *sympathisch* (likeable). Marius Happe from ad agency *Jung von Matt* spoke in Bochum about modern communication methods and how managing them, among other things, can be a way of protecting and strengthening a coach's position in the face of pressure. Building a brand has perhaps never been as important for a head coach as it is today.

At the time of the conference (July 2017), there were 890 *FLs* (*Fußball-Lehrer*) in Germany but just 56 jobs in the top three leagues. Happe's stats showed that on average a Bundesliga coach spent just 1.2 years at a club – a number that sounds like it would be more at home in the Premier League than in Germany. Whichever way you look at it, the competition is fierce, and it clearly extends far beyond the borders of football knowledge.

To be a head coach today, Happe believes you have to be the face of the club, your own brand ambassador, an innovator, tactically shrewd, a leader of players, and that you need to understand the fans, social responsibility and follow sponsorship obligations. Yet despite all of this, coaches continue to be judged by points and table position. The expectations are multidimensional. Perspective, knowledge, network, vision, and structure – how can one person possibly fulfil all these criteria in the modern game?

Part of understanding that is putting yourself in the right position to be successful. If you know your personality and how it differs from others, know what kind of football you want to play and how you want to lead, and recognise to what your abilities are best suited, then you have a far better chance of not only creating a brand that could help you as a head coach but also of getting the right job. Hannover's sporting director Horst Heldt said that he looked at how a head coach handled himself as being one of the key attributes.

The concept of 'creating a brand' sounds like it would be more at home in an Instagram tutorial, but consider the competition most people face just to get an interview. It's just as tough for a football head coach. You have to be memorable. Naturally, it's hard to have a brand without a successful end product (in football's case, results), but focusing on the processes that lead to the results rather than just the results themselves can not only be far more rewarding but also makes far more sense. Just like chance creation, it's not always about getting into the right position, but sometimes how you got there.

Happe cited the great example of Roger Schmidt, who was sacked by Bayer Leverkusen, and posed the question: 'Would he have been fired had he not said his side took a step in the right direction after a 6–2 defeat to Borussia Dortmund?' The media spotlight on Schmidt was higher at that moment than when he arrived, argued Happe. What you say and when you say it says a lot about you, and that matters in a job constantly in the public eye.

In fact, everything you do as a person says something about you, even if you don't say anything at all. Your lifestyle choices, the music you listen to, the clothes you wear. The same is true of a head coach, as Happe discussed during his presentation. Jürgen Klopp makes himself famous for his 'one-of-the-lads'-like appearance with his tracksuit. His glasses add a level of style and imply intellect, while his beard shows he isn't overly formal. Along with his charismatic personality and visible gesticulations of passion, Klopp's brand reflects his personality, and plays a role in his success. Pep Guardiola, in contrast, is more often smart-casual. The Spaniard is immaculately dressed, with shirts and trousers tailored as tightly as his style of play. He too is passionate, but in a more furious way than Klopp. It's symbolic of his need to convey as much information as possible in the smallest window of time available.

The role of the media has played and will always play an important role in the presentation of a coach. Before, the only media exposure head coaches used to get was at press conferences before and after the game, with the occasional interview. Now with an exhausting number of sponsorship commitments and media appearances, coaches are everywhere, and that's without even factoring in social media.

Interestingly, Happe's research found that most head coaches continue to communicate with classical media (newspapers, magazines, etc.) and tend to stay away from social media, a place which, to many, is full of pitfalls and easy-to-type hatred. In truth though, as Happe points out, using social media actually gives head coaches more chance to speak the truth rather than leave it up to journalistic subjectivity. You can't control how television or newspapers mould the story. On social media you can.

Thomas Tuchel joined Twitter on the day of his dismissal as Borussia Dortmund head coach, and his first tweet was about the account supplying 'first-hand information.' Embracing the new technology rather than fearing it can leave head coaches in a strong position, if handled correctly. Then again, Jürgen Klopp told ESPN in an interview in the summer of 2018: 'I think my smartest decision in life was not to use social media', and it would be fair to say Klopp's career has worked out just fine without it so far.

• • •

With the arrival of this young-head-coach trend, there is a fear that older coaches will be left on the shelf. The likes of Thomas Schaaf (57), Mirko Slomka (51) and Armin Veh (58) have all made regular media appearances in the absence of dugout opportunities. Veh has since returned to football, having been appointed Köln's sporting director in December 2017, as has Schaaf, who was appointed technical director at Werder Bremen in July 2018. But both appointments perhaps show the beginning of a trend, where the experience of a slightly older head coach is preferred in a different position at the club.

Slomka attended the ITK in Bochum, but after failing to convince at second-division Karlsruher SC he was out of a job after just 10 games. Since his success at Hannover between 2010 and 2013, he hasn't taken the chances that have come his way. As Frank Wormuth said in Chapter Two, 'The door is open to everyone, but you have to get in, and once you're in, you have to be good.' It's not the presence of younger coaches that is making life harder for older coaches, but rather the smaller window within which they have to deliver.

Horst Hrubesch has been more than good at almost every stage of his career. One of Germany's legendary players, Hrubesch won three German titles and a European Cup with Hamburg, and also lifted the 1980 European Championship with Germany. In the 1990s, he was a head coach in Austria and Germany, but around the turn of the millennium Hrubesch found his calling: youth football. Since then, he has spent time as head coach of Germany's U18, U19, U20 and U21 teams. In the summer of 2016, he guided Germany's Olympic team to silver. From January 2017, Hrubesch took over the Germany sporting director role aged 66, and in 2018, he was interim head coach of Germany's women's team, guiding them to 2019 World Cup qualification.

Hermann Gerland is a man of equally legendary status in German football history. Gerland was a fiery central defender for Bochum and played most of his career under Heinz Höher (the subject of the excellent book *Matchdays: The Hidden Story of the Bundesliga* by Ronald Reng). Gerland was Bochum head coach in the late 1980s, and spent time scattered around the country at various clubs before settling at Bayern Munich, where he coached the second team for about ten years before moving into the first-team dugout as assistant head coach. From July 2017, he was given the responsibility for Bayern Munich's new youth academy in the hope of unearthing and nurturing Bayern's next star. By the start of October though, Bayern Munich had appointed Jupp Heynckes again and Gerland was back in the dugout as assistant head coach. At the start of the 2018–19 season, Gerland had returned to the academy in search of the next great talent. In all that time, Gerland hasn't lost his *Ruhrpott* (Ruhr area) personality.

Along with Sammer and Ralf Rangnick, Hrubesch and Gerland were the star attractions at the ITK in Bochum, the latter pair perhaps even more so given their local history. At the heart of their conversation was how they have dealt with young players in the modern era, a different one to the one they played in all those years ago. 'Back in our day, the older lads always led the younger ones,' Hrubesch said. 'It's been that way my whole life. Even in my career as a head coach I've gone to the young players and taken them with me. They've paid me back and that was important to me. Honesty develops through trust, and if the lads pay that back then you'll be successful.'

'I have to say that I train the elite, the best players we have,' he added, 'There are a few rascals, but they're no different to us. They have the same goals and want to reach the top. They want to earn money and play in the Bundesliga. If you take the lads with you and give them the opportunity to take responsibility, you support them and forgive them their mistakes, then you end up where you want to be.' He continued by saying that in all that time he never felt football had stopped being his world.

'If I was of the opinion that Philipp Lahm would be a Bundesliga player, then I fought for those people,' Gerland said. 'I helped people. Bastian Schweinsteiger was mischievous at times, and that led to meetings that I sat in on. We stood there and said, "Basti is staying with us". We didn't run through the village with the prayer book back in our day. I also often did stupid things as a young man, and I remembered that. I gave the lads a talking to. You have to talk about these things and tell them they can't do such things.'

Gerland was tough with his players, but that line of communication was always open. It was always clear what was expected and what was happening, which is particularly important for youth players. Gerland's focus on the individual also had its advantages at youth level. 'At the academy level, the individual is important. The development of the individual is of greater value than the success of the team,' Gerland said in Bochum.

It was the combination of individual development and Gerland's capacity to fight for players that gave Thomas Müller the chance to rise. Müller scored goals in the third division for Bayern's second team – that's why he wasn't sold. At the time, Mario Gomez had just been bought and Luca Toni was the club's leading striker, but Gerland fought for Müller, and he played and scored. Hoffenheim, coached by Rangnick at the time, were interested in signing Müller but Gerland forced Bayern to push Müller's buyout clause up, and so Hoffenheim decided against it. Belief can change a life.

Gerland also fought for players that might not have been good enough for Bayern, but were good enough for other teams. He would call other teams and push for those kids to have a chance.

Once, on a trip in Berlin, during breakfast, Gerland went off to watch Tennis Borussia Berlin's U17s. He saw a young striker look sharp and invited him to a trial at Bayern's academy. When he asked for the scouting report, he was told 'nothing special', and so the striker didn't sign for Bayern. In the summer of 2017, Maximilian Philipp signed for Borussia Dortmund for €20m. Market prices aside, Gerland saw it as proof that he was right, that he could see things others could not.

Arriving at the congress with their A Licence or *Fußball-Lehrer*, coaches are given lots of engaging and informative material, as well as the chance to chat to coaching colleagues. Maybe it changes a coach's approach to training, maybe it changes the tone a coach takes with a player, maybe it changes nothing, but there's no denying the ITK gives coaches the chance to be better.

Key Lesson

One of the best traits anyone, let alone a head coach, can have is the ability to appreciate the perspective of others. Of course you won't always agree with them, but taking the time to try to understand them says a lot about a person. For a leader, it's imperative.

Once a year in a different city in Germany, a big group of coaches at or near the top get the chance to see, from one another, external speakers and some of the greatest minds in the game of football from a different perspective. It is perhaps the best way to develop a mature mind.

Vorsprung
(Edge)

---

*'It's a good life choice to see different
players from different countries.'*

– Lily Agg

In *The Will To Power*, the German philosopher Friedrich Nietzsche wrote about self-improvement and how suffering can lead to fulfilment. Nietzsche argued that we cannot realise the best version of ourselves or pursue the attainment of it until we have endured challenges. Only in time out of our comfort zone can we realise the truth about ourselves.

This is true in almost all walks of life, whether it be a profession or not. Teachers who live and work abroad, doctors who help outside of the world they learnt in, students who dare to change their location during the most confusing time of their lives – there is much growth to be found in change.

The same is true in football. But I wanted to know what it felt like to be coached in different countries, and what it felt like to coach in the women's game, where support is sadly hard to find. I wanted to find out whether adversity did create an edge. To do so I spoke to a German defender who joined an English club, an English striker who spent a season at one of the most successful clubs in the world and a coach who has overcome all the odds. All of them spoke about the changes they've been through and what they've learnt along the way, and it reminded me that it is often enduring rather than just enjoying that can give you an edge.

Perched amid fields of green, the dark stone of Lancing College looked more becoming of a world where gods and kings planned great battles than a boarding school in the south of England. As the train rolled on, the stone began to diminish in size, fading into the background behind a brighter, more modern structure. From the train it looks like a NASA facility without the spaceships, and once you find your way through the lanes you stumble across one of the most impressive training grounds in England. Brighton and Hove Albion have certainly come a long way.

It's January 2017. Brighton were looking to push on in the 2016–17 Championship season. I was waiting to meet German defender Uwe Hünemeier. The 31 year old had come through the ranks at Borussia Dortmund and played under Jürgen Klopp before leaving to join Energie Cottbus. From there he moved to SC Paderborn 07, where he played Bundesliga football in the 2013–14 season under André Breitenreiter (who would go on to coach Schalke and Hannover).

If you want the truth about quality coaching then it's best to ask those who have received it. Most pupils who love a particular subject will more often than not say it's because of the teacher, and football players are no different. There are many motivations for someone to work for a company, play for a team and be part of something bigger than themselves, but often the most powerful force is the charisma of the boss. The first steps towards creating a legacy start with a leader. The head coach is that leader, and their decisions affect both the player and the person. Hünemeier has experienced the impact of those decisions throughout his career – and it started with Jürgen Klopp.

'I only have positive things to say about Klopp,' Hünemeier tells me when we meet. 'He came around 2008. When he arrived, I was in the second team and after half a year, I was in the first team. I worked for him for a year and a half I think. I was around 21, 22, and on the verge of first-team football. I developed hugely, but it came to the point where he said to me, "You're too good to sit on the bench here. I would say now is the time to make a move." I knew the competition was too great, with Neven Subotić, Mats Hummels and Felipe Santana. I was fourth choice and couldn't find a way past them. He was always open and honest with me. "You're a good player, I'm happy that you're here but you'll develop more if you go somewhere else," he told me. I thought that was honest, and he asked again in the summer how things were looking and whether I had found a new club. I thought that was fantastic of him. It could have also been irrelevant to him to see what the players leaving the club were doing. He offered his help about talking to clubs. I thought it was notable. I was lucky to train under him. He was open and charismatic.' It's clear that many players in the game today love the kind of outward passion that Klopp displays. One look at Liverpool's celebrations during their Champions League run in the 2017–18 season are evidence of that. 'He gives every player the feeling that he is one of them. Lots of players see that emotion. It's what makes him Jürgen Klopp,' Hünemeier tells me.

Decisions impacted the defender again at Paderborn, as the head coach who signed him had been sacked by the time he arrived at the club. Nevertheless, Hünemeier quickly found his feet with new head coach Breitenreiter, and his words on their time together certainly shed some light on the coach who went on to struggle under the Schalke spotlight, before enjoying highs and lows at Hannover.

'He made it clear from the start that I was his player, his leader,' Hünemeier tells me. 'He gave me the feeling that I always had his support, regardless of what happened. I wasn't an easy player in training. I was always about winning and improvement. I wasn't easy for others, and there were a few exchanges with the head coach, but it was always about the task at hand. I always wanted the maximum. I took a huge step forwards with André Breitenreiter. The support he gave me in those two years and that I paid back with my performances moulded me. I still have a good relationship with him. He has been to visit me in Brighton. I was happy to have played under him because he's a good head coach – an honest one too, with great training ideas,' Hünemeier says.

Has one coach stood out so far in Hünemeier's career? 'Klopp is charismatic, Breitenreiter lived for football and of course Chris Hughton is different. He's quiet, but he's still a great person who you can talk with about anything. I think he's a great head coach and a lot of the English lads in the squad have said he's one of the best managers they've ever worked under,' Hünemeier said, delivering an assessment of a man who I haven't read a bad word about.

I was curious to know what differences Hünemeier had encountered when it came to the game since he had joined Brighton. Was there even a noticeable difference between playing in England and playing in Germany?

'Training intensity is a topic,' Hünemeier says. 'I think the English lads know they have it relatively good here, in terms of pre-season. I think more is done in Germany to make training intense,' he continues, with a knowing smile.

'David Wagner's arrival in Huddersfield has certainly got fitness coaches asking what the training there is like. We had a player who was on loan there last season and he told us that the training intensity was noticeably higher,' adds the defender.

'Sadly, I missed pre-season this year due to injury, but from what I hear it was hardly a pre-season that killed someone,' he says with a chuckle. 'It wasn't as tough as I know it from Germany. Pre-season in Germany is much harder. To train twice a day during the season would have some players rolling their eyes here. We talk about things like that, about the winter break and what it's like. One or two of the lads here would certainly want one. There's a lot of tradition though, Boxing Day and all that. It won't change quickly.'

From the 2019–20 season onwards, English teams appear set to be given a 10-day break from competitive games in January and February. This might not be a full winter break, but it is a start. Tradition won't be lost, and players will get some form of pause during an otherwise hectic time of year.

'There are differences between Germany and England,' Hünemeier tells me. 'What's better? Well, the German teams are fit and that's well known. Football in Germany is very physical, quick. It is that here too, but it's different. In Germany, the players are at peak fitness on the first day of the season. Here, I don't think everyone is at their level in the first three or four games, and so they get there through the games.'

While the Premier League is another level from the Championship, the starting fitness levels that Hünemeier mentions are intriguing. Is there less focus on preparation in England, and are German coaches changing that?

'There are no afternoon sessions. I think that's the case at most clubs in England,' Hünemeier tells me, adding that he has heard then-Huddersfield Town head coach David Wagner has changed things and brought in a more German style of training. 'I don't know how Jürgen Klopp does it at Liverpool. I think he too has made training more German. We hardly ever, never really, have double morning and afternoon sessions. If so then it's a muscle session after lunch.'

Liverpool's head of medical services, Andy Massey, told the *Liverpool Echo* about Jürgen Klopp's training intensity: 'Jürgen's philosophy is very much that we've got to run further, run faster, run quicker than every other team because if we can do that then the skill will take over.'

With a greater number of games in England, training has to be organised accordingly. Wagner's approach clearly didn't hinder Huddersfield – they won promotion to the Premier League at the end of the 2016–17 season – but with Brighton also winning promotion, it seems the lack of a German approach didn't hinder Hughton.

The increase in intensity in German training is partly because the fitness demands in German football have grown dramatically in recent years (largely due to the rise in pressing), but also because if the players are fitter and stronger than anyone else they are more likely to be able to perform in the key moments. One look at the way Klopp's Liverpool side played during their European run in the 2017–18 season was an example of how explosive a difference that next-level fitness can make. There are also individual examples though.

Towards the end of the 2017–18 season, Brighton's Pascal Groß scored the winner at home against Manchester United to secure the club Premier League football for another season. Groß had proved himself one of the signings of the season, not just at Brighton but also in the Premier League. Towards the end of 2017, I interviewed the midfielder for *11 Freunde* (one of Germany's biggest football magazines). Whenever Groß talked about his attacking talents he always mentioned his defensive qualities in the same breath. When another journalist asked Groß about where he got his energy, the midfielder smiled. 'I train hard,' was his response – a German trait if ever there was one in a footballer.

Uwe Hünemeier is no different. For the German defender, England's Championship proved more of a battle than he was used to. 'During international breaks, we don't work on our fitness like in Germany. In England, the break is seen as a break because you don't have a winter break and then when you have three to four days off, it's a chance to clear your head,' Hünemeier says.

'These are huge differences, but it's to do with the fact you have 46 league games here, plus the cup games which leaves you at 50, 55 games at the end of the season. That's a big difference. The training intensity is definitely lower because of the number of games. If you have a double-game week here, you can't have intensive sessions. It's final session, game, recovery, final session, game, recovery. For those who are playing, sessions between games are just a chance to sweat again. Even during weeks with no mid-week games the intensity is of course harder at the start of the week, but it's definitely lower than in Germany,' Hünemeier tells me.

Head coaches are different, as are their surroundings, but had Hünemeier been surprised by anything in England having grown up in the German system? 'Every head coach has their own style. One focuses on the opposition and what tactically awaits them, the other is more interested in their own strengths and isn't too worried about the opposition. It's hard to compare. The quality is high here and the exercises are similar to Germany – lots of small-pitch tournaments, full-pitch games, shooting drills. It's much the same. But in England there is more focus on muscle training, on injury prevention. Leg strengthening is of great importance. That was different for me. During my medical, I had to lift weights so they could see my strengths. In Germany, of course muscle work is done, but this is a little different. The clubs where I was, more was left to the individual. There was a muscle session every week, but more upper body, back, buttocks here,' Hünemeier says. More muscle here, more stamina there. They're the fine margins that make the difference right when it matters, and the head coach has to be aware of those developments, and be sure to have their staff look after players without overwhelming them.

'Training analysis has grown massively,' Hünemeier tells me. 'Every metre is followed. You're regularly checked to see if you're in top condition. I see that here with daily screening to check you've drunk enough. We do muscle work, stretching. It has become more complex. Nothing has been left to chance. Back when I started playing in the early 2000s, it was boots on and out you go, and that was it. It was relatively easy. There were no GPS systems or body-fat measurements. There were head coaches who weighed their players daily. I think Felix Magath was the type for it, but it was relatively easy when I started. It obviously got tougher and tougher. Then, you had lactate tests at the start of the season; now, that's something checked every single day.

You see how many metres you ran in training and during the week, and then at the end of the week, maybe you need to do some extra work to reach your weekly limit. Every player is roughly on the same level, which isn't easy if you don't play. The games are what matter because you pick up fitness that you just can't get in training. You try and compensate for that with extra training sessions and exercises,' Hünemeier tells me.

Every head coach wants to be successful, and part of achieving that extends well beyond the tactical approach the team should employ on a Saturday. It's navigating the complexity of different human beings and understanding what's best for them and the team. 'I was lucky to work with great head coaches: Bert van Marwijk, Jürgen Klopp and André Breitenreiter, and now here with Chris Hughton,' Hünemeier says. 'I think it's important the head coach is honest and always has an open ear for his players to keep communication open and get feedback. You don't always need it. If I don't play, I don't go to the head coach and say, "Why am I not playing?" I'm old enough to know. But to know you're training well even if you're not playing, that's important,' Hünemeier adds.

Undoubtedly there are differences in coaching styles between countries – the same is true inside one country, but to hear Hünemeier talk about different training methods and intensity sheds some light on the level of adjustment that players leaving Germany for England often have to make.

Players and coaches often see the Premier League as the ultimate challenge, but what about those who leave English football for the continent? Reece Oxford joined Borussia Mönchengladbach on loan from West Ham United for the 2017–18 season, and returned to the Bundesliga in January 2019 when he joined FC Augsburg on loan. Mandela Egbo, Oxford's former teammate in Germany, has also broken through into Gladbach's first team in 2018. In doing so, the former Crystal Palace youth player became the sixth Englishman to make his debut in the Bundesliga in the 2017–18 season.

Egbo spoke frankly about progression and what the move to Germany has done for him in an interview with *The Set Pieces*. The youngster said that 'coming to understand the German mindset' of 'every little thing not being as little as you think it is' allowed him to develop. Once again, it's also evidence of the ethos that even the small steps are an important part of the path to success, which Frank Wormuth talked about in Chapter Two.

It hasn't always been that way in German football though. Germany once believed, much as England did for a long time, that leadership and fight would be enough to see them through. At the 2002 World Cup, three leading players, a favourable draw and plenty of fight saw Germany make the final, but that wasn't enough to cover up the dire performance at the 2000 European Championships two years earlier. Germany realised fight wasn't going to be enough. Fourteen years later, Germany showed what deep-rooted change could do. Now, many of Germany's players have the right combination of skill and strength. As Egbo told *The Set Pieces*: 'Everybody here is technically secure and sound at what they're doing, [whereas in England] you can get out of being not so technically clean with pace and strength.'

Long has English sport suffered under the belief that the 'good old English spirit' would be enough. Grit and determination – they were the intangibles that would lead England to glory. As many teams in many competitions over the years have shown, though, it takes far more to win it all. The England men's rugby union team demonstrated that innovative thinking, the ability to perform under pressure, a strong philosophy developed over years and good players were integral reasons behind their victory at the 2003 World Cup in Australia. Recent success at international youth level leaves English football with the chance to forge ahead. Now is the time to nurture the current crop of young players. English football has arrived at its moment for change. They can ill afford to pass it up.

In Germany, youngsters are already getting that chance – and that's part of the reason that more and more young English players are joining Bundesliga teams. Jadon Sancho turned down the chance to be a part of Pep Guardiola's Manchester City in favour of a bigger role at Borussia Dortmund. The 17 year old's decision to choose regular game time over a Premier League winner's medal for a handful of minutes already appears more than justified. Sancho has since burst into life, assisting goals, dancing away from defenders and exciting with his skill and flair. English football hadn't seen anything like it from an Englishman in far too many years, and it earned him a place in the senior England squad.

There's a fair opportunity for young players to learn and grow in Germany. The spotlight is there, but unrealistic expectation is notably well managed. Gladbach's offering of opportunities to talented young English footballers continued into the summer of 2018, when they announced the signing of Tottenham Hotspur's talented 19-year-old winger Keanan Bennetts. Interestingly enough, Bennetts was born in London but grew up speaking German because his mother was born in Hamburg.

Danny Collinge, 20, moved to Stuttgart as a 16 year old instead of accepting a two-year scholarship from MK Dons because he wouldn't have been able to continue his studies at the English club. Collinge has since progressed through Stuttgart's youth system and now plays in their reserve team. In an interview with *BBC Sport*, the centre back revealed he wanted to keep studying because it was important to him and because he was thinking about life beyond football. 'In England that opportunity wasn't there for me, but in Germany I was given the opportunity to go to an international school and study for an International Baccalaureate.'

Collinge's situation is frustrating to hear about – a youngster shouldn't be forced to choose between his football development and his studies. Yet it led Collinge to make the move abroad, a decision that has clearly enriched him. 'I think a move abroad is difficult but it's so rewarding.'

Looking beyond your own borders is so often an enriching decision. Learning new cultures and routines, and meeting new people has a huge impact on someone's character, and that can then extend into the performance and growth of an athlete. I caught up with a 23 year old who had left England in September 2017 to join one of the most successful teams in Europe.

Lily Agg left Bristol City in the FA Women's Super League (WSL) to join four-time Champions League and seven-time German champions 1. FFC Frankfurt. The striker made a bold move, one away from a comfort zone. A new country, language and culture are certainly a test, but Agg is positive about the impact the move has made on her career and her life. 'I'm glad I've done it,' Agg tells me after her German lesson and before her afternoon training session. 'It's already benefited me as a person, not just on the football pitch. It's a good life choice to see different players from different countries.'

Agg played in Arsenal's youth teams before going on to feature for Brighton and Bristol City. Moving from one of the weaker WSL sides to one of the best teams in another country meant she had to adapt. She tells me that at Frankfurt there are a lot more small-sided games and passing drills, but not as much attacking work as she is used to.

While the head coach's preference and team strength play a role, differences in training and coaching are noteworthy because they can, and often do, represent the style of play in a country. 'We're expected to win most of the games, and we go into it preparing how we would and the other team almost has to plan to stop us,' Agg says of Frankfurt's approach to games.

Clearly the role of favourite changes the mental approach of coaching, but can winning really be coached? It would certainly explain why Germany have had such a successful women's team over the years. 'The attitude in the team, and maybe it is the German way, is that expectation to win,' Agg says. 'The fans get behind you and they expect. And people on the streets even. Frankfurt is in the paper, the women's team, and that's the main news,' Agg says with a smile before going on to tell me an inspiring story.

'I had my German class earlier and an American woman asked what we did, and I said, "Me and Kumi Yokoyama play football." The woman said that was awesome and that she would bring her daughters down to watch us. It's a different outlook, whereas sometimes in England it's still kind of behind I think, although it's getting better,' Agg tells me.

The enormous amount of respect the women's game receives in Germany boosts development. If a player feels more professional, then they're logically more likely to stand a better chance of developing. More than that though, it's a reminder of how important it is for the world to give women the chance to not just feel more professional but also *be* more professional.

In German football, doing something right also tends to mean being smart, and that is the idea that Agg explains when I ask about the biggest difference between playing in Germany and in England.

'I think German football is a lot smarter,' Agg tells me. 'In England, I'm used to everything being 100 miles per hour, turnover possession, as soon as you get it you want to attack. In Germany, I feel like teams set up smarter, whether they sit off or go to press. The build-up play

I've learnt at Frankfurt is that we build from the back a lot more.'

Granted, every player has a different experience at a club, but it is interesting to hear an ambitious 23 year old talk about the differences during a key stage of her development. 'There was a stat to do with the Euros. Something like 60 players from the Euros were from the German league, and it was the highest of all leagues,' Agg says, hinting at the obvious benefits of a move to Germany.

Twenty of the German players at the UEFA Women's Euro 2017 played in Germany, as did a further 39 players at the tournament. By comparison 42 of the players at the tournament played for English clubs – half playing for England and the other half playing for other countries. Both leagues have their merits and quality, but clearly there's a draw to playing in Germany, and Agg is an example of someone who believes that.

The personal and professional development that can occur by playing in a different league can result in huge strides forwards. Some of Agg's former teammates have called, asking her what's different and what the move was like. There is a certain level of intrigue about stepping outside of her comfort zone, and perhaps because a move to Germany is less about risk and more about reward. 'It's your ship to sink if you like,' Agg says. 'You have to make the most of it.'

Footballer or not, the decision to be part of a club, of a collective, is a pivotal part of development. As Julian Nagelsmann said on a *Bild* podcast: 'Life in a club, regardless of whether in football or somewhere else, is important for development, whether a sporting career is the result or not. You learn values and how to behave in a group, which shapes and adds to your life.'

However hard the journey, the personal and professional development Agg experienced at Frankfurt will have undoubtedly added to her life. After being unable to play in the first few weeks after her move due to illness, Agg scored a brace off the bench in Frankfurt's German Cup second round 6–0 romp against Bayer Leverkusen. Agg scored against SC Freiburg, impressed out of position against SGS Essen, and on the final day of the season – a home game against Bayern Munich – she swung the momentum back in Frankfurt's favour after coming off the bench with 35 minutes to go. Sadly, the home side couldn't convert that pressure into a goal and the game ended in a 1–0 defeat. I spoke to Lily afterwards, and while she still felt she had learnt from the move, the frustration at the lack of game time proved decisive and made other parts of the experience harder to appreciate. After scoring four goals in fifteen appearances, Agg signed for Charlton Athletic ahead of the 2018–19 season, hoping her experience abroad would give her an edge.

For both Hünemeier and Agg, perseverance in the face of a challenge is what gives them a better chance of growing – both as players and human beings. There are certain environments in which obtaining that progression is trickier, though.

After playing Bundesliga football for SC 13 Bad Neuenahr and MSV Duisburg, and making 13 appearances for Germany, Verena Hagedorn became assistant to the head coach of the German national women's team, Steffi Jones, in September 2016. In October the following year, Hagedorn was sitting in Bayer Leverkusen's dugout watching Agg score that brace for Frankfurt in the second round of the German Cup.

Appointed in April 2017 aged 34, Hagedorn took the job at Leverkusen – a team relegated from the Bundesliga to the then regionalised (north and south) second division – to return to the touchline, where she wanted to be more often. In doing so, Hagedorn has battled with all the challenges that face women in football, and speaking to her at the hotel attached to the BayArena it's clear to see how passionate she is about what she does.

'There aren't many women's clubs that can work professionally,' Hagedorn says, matter-of-factly. 'In the first division, that is the case, but often thanks to financial support from the DFB. Otherwise, not all clubs could afford a full-time head coach. That's why it's very difficult and not very lucrative for women to move into this profession.' It stands to reason that a sport with less interest, little television money and fewer job opportunities would have less financial clout, and yet it is upsetting to hear just how hard it is for women to make a career in a game that is supposedly the world's favourite.

Hagedorn doesn't see herself as a role model. Men's Bundesliga referee Bibiana Steinhaus, and Tina Theune – who was the first woman in Germany to become a *Fußball-Lehrer* and managed the national team to three European Championships and their first World Cup – are the names she cites as more accurate representatives of the role, before asking with some validity: 'We just want to be seen as coaches or referees, and if you do the job well, then why not employ a woman?'

In September 2014, French second division men's team Clermont Foot did just that, appointing Corinne Diacre. Diacre spent three years at the club before taking over the French women's national team. Diacre had replaced another woman as head coach, Helena Costa – the first woman in Europe to be appointed a head coach of a top-level club. Costa quit after just one day of training, saying she felt sidelined by men and that she had only been given the job to attract publicity. However, Diacre remains an exception to the rule.

'In the top flight here, there are two women who are head coaches – [at] Werder Bremen and Jena,' says Hagedorn of the *Frauen-Bundesliga* (the women's top flight). 'All other head coaches are men.' When I met Hagedorn at the end of 2017, she was just one of four female coaches in the women's twelve-team southern league in the second division, while at the same time just three of the ten head coaches in England's top flight were women.

'Of course it would be great if women could see they had a chance to be more involved, but because of the financial situation that's just not the case. And the men have a better chance of getting a better coaching licence at a club where they'll get money for it. If a woman has an A Licence, she's a long way from getting a paid job for it,' says Hagedorn.

Clearly, there are fewer jobs available in the women's game, but it is astounding to think that too often it appears the equally qualified female candidate loses out because of her gender. Sadly, this is an all-too-familiar story for many women in the professional world.

Phil Neville was given the England women's job in January 2018. Prior to his appointment the ex-Manchester United defender had a Pro Licence but had never managed a first team in either the men's or women's game. On top of that, his social media history includes sexist comments. The FA claimed that some of the potential female candidates they had considered did not want the job because of the increased scrutiny they would receive, but to suggest that none of those they did look at were qualified and keen on the job runs counter to the evidence. Dutch football coach Vera Pauw, one of the 147 candidates from 30 countries who was considered, told Louise Taylor of *The Guardian*: 'It's a problem all over the world where women coaches who are ready to flourish are actively pushed out of the game. There are too many male coaches who can't get jobs in the men's game but are then given chances with women's teams.'

In such conditions, it is difficult for women to get a head coaching job, largely because even a less-qualified man is more likely to get the job than the best-qualified woman.

In Germany, county associations and the DFB heavily support talent development in women's football, but the decision to run a women's football team as part of a club remains, sadly, a tough economic decision for many. 'You only need the monthly income of an average male player to fund that part of the club for an entire year,' says Hagedorn. 'It's peanuts, but on the other side of things the clubs aren't earning any money with it,' she adds.

Given the obsession with finance in football, it's hardly surprising that a mildly successful women's team that never makes a profit would be one of the first things to go when budget cuts need to be made. But what message does that send? The only way to change the financial loss is not to focus on it. Instead, look at the opportunity and equality that a women's team offers a club and its community. Manchester United announced in March 2018 they would be establishing a women's team (after disbanding their previous women's team in 2005). Seeing one of the biggest clubs in the world deciding to send the right message to its community and open a pathway for talented players in the area was, even if long overdue, refreshing.

Why women aren't paid as much as men is a concern that Hagedorn shares with millions around the world. In football, she believes the reasons for the difference in financial return are clear. 'The women's game isn't as fast or athletic, that's just what a woman's body gives, but that's why there'll probably never be that much hype about it,' Hagedorn says, before adding that the Netherlands' hosting of the 2017 Euros was a super example of how to improve the role and perception of women's football in society.

'Then there's also broadcasting. In the men's game, the rights are sold. In the women's game, the international games are shown, the league games once a week, but it's more a case of orientating yourself to the TV groups rather than the other way around,' Hagedorn says, pointing out the altar at which the men's game now kneels.

Despite the lack of interest, Hagedorn believes women's football has one great advantage. 'At the moment in women's football, perhaps by chance, we have the fortune of being a part of the largest professional association in the world. Our job is to develop the women's game. Thirty years ago, we fought for even permission to play.'

Athletic perception, television deals, interest, role in society and the sheer right to play are all issues the men's game doesn't have to worry about. The helping hand of the DFL (German Football League) and an obligation to develop young players are commonplace in the men's game in Germany. The women's game is just working towards getting on the same playing field. Hagedorn believes this is changing though, and more thought is being put into youth teams for *Frauen-Bundesliga* sides. 'It's growing, but it takes time and once again we get stuck on that topic: money,' Hagedorn says with a weary smile.

The young head coach took her *Fußball-Lehrer* with the likes of Germany's men's assistant coach Thomas Schneider, former Borussia Dortmund and Arsenal scout Sven Mislintat, former Bayer Leverkusen head coach Roger Schmidt, former Hamburg and Hoffenheim head coach Markus Gisdol, Stuttgart head coach Tayfun Korkut and former Augsburg and Schalke boss Markus Weinzierl. The course was, naturally, 'an incredible amount of hard work' but also 'a pleasure to be able to experience all of that and to see how the world works there – it's different from the women's game.'

'We have support from the club, that says they want us, and that's already a lot,' Hagedorn says, reminding me further of the vast difference between the two football worlds.

If we can't make the women's game more professional then the financial hurdle will continue to be a stumbling point for many female coaches and players trying to make their way in the sport. Things are improving in the women's game, but with that raised level of opportunity comes a slippery slope – and given Hagedorn is already climbing this hill in the proverbial rain, it's clear just how tough her job is.

The women's game, which has now been officially 'allowed' in Germany for nearly 40 years, has made substantial progress in the years since Hagedorn was a player. Coaching women, though, especially for someone in Hagedorn's position, remains a fine art. 'You have to *kitzeln* it,' Hagedorn says, using the German word for 'tickle', in terms of coaxing out talent or motivation. It's the deft touch of leadership that so often makes the difference.

Between the lines lies the feeling that in this world of slender opportunities and financial discrepancy, players and coaches can ill afford to take things for granted. Things are better, but there's still a long way to go. 'In women's football a lot of success comes from physicality, because the discrepancy is still huge, particularly between the leagues. Perhaps not so much between international teams, but between a team that is professional and one that can't be due to time or funding issues, then the number of training sessions are vastly different and then you have players who are fast against those who aren't, and that's sometimes the difference between winning and losing,' Hagedorn says, likely referring to games such as the cup defeat to Frankfurt.

Hagedorn has seen the game change to become vastly more professional since her time as a player. Going from being a Germany international at the turn of the millennium to a Germany coach 15 years later seems to have given her an extra level of motivation. 'You have to reach that level to get everyone working towards a goal. That's why we're all here, really, isn't it?' Hagedorn says, rather profoundly. At the end of the 2017–18 season, Hagedorn appeared to have got her team doing just that as they secured promotion to the Bundesliga.

Unsurprisingly for a German coaching academy student, competence and the transmission of that competence are right at the top of what makes Hagedorn a good coach. 'You need the knowledge because players ask "why?", and that's a good thing, perhaps a little different to a few years ago when the coach said do and they did,' says Hagedorn, referencing the idea of Generation Why.

Hagedorn is relishing the chance to make decisions at the top and take on responsibility. When we spoke, promotion was a goal, but the greater focus was on her desire to create a 'philosophy of development' built around solid work. 'If you build something properly, then I think in the women's game you have the chance to lead a club for a long time,' she says. It was fitting that in 2018 promotion became a reality when Hagedorn guided Leverkusen back into the Bundesliga.

With Leverkusen's promotion, Hagedorn achieved the ultimate: the instillation of a developmental process that led to success. 'In the men's game, Freiburg have realised their role. They're a development club, sometimes in the top flight, sometimes in the second division, but they stick to that – because they don't work beyond their means,' Hagedorn tells me, emphasising that in both cases, tangible success such as promotion doesn't have to be the goal for it to be the end result.

Despite all the difficulties that lie in her way, Hagedorn is relishing the work she does. 'You want to implement something and when you're handed the responsibility of doing so, then what more motivation do you need?' she asks. 'I don't think about hours or money or length of contract. Of course you have the hope that the other side of things automatically sorts itself, but it's a luxury to work in this environment.'

Whether a player moving to a different country or a female head coach trying to make the most of modest means, taking on challenges can lead to great personal, professional and sometimes even social change.

Key Lesson

Looking beyond your own routines and opting for the greater challenge can lead to great reward. Both Uwe Hünemeier and Lily Agg benefited from moving abroad, and it seems Verena Hagedorn has developed a steely determination to overcome the hurdles in her way.

Growth is at the heart of our time on the planet. We must learn, challenge ourselves, overcome adversity and continue to be resilient. One coach told me that having spent 12 years battling relegation as a player and then doing the same later as a head coach made him appreciate the value of winning more. 'I know how wonderful it is to win because I know how miserable it is to lose.'

5

Initiative
(Initiative)

'This is the blind spot in football.
Seeing this in games isn't ingrained yet.'

– Stefan Reinartz

Germany is big on the idea of 'the team behind the team'. Much was made of the key role the philosophy played in their 2014 World Cup success. From physiotherapists to video analysts and yoga instructors, the structure of the group behind the team seemed to play a big part in Germany's success. How much is too much remains a fine line when it comes to support staff, though. In the same tournament, England had a record number of support staff but failed to make it out of the group. Four years later in Russia, Germany's team behind the team seemed to grow too big and was perhaps one of many factors that led to the team crashing out in the group stages. Either way, the size and skill set of the team behind the team has to be just right for the benefit to be seen on the pitch.

Part of that is knowing what information to pass on and when, no easy task given the phenomenal amount of analytical information now available in football. One analytical tool rising to prominence in Germany is called Packing, and I travelled to the northern outskirts of Cologne to find out more about a sensation that Thomas Tuchel loves.

After retiring aged just 27, Stefan Reinartz attended an event at Cologne's sports college and was told in no uncertain terms that statistics were not significant in football. In that moment in 2014, the first seeds of an idea were planted. Together with friend and fellow pro Jens Hegeler, Reinartz wanted to prove more telling statistics were necessary. The company Impect was created, and Packing was born.

Reinartz, who was crowned a Bundesliga and European champion at U19 level, went on to make 163 Bundesliga appearances for Bayer Leverkusen and Eintracht Frankfurt, as well as three appearances for Germany. He believes everyone is obsessed with pass percentage, but in truth it is one of the most misleading statistics around. A player simply having a high pass percentage doesn't mean much, because it doesn't tell you where the passes were played. There's an obsession to reviewing the number of hours clocked by staff in the office in the hope of finding answers to productivity, but like pass-accuracy stats, this too is misleading. German-American political theorist Hannah Arendt differentiates between labour and work – the difference between the profit we turn at the end of the week and the creation of something durable. In *The Human Condition*, Arendt argues that it is how we act with what we create (our work) rather than adding up our hours (our labour) that can lead us to a greater human understanding of what we do. Reinartz found his in the creation of Packing.

One statistic that won Reinartz over was the comparison between Mats Hummels and Sokratis when the pair played together at Borussia Dortmund. Sokratis had higher pass accuracy (88.1 per cent) than Hummels (84.6 per cent), but Packing revealed Hummels had in fact taken far more players out of the game with his passes (73) than Sokratis (41). Hummels also took out six defenders per game, a brilliant rating for a defender – more than defensive midfielder Julian Weigl. Sokratis had taken out just one defender.

Players 'taken out of the game' by a pass are those no longer between the ball and the goal – that is those no longer capable of defending the goal. It's called 'Packing' because those players taken out of the game are 'packed' and out of play. Defenders are defined as the last five outfield players (six with the goalkeeper). 'For us, it's about getting past the last five opponents,' Reinartz says. It is unremarkable that beating defenders improves your chances of scoring, but the ability to put this into numbers is more than just a trend. It's a coaching revelation and it fits every style.

'Possession, distance covered, shots. They all have very little if any significance for results in football,' Reinartz tells me, while showing me the evidence to back it up. With only 10 games left of the 2016–17 Bundesliga season, a look at games that ended with winners and losers revealed only 54 per cent of the winners had more possession, and only 61 per cent had more shots. However, 88 per cent of those who won took out more defenders, an impressive and also somewhat logical statistic when highlighted.

'My generation was really brought up on the concept of playing through rows, playing vertically. So it was clear to me that pass percentages have no significance, because they don't take effectivity into account. It's hard to measure rows because football is not like table football. So it's about taking opponents out of the game,' Reinartz tells me. That is the core focus of Packing – not how successful you are at passing the ball, but how many players you take out of the game when you do pass.

'In almost every sporting event you can see how good you were, athletics in particular. In long jump, you jump 7 metres 52 and afterwards you say, "That's not so great, I normally jump 7 metres 70." In football, it's bloody difficult. Strikers can be measured by their goals: "he scored, great, he didn't, rubbish", but that too doesn't tell the full story,' Reinartz says.

'It's hard to know as a player whether you've played well or not after a game, because there is no objective feedback. At best, the coach can tell you, but he doesn't have that much time to tell every player what was good and what was bad. Even if he did that, it's only an opinion, albeit an important one. Perhaps as a player you see things differently, but there are no criteria.'

That is what Reinartz hopes to change with his stats. Impect are already working with Borussia Dortmund, Bayer Leverkusen and Borussia Mönchengladbach among others. Since I spoke to Reinartz, Impect confirmed in an online interview with *inews* that they were in talks with two top-six Premier League clubs. Former BVB head coach Thomas Tuchel was very excited when Reinartz spoke to him, because it is exactly the kind of tool he likes.

'We talked during his pre-Dortmund sabbatical,' says Reinartz. 'It's the best time to speak to a head coach. It's exactly his style of play, although you could say it's everyone's style because you can't win if you don't play the ball past the opposition. But his style, playing vertically through the rows and having players open to receive the pass, fits this approach perfectly.'

'Tuchel speaks to his players about this,' Reinartz adds, citing the example of Julian Weigl. I interviewed Weigl for *Deutsche Welle* just before the start of the 2016–17 season, and asked him whether he wanted to play fewer safe passes (in essence, whether he was looking to play more passes through the rows). Weigl acknowledged that indeed he did want to play more passes into the final third, with Packing numbers seemingly playing a part of that development.

Reinartz told me that Tuchel told Weigl, 'Look where you are now. This is where you want to go', referring to other midfielders with much better Packing stats. In 2016, Weigl averaged 42 opponents removed per game. The Bundesliga average was 28. Granit Xhaka was averaging 62 per game, the best of any defensive midfielder in the Bundesliga, while Toni Kroos averaged a whopping 82 for Germany. It was clear where Tuchel wanted Weigl to go in terms of development.

'It was the same with Sebastian Rode when he arrived. He had average stats. Tuchel showed him and said, "Here is where you need to be if you want to play",' Reinartz added. 'For most coaches at the moment, it's the players who make these passes possible that are the hot topic of discussion,' Reinartz says. 'It's under appreciated.' Reinartz shows me a clip of Toni Kroos playing a delightful ball to Sami Khedira in Germany's game against Ukraine at the 2016 European Championships. Kroos's pass takes nine players (excluding the goalkeeper) out of the game in one move, but, as Reinartz reminds me, there are two players involved in this move. For every player that makes the pass (and it must be a pass that is controlled), there must also be a player available to receive the pass.

Mesut Özil continues to be the scapegoat when his teams play badly – to damaging effect in the aftermath of the 2018 World Cup. Bayern Munich's President Uli Hoeneß might have delivered the most damning comments when, after Özil had stepped away from the team, he told *Sport Bild* he was glad the episode was over because 'He had been playing shit for years. The last tackle he won was before the 2014 World Cup ... Whenever we played against Arsenal, we played through him because we knew he was the weak point.'

Hoeneß's rather sweeping statements on Özil's performances were poorly phrased and poorly timed, and missed the point. The conversation about Özil and teammate Ilkay Gündoğan's photos with Turkish President Erdoğan is complex and full of nuance, but Hoeneß's decision to focus on the sport is made all the more baffling by his incorrect assessment of Özil's performances. One look at the Packing stats proves just that.

On first glance at a clip of Germany's best chance in their Euro 2016 semi-final defeat to France, Özil appears to do little more than play a two-yard pass. However, a closer look shows that his movement in between five French players earlier on in the move allows Kroos to feed the ball forwards to him, taking out a handful of opponents in the process.

'That is of extra value to us. In order to take out that many opponents, you need a passer of the ball but also a receiver. This is the blind spot in football. Seeing this in games isn't ingrained yet. All the coaches, managers, scouts we've spoken to all say they need players who can receive the pass in interesting areas of space (i.e. those areas where most opposition players are taken out of the game),' Reinartz adds.

In the 2016 Euros, Özil ranked number one of all midfielders as a pass receiver according to opponents taken out of the game. He constantly made himself available in tight spaces, and he is able to control the ball and create something in those spaces. In 2018, Germany suffered as a whole, but Özil continued to show himself in between the lines as a pass receiver. Collectively though, Germany's Packing statistics in Russia were telling. While they bypassed 40 opposition 'defenders' in their three 2018 World Cup games, the number of Germany 'defenders' bypassed was 51.

The beauty of Packing is that it also works the other way around. In that 2016 semi-final against Germany, French striker Olivier Giroud was denied by an epic Benedikt Höwedes tackle that blocked his shot and which, in the process, brought nine German players *back* into play. Ranking players according to how many players they bring back into the game also works as a coaching tool to demonstrate where areas of improvement are required.

Reinartz's comparison between Bayer Leverkusen's Karim Bellarabi and Özil further highlights the importance of Packing from a coach's perspective. 'If these two were playing in the park, Bellarabi would destroy Özil. He's faster, a better dribbler and has a better shot. And yet, Özil is a world-class player whereas Bellarabi is a good player at a good club. Where is the difference? Mainly in the fact that Özil makes himself available for the pass in good areas.' That much is seen in statistical form. In Germany games at the 2016 Euros with Özil, 66 players were taken out of the game. Bellarabi has 'only' taken out 31 players in all his appearances for Germany. 'If you want to put it bluntly, you can play twice as many attacks through Özil as you can through Bellarabi,' Reinartz explains.

Reinartz tells me about one of his old teammates who often struggled to bring the ball under control, and so was coached to improve his control, which led to him drifting wide. As a result, he was rarely available to receive a pass that would take out opponents. Reinartz believes this is a mistake. Coaching a player out of this movement for the sake of control is wrong and affects the entire balance of the team. 'The problem is when you are open in these spaces, they are often hard-earned. The likelihood of you losing the ball is higher there than on the sidelines. Most ordinary players lose a lot of possession here. If you don't make it clear to a player how important it is that you make these moves regardless of how often you lose the ball, then the player will automatically show himself less in those spaces,' Reinartz says.

Explaining this to coaches at an event when faced with the usual, 'why more stats?' counterargument, Reinartz's compelling evidence was concrete numbers that could be used to highlight and improve both players' and teams' performances.

Along with the Hummels/Sokratis comparison, there was another favourite example for Reinartz: Germany's historic 7–1 win against Brazil in the 2014 World Cup semi-final. In that game, Germany took out 402 opponents and 84 defenders (Brazil took out 341 opponents and 53 defenders). The Bundesliga average in the 2016–17 season for defenders taken out of the game was around 36. Taking out 84 defenders per game is extreme, but so is Brazil's 53. 'Looking at these stats only, and if I didn't know the result, I would have said 6–2, 6–3,' says Reinartz, pointing out Brazil's wastefulness on the day.

In the Bundesliga, there is perhaps no better yardstick for all-round striking ability than Robert Lewandowski. With 10 games still left of the 2016–17 season, the Polish striker was already averaging 18 players removed per game as a pass receiver. Such a close look at the movement Lewandowski offers between the lines and in the midst of the opposition's defence shows that measuring strikers by just their goals is never enough.

Naby Keïta is as good a player as there is. With 10 games left of the 2016–17 Bundesliga season, the Leipzig star, who has since moved to Liverpool, was already averaging 10 defenders removed per game. Former Borussia Dortmund winger Ousmane Dembélé was in the top five of the same category with eight, a remarkable tally for a player aged just 19 at the time. From a team perspective, the stats are also revealing. Hoffenheim finished fourth in the Bundesliga that season, somewhat surprisingly, but they were also the fourth best in the league for defenders removed per game – averaging 43. Borussia Dortmund were third in the final league standings, as well as the rankings for the most defenders removed per game (46). RB Leipzig were surprise second-place finishers, and the fact they averaged 48 defenders removed per game is part of the reason why. Bayern won the league and had the most defenders removed per game (averaging 50). Hertha and Frankfurt were in the bottom four when it came to removing opposition defenders (both averaging only 34), but in the top five when it came to prevention (fewest of their own defenders removed per game). Frankfurt, under Niko Kovač, were in fact joint-first (with Bayern) on the latter measure, allowing on average only 35 defenders removed per game.

'This is a coaching tool. It's nothing to do with what players do with the ball. It's about what runs they make. So, as a coach, you can teach that to players because it's not about their technical abilities,' Reinartz says, slowly revealing the early signs of a man who might well be suited to coaching himself one day. This tool is variable. The aforementioned case of Julian Weigl is the most obvious example of Packing as a coaching tool, but it doesn't have to be used so directly.

Reinartz tells me how the Hoffenheim coach Julian Nagelsmann worked with the software company SAP on *Deckungsschatten*, which literally translated means 'discovery shadows'. 'So for example,' Reinartz says, 'I have the ball, you're an opponent and just behind you is my teammate. I can't pass to him because you are throwing a shadow over the pass – everything in the dark is not an option.

Bellarabi is often in the shadows. Nagelsmann looks at how much time his attackers spend in the shadows and how often they're "in the light" and therefore available for the pass.' More coaches are using a basic framework and are then giving their players creative licence within that structure. 'It's not like Guardiola, who gets every detail, every pass. It's more about instructions where the player then has more freedom to decide how to execute the instruction,' Reinartz explains.

Packing can also be used as a motivational tool for coaches. After every game while coaching at Gladbach, André Schubert used to hang out a list of how many opponents his players had removed during a game, thus creating a changing-room competition. At Eintracht Frankfurt, one of the video analysts said he wanted to hang a similar list in the changing room for the players because it was a type of coaching.

Even in defeat, this tool shows that your team is playing well. Looking at Eintracht Frankfurt's form across the first 22 games of the 2016–17 season, their best game was away against Hamburg. They played 23 more defenders out of the game than their opponents and scored three more goals, classifying it as a deserved win. Other games where Frankfurt played more defenders out of the game than their opponents but scored fewer goals – as was the case against Darmstadt – ended up in the 'unfortunate defeat' category. Then there were the games where Frankfurt played fewer defenders out of the game and scored fewer goals – deserved defeats (such as against Leipzig) – and games where they took fewer defenders out of the game, but won – lucky victories.

A string of fortunate victories might indicate a pattern, and with this tool that pattern is now tangible. This was the case for Bayer Leverkusen in the 2016–17 season. They were due the hammerings they eventually got in February and March 2017 as a 4–2 loss to Atlético Madrid was followed by defeat to Mainz and then a 6–2 loss in Dortmund.

'Most coaches see themselves as coach of a team,' Reinartz says, 'which is true. Tuchel says in interviews a lot that he is also a companion for the players. You are also coach of every individual player. They are all competitive sportsmen who earn lots of money, who have agents. Each one is like a small business. If you look at tennis and the amount of feedback they get from their coaches, you see it's not possible in football. But I think it will go in this direction, giving each player more attention because you have to improve each player. Even if coaches say they try to improve each player every day, it's impossible. You can't be coach of a team and at the same time improve every single player.'

With the increasing amount of scrutiny on the daily work and life of a football head coach, it seems inevitable that staff sizes will increase so that every part of the job can be fully attended to. 'You have two goals as a club,' says Reinartz, a man who has been on the inside. 'You want sporting success tomorrow, but also to develop players over years. We will likely head in the direction where one coach is employed to win the game, while another is employed to develop talent.'

Reinartz hasn't ruled out taking up a coaching job in the future (he was a second assistant coach of Bayer Leverkusen's U17s at just 23 years old), but in creating this tool he has done more than show his ability. He has opened up another domain in the already crammed circle of analytical coaching tools.

'We can now measure a performance better and set a benchmark. Perhaps less of an issue at the top level, but in youth football it's pivotal to set the approach and show the importance of movement in key spaces. Now I can give that to a player in the form of a number,' Reinartz says. Soon, Impect are hoping to be able to launch an online database where managers can log in and check their selected stats.

What happens at youth level can make a significant difference, with players emerging smarter and better than the average player of their age, and Germany have proven experts at that since their overhaul at the start of the millennium.

'For a coach to be able to explain: "This is what I want, to get past the opposition, so that's why these passes make sense and those don't" to a player at youth level is hugely important. That's why coaches at youth level think highly of this tool: because it means they don't overwhelm individuals with thousands of explanations of how to solve situations. It's a global form of coaching, and where things are heading in Germany at the moment,' Reinartz says, proudly.

It's one of the reasons why Germany continues to produce such talented youngsters – players who can handle pressure and who don't just want to turn up to training sessions but are also yearning to understand more. 'Often you don't get much feedback. Of course the danger is overburdening players with stats, but at the moment players get far too little or hardly any feedback for their performance, which is terrible for players in a competitive sport. This young generation, particularly in Germany, wants lots of input. They want to know about their game, and how to improve,' Reinartz says, reinforcing the concept of Generation Why.

Naturally, there is a difference between the generations, but Reinartz recalls an example from his 11 months at Eintracht Frankfurt at the end of his playing career to show that while statistics don't provide all of the answers, they can help paint a clearer picture.

'It was the second game of the season and we were playing against Augsburg. The team didn't play well, but I did. I played in holding midfield with Marco Russ. In that game, I took out 75 opponents, including 14 defenders. If I played that way every weekend then I might not have played at Real Madrid, but I definitely wouldn't have been at Frankfurt,' Reinartz says with a smile. 'Russ took 12 opponents out of the game, and zero defenders – terrible for a holding midfielder. Armin Veh, the Frankfurt head coach at the time, said after the game, "Both players can't play together because they are too similar." I thought, "Which game did you watch?"'

With Packing, football coaches in Germany can take the game they watch and analyse it in a new way, and the concept has already started to spread. One glance at players like Julian Weigl, Joshua Kimmich and Sebastian Rudy, and it's clear to see what kind of an impact the use of the statistic is having on coaching. And it won't stop there either. Lukas Keppler, Reinartz's fellow managing director at Impect, told *inews* that the company is looking for 'way more than just the two numbers of bypassed opponents and defenders'.

There are an endless number of analytical tools in football, but those that add learning and clarity to the streams of figures in the sport are of benefit to everyone. Reinartz's development of this tool says a lot about him too. As Christoph Biermann correctly observes in his wonderfully insightful book *Matchplan*, Reinartz was not just a player who wanted to play the game, but one who also wanted to understand it. In creating Packing, he also gave others the chance to understand, and that is a rare and brilliant thing.

Key Lesson

Reinartz was motivated to prove that if the statistics are right then they can be significant. Great teachers don't just accept the evidence they're presented with – they go deeper, they challenge the status quo, they take the initiative to find the best possible version. It was this approach that led Ralf Rangnick to challenge systems and Christian Heidel to lead a cultural revolution. Sometimes these attempts aren't successful, but that is part of taking the initiative; even in failing, the attempt often enlightens and the end result is a changing of the game. But when they are successful, the change is even greater. Reinartz has done just that. He took a blind spot and made it into something tangible.

Erfinder
(Innovator) Part 1

---

*'We want to create chaos,
but we also want to control it.'*

– Helmut Groß

As we stand outside RB Leipzig's academy while the fire alarm goes off, Helmut Groß smiles at me and says that now I will get to know everyone at the club. Moments ago, one of Germany's greatest football minds, and a close advisor and friend of Ralf Rangnick (at the time the club's sporting director), had explained the benefits and challenges of a modern-day football club staff to me. The 70 year old, whose sharp blue eyes still glint, is also keen to point out that a tactics board stands in the corner should we need it.

Groß spends the next two hours – fire alarm break included – talking to me about his role in the development of coaches in Germany. Through an endearing Swabian accent that makes him occasionally sound like Germany head coach Joachim Löw, Groß talks about the importance of looking beyond your own boarders, the value of youth football and the difference cognitive thinking makes. This is the man who has influenced not only Rangnick, whom he worked with at Stuttgart, but also Markus Gisdol, Roger Schmidt and Thomas Tuchel – the generation before Julian Nagelsmann and Domenico Tedesco. Tapping into his knowledge is a privilege.

'I think those head coaches that are interesting are the ones that looked outside of Germany. In our time, we always learnt more from Arrigo Sacchi in Italy, Valeriy Lobanovskyi, and later the Spanish. And for a time, the French, who were European champions in 1984 with ball-orientated zonal marking,' says Groß, before adding with a smile that back then it was called 'zone-tied man marking' because they didn't know what else to call it.

Groß adds legendary Austrian coach Ernst Happel to the list of influences, as well as Switzerland, a country where coaching styles were successfully mixed. An open and receptive football mind is what interests Groß about Germany's batch of young coaches, 'the ones that look abroad and do not just focus on Germany'.

Germany's chief scout Urs Siegenthaler was once asked in an interview with the *Berliner Morgenpost* about his fascinating theory that a country plays like its mentality. Siegenthaler's response was an extension of what Wormuth mentioned about his time with Joachim Löw in Turkey in Chapter Two. 'You also have to look at the country, the people and their mentality in order to understand the opposition better,' he told the paper. 'If you travel through Mexico, Sweden and South Korea, it's obvious where the differences are: their culture. Mexicans are gleeful for life. If in doubt, they seek their salvation in football through attack. They have the mindset: we score more goals than we concede. That's difficult to calculate. The Swedish are completely different. Ride a motorcycle through Sweden. Everything is organised, no one breaks ranks, everyone follows the traffic laws. The Swedes are normally chilly. That's how they play football too: controlled and decent. And then there are the South Koreans. These are hardworking people, who are very disciplined. They take on tasks almost obsessively.'

While cultural aspects do not always reflect the sporting approach, their incorporation into scout reports show an understanding for the human aspects of coaching. At the 2018 World Cup, Mexico certainly did seek (and found) their salvation in attack, and while Sweden were perhaps not as organised as their country's traffic laws, they made life difficult for Germany. The central thought around the red-and-blue circle and the four trigrams on the South Korean flag is perfect harmony and balance. While South Korea weren't perfect against Germany, they were a brilliant team. They raised their game as individuals, and taught Germany a lesson on what togetherness translates to on the football pitch.

Many coaches look abroad for inspiration, and Groß is no different. Working at Stuttgart during the early 1990s, Groß and Rangnick were able to develop their philosophy at youth level thanks to the reform of youth football and the introduction of academies in Germany. 'When he was president of the DFB, Gerhard Mayer-Vorfelder pushed through the academies to make it a must for first- and second-division sides to have academy teams. That meant we needed good coaches as well, of course. This was also part of the development; that the coaches would have an optimal education in terms of coaching. They had to be full time, that wasn't always the case beforehand. Although back then, depending on the job they had, they weren't always the worst ones,' Groß says, intriguingly. 'But a full-time coach, normally with a sports science degree, was the foundation of a good career. And in academies they developed players.'

Like Frank Wormuth, Groß, who worked as an adviser at RB Salzburg and Hoffenheim before joining RB Leipzig in 2012, believes if something is to be done, it should be done right. If the outgoing effort is great enough, a certain level of quality is expected in return. 'In Germany, whenever something costs money, then you take it more seriously, you want something in return,' Groß says. 'That's why a different kind of quality was born in terms of education. At the same time as young players started to develop, so did young head coaches. German football has benefited from that in the past, and hopefully still will in the future.'

When Jürgen Klopp was appointed head coach of Mainz back in 2001 and proved a success, it gave German clubs 'permission' to take a risk on a younger, perhaps internal, coach. While they can't always be the answer, the decision coincided with the sprouting of Germany's academies, and that meant more intelligent players demanded a different kind of coach. Despite the success of Klopp and those that followed, Groß believes the numbers aren't high enough. 'For me, the rate is still not good enough. It's still only individuals – Nagelsmann, Tuchel – who have made it through.'

Groß knows another member of Germany's talented young head coach movement: Roger Schmidt, whom he used to work with at RB Salzburg. 'In his second year at the club, he said: "If that's the way they want it, I'll show them it can perhaps be even better." He exaggerated the approach, and in the exaggeration of our philosophy came the progress. I have to exaggerate in order to develop, and then I have to review which exaggerations led to a nosebleed and which brought advantages. The main advantage of exaggeration is it surprises opponents. In Roger's second year at Salzburg that's what happened, and led to his legendary win against Ajax in the Europa League. Ajax play that classic Dutch football and the essential approach of Dutch football is almost the exact opposite of our philosophy. If we could pick out an ideal opponent then it would always be a team that plays Dutch football,' says Groß.

'They had a huge edge thanks to Johan Cruyff, but they stood still. It's almost impressive how after every defeat they say, "we don't need to change our style, we just need to do it better". Back then, against Ajax, their approach played into our hands. They lost 6–1 on aggregate, but supposedly only because they didn't implement their philosophy well enough. That is deadly for the Netherlands,' says Groß, who believes the same is true of England.

'We can always find a way in against the Dutch because they always try to play their positional style, independent of whether we try to prevent that with purposeful chaos. Because chaos is exactly what the Dutch don't need. They want their system and their organisation. We want to create chaos, but we also want to control it.'

Control is the keyword for coaching. What can and can't a head coach control? When do they take a step back and let things control themselves? Cognitive training is one of the hardest parts to manage. Groß tells me how he and Rangnick have nurtured and developed their approach over the years.

'The cognitive skills we develop are designed to release ourselves through the chaos, and we can take advantages from that. And, in return, the opposition sinks into chaos. That's linked to those cognitive skills – such as quickly recognising situations, anticipation and quick reactions – but it's also linked to the desire to work at an extremely high physical, very intense level. Those two things, the intensity of the game (playing with high dynamism) and thinking and reacting quickly, they're the main features.

'When we've had the smallest failure, such as not getting promoted, then people say, "We told you that wouldn't work. The way they're exaggerating and making chaos." Then they always said we were tired in the seventieth minute and that we had challenged ourselves too much. There are ways to recover during a game, and what's decisive is whether you're successful following this method. In the moment when you're leading in the seventieth minute and successful, there are happy hormones in your head that give you that second wave. Then it's irrelevant how tired you are physically because the brain will keep going. But if it goes the other way and you suffer surprise disappointment, then paralysis sets in and you notice the intensive physical aspect,' Groß says, before adding proudly, 'That's rare with us.'

So, is it cerebral thinking from both coach and player that have allowed German football to take a step forwards in recent years? Groß believes so, but isn't sure every coach is aware of it. 'You always notice that it's decisive how you grow up with football. If I grew up with a Dutch football philosophy, then my cognitive skills are connected to that. It's often about calmness and width and safety – apparent safety. As a player, a coach, a fan or even a journalist, I develop certain cognitive skills that fit that style. And if someone does something completely different, then I'm uncomfortable. I bristle. Former footballers don't want to admit they did the wrong thing or something different. That makes people agitated, so they start to form counterarguments,' Groß says.

Admitting mistakes is difficult. In football it's almost impossible. Head coaches often do so to take the pressure off their players, but coaching staff have to overcome a great deal of vanity to achieve success. That can make accepting error and seeking solutions – a healthy part of improvement – trickier. If even a fraction of any team hasn't adapted to this mindset, trouble can occur. 'It's often those that like to keep the ball, play the short pass,' Groß tells me. 'I always say they long for calmness, or slowness, because their entire cognitive thinking is aligned that way. They have a certain level of intensity and if the play speeds up, it gets uncomfortable.'

Groß proudly declares that Leipzig 'create speed and chaos', and that can cause problems for everyone – including those watching. Groß tells me that famous commentator Marcel Reif once said, 'It's great what they're doing, but it's missing someone holding onto the ball for a moment or two.' Being different (as we'll see in Chapter Twelve) is a key part of development. To succeed as a leader, a coach, going your own way, breaking away from the safe option is often very necessary, and often it's young coaches who tend to do it. But resistance can accompany that path, as Roger Schmidt found out at Leverkusen. Schmidt's desire to play extremely intense football, the kind that makes the opposition uncomfortable, put Leverkusen on a rollercoaster ride. But the dips in form started to become the norm and eventually cost him his job. Groß thinks such opposition no longer exists in Germany.

'I think in 12 games, Leverkusen hadn't conceded from open play – only from set-pieces. Set pieces are situations that can be handled similarly in every philosophy. Then they lost after 12 games, I think two games back to back, and then, because they lost those two games, people said the philosophy was far too attacking. They can't defend. Even though in 12 games beforehand, they hadn't conceded from open play at all. People weren't interested anymore. That can be frustrating.'

Such criticism can lead to headlines, which can lead to doubts. That in turn can be damaging and it can divide a team, too. 'Of the twelve regulars, five said they wanted to play like they did before, even though they were successful, even though they were in the Champions League. The moment a small crisis arrives, the same thing that made the team successful in the first place is blamed for the arrival of the crisis,' Groß tells me.

I remember Leverkusen under Schmidt. I too thought that the team's defensive shape and focus was lacking, but quite frankly, what do I know? As a journalist, it's my job to question and review but this process shares a fine line with the presumption of knowledge. Only very few tend to know what is really happening in a dressing room, let alone understand the game anywhere near as well as a head coach does. Without that knowledge, pretending to know the other side is a dangerous and uncomfortable slope, because it too often fails to take into consideration one of the hardest things for head coaches to manage: a playing philosophy.

If the head coach feels they are standing alone, particularly when the pressure increases, then questions also need to be asked about the structure of support in the club. Head coaches are rarely, if ever, the sole reason teams underperform, and while Groß admits that Schmidt's decisions changed when the pressure grew – something anyone who watched Schmidt's final months at Leverkusen could see – there's clearly a line that the club has to take about their future and their philosophy.

'It's the same at the traditional clubs here in Germany. They think the same way as the English. Even Bayern Munich, who just signed Jupp Heynckes as their coach, will certainly make their next head coach in the direction of Pep Guardiola,' Groß tells me, referring to the interim appointment of Heynckes after the decision to appoint Carlo Ancelotti didn't work out as desired. 'Preferably, they'll get an experienced, conservative head coach who appreciates the old values, but he should still have a playing philosophy like Guardiola. That's what they dream of! And that's what tears them back and forth.'

The appointment of Niko Kovač, a former Bayern Munich player and Croatia head coach, in 2018 combines some of those qualities. His tactical masterclass in the 2018 German Cup final, which saw his Eintracht Frankfurt side beat future employers Bayern 3–1, demonstrated his intelligence, but handling a group full of superstars as well as the club's remarkable expectations is another matter.

Almost every football club has this age-old battle when it comes to appointing a head coach – experience or youth? There's an argument to be made that that needn't always be an either/or decision. A change in perspective about what counts as experience and a broader level of competence in young coaches means that many coaches, although not enough for Groß's liking, have the ability to be both relatively young and experienced, thus capable of nurturing the so-called 'old values.'

The eighteenth century German author Goethe touched on this concept in *Sprüche in Prosa (Sayings in Prose)*: 'To become aware in time when young of the advantages of age; to maintain the advantages of youth in old age: both are pure fortune.' To think and grow beyond the preconceived limits of your age, whether that is back to younger years or towards years you have yet to live out, are huge assets in both life and coaching. But, as Groß says, you also need talent to be successful, and that's why some young coaches have progressed more than others.

Groß went on to reiterate the point that many coaches I spoke to made about youth coaching counting for much more than many give it credit for. 'People focus on Julian Nagelsmann and Domenico

Tedesco because they're so young, but they're also very experienced head coaches,' he told me. 'They've been coaches for ages, starting from youth football. And in truth, 80 per cent of what I do is the same whether it's with youth footballers or professionals. Thomas Tuchel was also a youth team coach. Jürgen Klopp went straight from player to youth team coach.'

David Wagner achieved historic success at Huddersfield Town after 150 games in charge of Borussia Dortmund's reserves and 50 games in charge of two youth teams at Hoffenheim. Similarly, Daniel Farke got the chance at Norwich City after coaching Borussia Dortmund's reserves. Most recently, Daniel Stendel was named Barnsley head coach and the 44 year old's appointment is perhaps the best example. On the face of it, Stendel arrives in Barnsley having managed only 34 first-team games at Hannover. However, like many coaches in Germany, Stendel's experience stretches far beyond that. He coached Hannover's U17s for 125 games and the club's U19s for 82 games. He got his *Fußball-Lehrer* in 2013, which means that three years before he was Hannover's interim head coach, and five years before he was appointed as Barnsley's head coach, Stendel was working with the highest coaching qualification. Stendel made a strong start to the 2018–19 campaign, but whether he can create a lasting bond with the Yorkshire club and the community remains to be seen. His appointment though, is recognition of the value of youth coaching and the latest example of how changing a club's culture sometimes requires changing the lens through which you view the sport.

The landscape of German coaching might have looked drastically different had Julian Nagelsmann become head coach at RB Salzburg, something Groß admits they were interested in doing during Rangnick's three-year stint (2012–15) as the club's sporting director. 'He has a convincing charisma. When he says something, he can express it clearly and simply, and that sounds obvious but you can see the players are convinced and that they don't think, "He's too young." These are things that some people have and others don't.' Ironically, Nagelsmann agreed to become RB Leipzig's manager for the 2019–20 season.

Having a clear philosophy is just the starting point for any head coach, or leader. The ability to implement it is what separates the best from the rest. 'Very often, even in Germany, what coaches say and plan isn't always implemented. First I have to control it in my head – what I want – and I also have to be able to show it, and teach it to the players so they can internalise it. That's where an ordinary head coach differs from a very good head coach – one who can put it into action. And they're still rare, even in Germany, I think,' Groß says.

The strangling of time at the dirty hands of success has left much of the sporting and business world gasping for comprehension. What is an acceptable measure of time in football anymore? What is an acceptable measure of success? A handful of goals in a handful of games for a striker and a social media wildfire later, they're the hottest thing on the market. The same is true for coaches.

Nagelsmann's success at Hoffenheim, whom he turned from relegation candidates to Champions League qualifiers, is impressive, and it wasn't long before rumours about him taking over at Bayern Munich or Borussia Dortmund came about, at least until his move to RB Leipzig was announced. Yet they ignore all the factors that play into the success of a head coach and forget the basic principle that success in one place doesn't guarantee it in another. The best coaching talents do not to take a misstep.

'Of course it's painful, when you lose your footing on the career ladder, but if you look at it confidently, then you know what you can do as a young head coach,' says Groß. 'It's only those that land on a level that they don't belong on – if they fall off quickly and keep falling ... then there are no offers for a year, they're in the stands waiting for a job. That's tough. But that's because they had more success from fortunate circumstances rather than their ability,' Groß says, aptly. 'But if someone arrived at a certain level with quality and is convincing, then they don't fall as far. They have a tough time for a quarter of the year. Roger Schmidt, for example. He could still pick out what he was going to do next. That wasn't obvious to him during his tough time in Leverkusen. That's when you think, "Oh dear" and you want to stop all together, but in that moment that's when you realise where there are options.'

Despite the third wave of young coaches in Germany, Groß believes the same as Frank Wormuth: for those clubs more afraid of losing their position, the value of a name still tends to outweigh the right person for the job. It's the same thing that haunts the Premier League.

'In Germany, many clubs still lean towards a conservative approach, because they know it sells better in the media. But at least we've come to the point where things are 50/50,' Groß says, with a wry smile. 'The other half is cheering for young coaches and we've got be careful they don't say: "The main thing is that they're young". It's not dependent on age. It's dependent on what they can do and what experience they've had, and it's based on success too,' he continues, raising a point that other coaches I speak to also discuss.

'Success is not just related to a head coach, but also players,' Groß continues. 'In Brazil there are coaches that were World Cup winners but former players say they were never taught anything by them. Look at Carlo Ancelotti. No one knows why he won titles, in terms of content, but he did win them so he must have done something superbly. There are coaches who coach those types of teams, with players like Ronaldo, but to train those teams you have to have certain skills – and to me those skills remain somewhat hidden.'

Groß has an analytical mind, one that comes from his first profession: bridge building. Before football became his full time job, Groß spent half a day working on the site, half a day helping Rangnick with Stuttgart's U19s. It has created a mind that constantly seeks a method but has also allowed him to appreciate the bigger picture. It is true that the method of some coaches is hard to see, but Groß is equally aware that they must have done something right to win (even if it isn't clear what). Pivotally, the idea that victory was made possible by a number of factors combining at the same time is one that is perhaps underappreciated in football. So often the winning of a trophy is because of the striker's 25 goals, or the head coach's innovative thoughts, or the signings made in January. In truth, it is the combination of all those things and a slice of good fortune. And so employing a coach based solely on their previous successes is irresponsible. The question that needs to be asked more often is whether the coach is capable of replicating that success by aligning new or similar pieces of a different jigsaw.

One of the biggest pieces of that puzzle is staff – the team behind the team. As the financial circle of football has grown, so has the pressure. To manage that, as an individual and a collective, has become an increasingly trying task, and so having the right people around is important for both the sporting development of a team and its well-being. In an ever-expanding staff, psychologists, fitness coaches and video analysts all play a key role now even though not so long ago some of their jobs didn't even exist (more on that in Chapter Nine). 'You have to lead a huge staff well and use them,' Groß tells me. 'For many head coaches, it's a burden. They come to the club and say: "We've never worked with a psychologist. We don't need that." But to take those people with you and have them working towards a common goal, that will be more and more important for a good head coach.'

Leadership and management of the team behind a team is a role not to be underestimated in modern sports management. One elderly coach told me they were a goalkeeper coach and a scout at the same time as being head coach back when they coached. At that time, the bus driver helped out, and the whole staff consisted of five people. Football has grown into a financially greedy, culture-driving machine, and everything explodes around it. Now, some teams need two buses to transport the team and everyone involved with them.

If everyone off the field is working together to help those on it, then the likelihood of success is far higher. All it takes is one person to have a different view of the future and the collective goal can be lost. Just like the team on the field, the group off it also have their own struggles, concerns, and issues that need considering. And on top of that, the head coach cannot forget their own well-being (remember Chapter Three) or their role at the club.

'The head coach also has to be stable himself, not that he needs a psychologist in order to be able to deal with the psychologist,' Groß quips with a soft chuckle. He mentions that the former RB Leipzig boss Ralph Hasenhüttl, who joined Southampton in December 2018, integrated himself into the team superbly. 'You have to be able to do that. I think you can only learn how to do some of that. You have to be an open person, who knows a great deal and can be smart. It helps to have had experiences elsewhere, but some pick it up very quickly, like Nagelsmann or Tedesco. The experience they got from coaching kids can still come in handy as building blocks when you make it to the top as well. A head coach has to be diverse, but the most important thing of all is being a leader.'

Groß told me that Hasenhüttl's greatest strength was his empathy, and that during his time as head coach, everyone at the club was 'emotionally connected' to him. Perhaps Hasenhüttl's great strength was coming from Ingolstadt 04. When Hasenhüttl and his band of unknown heroes arrived in the Bundesliga in 2015 – just 11 years after Ingolstadt were formed by the merger of the wonderfully named MTV Ingolstadt 1881 (of the fourth division) and ESV Ingolstadt-Ringsee (of the seventh division) – little was known of the team from the small Bavarian city, which is home to a host of company headquarters. Despite the financial backing of one of those companies (Audi), Ingolstadt didn't quite march up the leagues the same way RB Leipzig or Hoffenheim did. It was only when Hasenhüttl arrived in 2013 that the wheels really started rolling. Hasenhüttl's team weren't spectacular, but they were consistent and they had a playing style built around collective strength. What sets Hasenhüttl apart is that when he arrived at RB Leipzig, he had to adapt to joining a team with much more individual quality. He had to adjust to having 'more of everything' at his new club. 'That's an important point for a coach, bringing the team beyond the level of the individual,' says Groß. It's also one of the reasons that Hasenhüttl spent little time out of work before joining Southampton.

Like any head coach or leader, Hasenhüttl had to be sure that however many people are involved in the process, he was still the head coach. 'For all those people, 50-odd if you include the kit man and everyone, the head coach has to be recognised as *the* one. Not everyone has to like him, but everyone has to say: "Thank God he's here, I know what we have in him." When that breaks, then you have to separate yourself from those people,' Groß says.

Being well liked by everyone as a head coach is a rare thing indeed. One assistant coach told me that when the head coach he was working for announced his departure, virtually every employee from groundsman to media came to ask the head coach to stay. Why? The head coach had always made time for every person. They had approached every member of the organisation on the same level, never from a superior position. They recognised something that another young coach told me: 'You have a special job, but that doesn't make you special.'

Trust means the work remains at the forefront. Head coaches and sporting directors or those in senior management positions don't always see eye to eye – as is often the case in business or schools – and that's part of being in a team, but if they can trust one another then the focus remains on the team and its success rather than an individual pursuit. 'If you have to constantly correct the coach or if you have the feeling you have to observe them all the time, then it's nothing,' Groß says. 'There has to be trust. I have to know it works even when I'm not there.'

'If the aim of the collective becomes more important than the individual's then success, in this context, is greater. Only at the very top is a certain level of inflated self-belief required,' says Groß. 'Vanity is a necessary impulse, but only for those that sit at the top of the hierarchy. That's when vanity can have its advantages.'

In a tug of war, if the coaches of the team start shouting different instructions in an attempt to steal the limelight, the chances of the team winning are reduced. If they have one unified voice – perhaps with just the head coach communicating what the staff have agreed on – the team is not only more likely to understand how to win, but more likely to win. In doing so, you also make the coaching staff more accessible for those that need them the most – the players.

'To lead the staff so that the players let the staff in. For example, not every player wants to go to the psychologist. That's a special part of leadership, to tell players they have to let people in who want to help,' Groß says. The challenge of understanding what each player needs and helping them understand why they need it is also a skill. 'That's the advantage of younger players, who are a bit more impartial. Older players say, "I never did that. I'm not starting now,"' Groß says, reiterating the idea that Ralf Rangnick spoke of in Bochum.

On almost every important decision, even if he is clear in his decision, Rangnick will likely call Groß just to talk it through. Granted this is made possible because their friendship spans many decades, but it is also because Groß has never wanted to be anything more than he is. 'Ralf always says I'm the most modest person he knows. I take that as a compliment,' Groß says, with the soft smile of someone who has done great work that only very few people know about. He doesn't get questioned, but it means he can focus on his work more – because

Groß has put the team's success before his own. 'It's only a small aspect of it, but those who aren't in the limelight often are trusted more by others. People tell me things they wouldn't like to tell the head coach, because they know I won't do anything with it,' Groß says.

Groß and Rangnick have had success over the years for a number of reasons. Clearly, an extensive turnover in an already wealthy transfer market has helped develop the club and improve the profit column, but the development of individuals around a team philosophy has also led to strong bonds with young players. 'We've had players who have been on international duty and sent texts saying: "Hope the international break is soon over so we can play real football again". They want to play our style, and some of them struggle with their national team,' Groß tells me.

Whether it's managing staff, the steadfast belief in a philosophy, or a place to use innovation, the approach Groß has to coaching is intriguing. Whenever I mentioned his name to other coaches I spoke to for this book, Groß was revered. At the time of our meeting, the 70 year old humbly told me he'd continue to offer his advice if it was still desired until the end of the 2017–18 season but admitted that by then, 'it really has to be the end, because you even start to look a little oddly at yourself' otherwise. 'I've had to learn a great deal over the last few years, not because someone demanded it of me, but because I saw that people wanted to listen to what we were saying,' Groß says, before admitting the key caveat: success is a drug that is hard to stop craving.

Groß might have been mute on how much he'd be involved in seasons to come, but the future of German coaching is something he was clearer on. 'I used to say, the best head coach in the world is the best doctor, the best physiotherapist, teacher, psychologist and so on. There are no limits to the top,' Groß says matter-of-factly.

While the modern head coach doesn't need to be able to do everything (now that such an enormous staff is usually in place), an understanding and respect of everyone's role in success is pivotal – remember what Frank Wormuth said: 'Our main goal is to make conductors who don't have to be able to do everything, but should be aware of everything.' Groß believes some coaches don't know why they're successful, why they won a game. In such moments, the importance of the staff

– particularly the video analyst – is clear. Nevertheless, the human elements of coaching success must be remembered.

'The sulky coaches of the past don't work anymore today. You hear it with Julian Nagelsmann or Domenico Tedesco, that the players have the feeling the coaches are their big brothers. That just means that empathy is there. That's important. We have to be careful that this isn't lost, that we don't become too analytical. I know Thomas Tuchel enough to say he's a warm, likeable, empathetic and incredibly honest person. Yet I see him in his interviews and can understand that others think he's a little colder, that he only thinks analytically. That's not the truth,' Groß says.

'Over analytical' is a trait that is often assigned to coaches like Tuchel or even Pep Guardiola. It doesn't always mean the coach lacks a connection to his players. Perhaps that connection is just hidden, more private. 'You can't just have a formula,' Groß says, somewhat ironically considering Rangnick's equation for the assessment of competence in young players. While that approach has value, the key is knowing when to apply it and when not to. Groß, a man full of stories who has been one of the central brains behind the development of one of Germany's leading playing styles and a host of talented coaches, certainly knows that.

Key Lesson

- To not be deterred by external perceptions of age and experience.
- To recognise the importance of managing your team.

As Groß and countless others have said: quality shines through. And the experience a lot of young head coaches have by the time they reach the top job at pro level deserves greater recognition. All development towards the top is of value, even if the moving parts are different to those at the peak.

To lead and inspire a group, but also to manage it, requires a great deal of competence (remember Chapter Two). In sport, business or life, those who don't recognise the value of the team around them tend to stumble. Great leaders always recognise they were not alone in reaching the top.

7

Erfinder

(Innovator) - Part 2

'The problem in Germany was that
we were world champions in 1990.'

– Helmut Groß

When he appeared on national television in Germany in 1998 explaining his football philosophy with a tactics board, Ralf Rangnick's impact on German football began to grow. Aged 40, his delivery was clear, the belief in his own philosophy unwavering. 'The back four is just a means to an end, because what we really want to play is an extremely distinct type of pressing,' he said on ZDF (Central German Television), before adding: 'Perhaps another myth that still exists in Germany – the back four is played without a sweeper.'

Rangnick was changing the game, even if the players and coaches of the time didn't approve or agree. What he said next, though, was telling. It's a reminder of the change that has occurred on the pitch and in the dugout in Germany over the last 20 years, but also how easy it is to forget – in this age of endless information – the events of past eras. 'It is often said that in Germany, specifically in pro football, there's not enough time, but I don't seen any difference from other countries,' Rangnick continued. 'I think the pressure on football head coaches is just as great in Italy and in the Netherlands,' he said, before adding: 'I think we have the problem in Germany, and this is why it might take a little longer to transmit this type of football to a team, because many players have been taught a completely different way.'

Nearly 20 years later, German football development and intelligence is higher than ever. German clubs certainly don't have the same success on the European stage as their Spanish counterparts, but they're producing a host of talented coaches and players. Rangnick was an amateur player, who even played in England for Southwick FC during his studies. As a coach, Rangnick worked for Stuttgart at youth level before making his name by helping SSV Ulm 1846 rise unexpectedly up the divisions. He had stints at Stuttgart, Hannover and Schalke, but enjoyed more success at Hoffenheim, whom he led to the Bundesliga via two successive promotions. Surprisingly, he then left in 2011 for a second stint at Schalke, whom he led to a historic Champions League semi-final as well as winning the German Cup in 2011, before leaving after just seven months due to burnout. The following year Rangnick became sporting director at RB Salzburg, and later RB Leipzig. He returned to the dugout to guide Leipzig into the Bundesliga, before returning to the sporting director role. For the 2018–19 season, though, Rangnick was back as head coach of the club before Julian Nagelsmann takes over for the following campaign.

There's no denying that the financial benefits he has had at certain clubs have not only smoothed the road but also made some of the innovation possible, but Rangnick's coaching style and philosophy have nevertheless been hugely important for German football. Intense, driven and intelligent, Rangnick is one of the great innovators – the Steve Jobs of German football.

Speaking to Helmut Groß, it is clear just how much of a difference Rangnick has made to the current football landscape. 'The fact that so many young coaches are getting chances in Germany is linked to the older coaches,' Groß says with a smile. 'I think that in the past in Germany – and I think the same could be said for England – we worked too conservatively. People with innovative ideas were rare. Ralf Rangnick established the back four in Germany – in pro football – at the end of the 1990s, 1998 I think,' Groß says, correctly recalling Rangnick's famous words on ZDF.

'Rangnick started using the idea in youth football back in 1984. It took 15 years before someone was bold enough to pair zonal marking with a back four, and the established coaches of the time were furious. Rangnick never said anything negative about the football others were playing, just how he wanted to play, and then Germany sat up and said, "He thinks he's reinvented football." This phrase is still used today, even under coaches themselves. If a young coach says something, then the older one says, "He thinks he has reinvented football." That shows that it was very difficult as a young head coach with new ideas. For example, Arrigo Sacchi at the end of the 1980s had huge success with a back four, 4-4-2, an offside trap and a focus on the ball. In that time, Sacchi had such success that it couldn't be overlooked, and his successors, Fabio Capello and so on, were triumphant with the same approach, but it had no effect on Germany. The problem in Germany was that we were world champions in 1990 and we did that without a game plan. It was Franz Beckenbauer's football, he wanted every player to show their quality on the pitch, but a national team head coach is always a little excused because he picks a selection from a group he doesn't have every day. So it has to come from the clubs and they have to pick a philosophy that doesn't just serve the mainstream but is also innovative.'

Being bold and going against the norm takes a certain character, and that is still true today. After Manchester City beat Manchester United in the derby in early December 2017, City manager Pep Guardiola said: 'We showed that this kind of football can be played in England. People say it can only be played in Spain, but we showed it is possible to have the courage to play.' That season, Guardiola led Manchester City to the Premier League title with a record tally of 100 points. Granted, Guardiola was in a fortunate position to buy the players who stood the best chance of executing his style of play, but the base idea of courage being a weapon remains. Before that though, you have to know how to wield it.

'In Germany, it's often said when head coaches have a philosophy, that the coach only has a Plan A. He lacks a Plan B,' says Groß. 'What Rangnick and I have developed in a playing philosophy – we believe anyway – is a Plan A to Z. That means there can't be any problem that the game creates that we can't find an answer to. The solutions are, largely, different to others, but it's not like we have a gap somewhere. We've been doing it too long for that,' Groß says.

Rangnick's work with Hoffenheim's then youth coordinator Bernhard Peters from 2006 to 2011 led to a powerful combination of innovative sporting minds. Peters was a former head coach of Germany's men's hockey team and led them to many World Championship titles before moving to football. Exchanges across sport and finding another way to look at the game, even if the rules are different and the ball a different size, can only enhance understanding. It is one of the many reasons Rangnick is such a revolutionary coach.

'At the end of the 1980s in Germany, stretching was huge and Ralf Rangnick was someone who opened up to new ideas and integrated it into his training. He's also a qualified teacher. He has a sports degree in physiotherapy, something which helps. He's an excellent speaker, which is also needed. He's a good analyst and has a great memory. What we worked on in three hours, we explained to Rangnick in 15 to 20 minutes. Well, we showed him. We didn't have to explain it to him,' Groß says with a smile, realising the importance of the right words. 'With his rhetoric and teaching skills, he would talk to the team as though he had been with us for the entire three hours. He knew every detail, and that's a huge skill.'

In Germany it has been proven that it takes not a generation of revolutionary minds but one wildly bold one to break through the old guard and reimagine their field. Beethoven did so with his bombastic crescendos two centuries ago. German artist Joseph Beuys declared to post-war Germany 'everyone is an artist'. Rangnick – and perhaps Groß as well – has joined this group of innovators who shook up worlds stuck in their ways. He is the courageous mind to change the game, and, somewhat ironically, his innovation has spawned a generation of broad-thinking coaches in his mould.

As with any revolution, circumstance plays a role. Rangnick's arrival at Hoffenheim in 2006 was well timed in terms of changing perspectives – thanks also to the work of other inventive minds like Peters and eventually Lars Kornetka, who became the club's video analyst in 2007 (more on him in Chapter Nine). Rangnick also benefited from the financial support of SAP (Europe's largest software producer) at Hoffenheim, and Red Bull at RB Leipzig. There are almost certainly other coaches out there brimming with ideas but not the means. Even Beethoven's extreme talent benefited from the patronage of nobility. Having a skill is one thing but being in the right environment to implement it successfully is another.

At Leipzig, Rangnick and Groß are continuing to develop and make headlines for the ideas they conceived at Stuttgart and gained national success with at Hoffenheim. One of those started with the work that Kornetka does. 'For every youth team here, we have an extra video analyst,' Groß says. 'When we arrived there was one for the whole club, but now we've got three for the first team and five for the academy. That is so important. The assistant coach has to be in symbiosis with the video analyst. It's hard to separate the two really, but if you had to choose between an assistant head coach and a video analyst, I would say the video analyst is more important,' Groß says.

'These are the kind of things that Rangnick encouraged, things from the physiotherapist. In that field, we've increased the size of the staff there by eight. Now we've got two fitness coaches. Before we only had one, and before that you never had one really. For our style of play with this high intensity, it's necessary to have that many. We have less time on the pitch to recover than others, and that's an important part of our philosophy. In both phases, where the opposition has the ball and where we have the ball, we want to control the game. And to have control over the game when the opposition has the ball means you have to invest a lot of energy.

Groß continues: 'In 2010, we did a scientific study. We wanted to know whether our ball-orientated forwards defending led to winning the ball back quicker than zonal marking or man marking. The professor we were working with measured the sprints in 1,000 situations in 100 games and noticed, unsurprisingly, the more you sprint and the more players there are who sprint, the quicker you win the ball back. This is not an amazing insight, but he noticed – and we knew this but he was the first to prove it scientifically – that if I win the ball back with lots of sprints, then I have a greater chance of scoring. He proved the connection between scoring or success in attack and the way I win the ball back. Since then, with more work we've been trying to perfect it. The newest task, and we've got a super computer guy who finds values in things that are not so visible to others, is to analyse energy, so high-dynamic movements – sprints with at least 15 miles per hour and acceleration of more than two metres per second – for all goals from open play. He's looking at the phase after winning the ball back until the shot on goal. And we compared the attempts that didn't lead to success – I think that was over 400 – to the 51 which led to goals in terms of energy.

'Looking at the entire energy from the winning-the-ball-back phase and the scoring phase, the total energy used by the opposition is a little lower. During the winning-the-ball-back stage, the opposition invests, let's say 30,' Groß says, inventing 30 as a value so as to make the concept more tangible. 'We invest, in that stage, 65,' Groß continues, using 65 to show that Leipzig invest more than twice as much as the opposition. 'But in the shot phase, the opposition sometimes invests more. Overall though, we invest more.

'The main difference is the allocation of this dynamism. That shows how important the intensity in the winning-the-ball-back phase is for us. Many of our opponents don't know or believe this – thankfully. There are more, of course. Julian Nagelsmann recently won 3–1, and they [Hoffenheim] score quite a few goals, but he said after the game that he was particularly happy that his team finally scored a goal after *gegenpressing* again. That's what it's about. Those are the most important goals. We score, proportionately, twice as many goals after *gegenpressing* than others. As a result, we are worse at set-pieces than others. We've got room to improve there,' Groß says, correctly pointing out a weakness that continues to haunt Leipzig from season to season.

Groß's explanation of the 2010 study is an insight into the kind of detail that some clubs are going into in order to find the edge over their opponents. Not all clubs have the means to do this in such detail, but the concept of innovation, of finding ways to get that extra few per cent out of your team, is apparent in German coaching. And Rangnick's boldness was enough for Groß to liken it to some of the great names in the football revolution.

'It was close to what Valeriy Lobanovskyi did with Dynamo Kyiv, and Sacchi,' Groß says. Funnily enough, Rangnick once faced Lobanovskyi's Kyiv in a friendly in 1984 and was inspired by their pressing game. In a 2011 interview in the *Daily Telegraph,* when he was Schalke head coach, Rangnick spoke about that meeting. 'I thought we must have at least three players less than them. I had to count to make sure that it was 11 versus 11. Their mobility and energy, and the way they'd been arranged to play was amazing, so I spoke to Valeriy and got an insight into his ideas,' Rangnick was quoted as saying.

Many had seen the legendary play of Lobanovskyi's team, but it was Rangnick who used his inspiration to develop his own philosophy. 'They weren't unknown things,' Groß tells me. 'It was even clear on television. Kyiv won the UEFA Cup Winners' Cup in 1986 and Lobanovskyi was also Soviet Union head coach at the same time and at the Mexico World Cup, he had the best team by some distance. They pressed, despite the temperatures. It was evident, and we could have taken note in Germany. But we didn't. Instead, we won the World Cup in 1990 with man marking and a sweeper.'

Even though Rangnick was met with resistance in his early years, his achievements speak for themselves. The 60 year old is no closer to putting his feet up though, as he returns to the coaching dugout as head coach of RB Leipzig for the 2018–19 season. Speaking at the ITK in Bochum while in his role as sporting director of the club, it was clear why Rangnick is a man who struggles to take a break. He has always been fascinated with developing younger players – and clearly has a good eye for which ones can develop faster than others. How to get the most out of young players is the way forwards, it's his mantra, and that's exactly what he spent an hour talking about on the final day of the congress in 2017.

During Rangnick's time as Hoffenheim head coach he looked set to sign Mats Hummels from Bayern Munich, but the centre back joined Borussia Dortmund instead. Rangnick also nearly signed Thomas Müller, but as previously mentioned the combination of Hermann Gerland's efforts and the raising of the buyout clause left Hoffenheim unconvinced, a decision Rangnick obviously regrets.

Developing young players has a host of obvious benefits for Rangnick's philosophy. The obvious physical benefits of faster recovery and greater physical capacity are matched with the tactical benefits – the sponge-like minds of young players can take more on board, making the players easier to convince of a playing philosophy.

Rangnick also feels working with younger players makes it easier to review errors through video analysis. Their willingness to implement new tactics tends to be greater, and they're more open to learning from their mistakes. Ultimately, Rangnick believes the coach's work is less complicated when players think a little less critically when it comes to tactical tasks. Perhaps there's a truth to increased effectivity by reducing critical thinking when it comes to tactics, but part of the reason Germany has been able to produce so many talented players since the millennium is because 'Generation Why' has understood the value of why they are doing something and not just how to do it. Critical thinking is in many ways a key ingredient to the successful development of players, and without it, players are more likely to become purely products of a system rather than a combination of technical skill and expressionism.

Granted, the last point sounds a little like the will of an iron-fisted ruler, but it certainly suggests reasons why Rangnick's strong, clear philosophy can and often does work so well. There are negatives to such an approach, as some players can be overwhelmed by the tactical complexity. Such consistent and disciplined application can be hard to uphold – and that's why not every player Rangnick (or any other head coach with a successful philosophy) buys turns into a top player.

When RB Leipzig signed much-hailed Scottish talent Oliver Burke for €15.2m in the summer of 2016, then head coach Ralph Hasenhüttl said the winger had 'an empty hard drive' in terms of his work off the ball. Almost exactly a year later, Burke joined West Bromwich Albion in the Premier League. Burke is proof that not all young players can adapt to the club's strategy and that a number of factors affect the success of a young player's ability to store information on their 'hard drive'.

One bad step doesn't always have to be the end, though. In fact, it often shouldn't be. Leipzig's French defender Dayot Upamecano had a poor game in a 3–2 away win against Mainz near the end of the 2016–17 Bundesliga season, and was taken off after just 41 minutes. After that, he played five of the last six games, gradually improving, and since then he has blossomed into one of the best young defenders in the world. Still only 20 years old, Upamecano was fast approaching 70 appearances for RB Leipzig by the end of November 2018.

Abandoning players after poor performances doesn't help their development, and even if they have less experience with stress and disappointment, they have to be given the chance to handle it. That's how characters are formed. Whether or not pressure and errors can be handled in such an intense environment comes down to the individual, but also the environment in which that person is learning.

While Rangnick didn't put a label on it, what he is cultivating is an 'error culture'. Interestingly enough, Germany head coach Joachim Löw used that exact term ahead of Germany's November 2017 friendly against France in Cologne. The country's head coach was keen to see players make mistakes and learn from them, emphasising the development the player undergoes in the process. On top of that is also the personal progress the individual makes, which plays a huge role for Löw when selecting a World Cup squad in which not every player's role is to play. The selection of Freiburg striker Nils Petersen for the 2018 World Cup training camp over Sandro Wagner (then at Bayern Munich) was a surprise. Wagner's response was one of frustration, but it also revealed some character traits that perhaps vindicated Löw's decision.

At club level, though, playing is paramount to development. It would have been easy for Leipzig to discard Upamecano after a poor performance or two, but at just 18 years of age the young man deserved a chance to find out what kind of person he is, because that will have a bearing on what kind of player he will become. On the opening day of the 2017–18 Bundesliga season, Upamecano had a nightmare against Schalke. However, by the end of the season he was excelling. As far as Rangnick is concerned, Upamecano will be able to play for any team in the world in the years to come.

And herein lies an obvious but often overlooked characteristic of the Bundesliga – young players play. When England and Germany met at Wembley in November 2017 both squads had an average age of 25.3, but the top-flight appearances of England's admittedly injury-ravaged squad totalled 2,746, considerably fewer than Germany's 4,130. Similarly, at the 2017 U21 European Championship, Germany's 23-man squad included a remarkable 18 Bundesliga regulars, whereas just three of England's players consistently played in the Premier League.

Quite simply, Germany's young players get the chance to play. England's youth teams had a fantastic summer in 2017, but the concern is whether they'll get the chance to play in a league desperate to retain its status as the biggest and brashest in the world. If they don't, then there's a chance they'll trust themselves and their quality and follow in the footsteps of the likes of Jadon Sancho, Reiss Nelson, Mandela Egbo and Danny Collinge. In a January 2019 piece in *The*

Independent, Chief Football Writer Miguel Delaney listed a host of teenage players that are of interest to Bundesliga teams. Delaney added that families are becoming aware of the difference in opportunities and are increasingly feeling that the key years of development are better served abroad.

At the coaching congress in Bochum, Rangnick showed a film of two of Leipzig's biggest talents from recent years, Naby Keïta and Emil Forsberg, while they were at their previous clubs, and explained what he saw. Forsberg's highlight reel included some great dribbling and goals, but his pressing off the ball at Malmö was non-existent. As part of Leipzig's tactical approach the Swedish winger has added this attribute. This improvement in his positioning has enhanced his overall quality, as it makes him even more dangerous in transitional play.

Rangnick admitted he was flabbergasted that no French club had been interested in Keïta, at a time when the youngster was playing in Ligue 2 for FC Istres – hinting that perhaps the French scouting system was in need of some improvement. Like a proud father, Rangnick said: 'There are few midfielders capable of such skill,' while a clip of Keïta winning the ball back and driving forwards through midfield during his time at Istres played on the big screen. It's remarkable to think how much Keïta has developed since then, and how exciting his potential at Liverpool under Jürgen Klopp is.

Cognitive factors affecting the development of young players seem to be Rangnick's speciality. Rangnick believes younger players can reset their emotions quicker than older ones, but that learning how to handle criticism is a skill that can be developed. In such situations, young players seek their happiness through sport, which coaches should use. If the player's mentality is right, they're not immediately offended and so try and improve themselves on the pitch. They train harder, so they don't get into that situation again.

According to Rangnick, one key difference between younger and older players is their motivation. Older players are keen to return to their previous reputation, but younger players just want to get better. To do that, they also have to battle professional development with personal growth – and both under a huge spotlight. Young players do want to get better, but today there's no 'just' about it, there are far more factors at play now and they are, in many cases, affecting the mindset and expectation of young players.

Rangnick believes in-demand talents must expand their social intelligence because the influence of meaningful others such as agents, parents, friends and advisors is much greater on younger than older players who know what life is about, know what they want and how to get it. While again some of this can be read as a tough approach, there is a vast degree of knowledge attached to Rangnick's words. He knows how to improve his players, but he's also trying to make sure they make good decisions for themselves.

Rangnick has limited the choice of cars players can buy based on their experience as a driver. If you're older than 24, you can get a 'fast' car, but if you're 18 to 21 you're limited to a car with a lower maximum speed. It may sound dictatorial, but in the current football climate with many fighting to find that extra percentage – off the field as much as on it – there's some reason behind it. It's also refreshing to hear that these suddenly wealthy young men are given guidance in off-field matters.

All of it comes down to a clear plan, and the creating and nurturing of a team bond. Rangnick said he was delighted to come back into the players' lounge after a training session once to find five players (Yussuf Poulsen, Fabio Coltorti, Dominik Kaiser, Marcel Halstenberg and Marcel Sabitzer) playing the strategy game Catan. While it all sounds too perfect a picture to be real, Leipzig's performances, more often than not, do suggest a strong bond off and on the field.

All of it takes a great head coach to put it into place, though. Ralph Hasenhüttl is certainly one of those. The Austrian had a modest playing career, but as a striker he did make eight appearances for his country. In his career in the dugout, after coaching at Bavarian side SpVgg Unterhaching, he led VfR Aalen to promotion to the second division, where his work caught the eye of Ingolstadt. From there, he guided the relatively new club to Bundesliga promotion and then got his chance at RB Leipzig. After a successful debut campaign, Leipzig failed to qualify for the Champions League at the end of the 2017–18 season. In May 2018, Hasenhüttl opted out of his contract a year early after Leipzig didn't offer the longer-term contract extension he was looking for, and by the end of the year he was head coach at Premier League side Southampton.

In the tenth issue of *Socrates – Das Denkende Sportmagazin* ('The Thinking Fan's Sports Magazine), Hasenhüttl was interviewed by Felix Seidel and delivered some insight into the kind of head coach he is and wants to become. 'If I go after something I don't set myself any limits. I always think about the maximum, the optimal. And if that happens then it doesn't feel like a dream come true, but more like the payoff for lots of effort. This mindset has changed over the years, though. As a footballer I had limits. I don't see that being the case as a head coach.'

With RB Leipzig, limits certainly aren't one the ingredients, but it was profound to hear a head coach talk about the same being true for himself. Hasenhüttl's assessment of how important development is is exciting for a journalist, let alone for the fans of the club lucky enough to have him as their head coach.

'I want to learn as much as I can so as to be a better head coach,' Hasenhüttl told Seidel in *Socrates*. 'Because what is the foundation for the best coach? If you win lots of Champions League titles, you're definitely a very good head coach. But I don't know if you're then the best head coach. You might have the opportunity to achieve these successes with top teams. More essential for me are the questions: How far will you go as a coach? How much development can you grab hold of? How much do you learn? What do you know? And when is the moment when you combine and convey all of that with your physical fitness so that you become the perfect head coach? That's very exciting. I don't know where the end of my development is as a head coach. It'll probably never end. But perhaps the moment will come where I don't have that internal drive to demand 50, 60 games from myself a year.'

Hasenhüttl is an intriguing character, whose playing philosophy is successful. In the same interview, he admitted he has an emotional personality because he follows the mantra: 'The fire you want to light in others must burn inside you.' Rangnick is a quieter, more meticulous personality. At the end of his talk in Bochum, his professor-like approach blossomed as he explained the formula he has for young players:

Natural born talent + acquired skill × mentality = competence

Using an out-of-10 rating in his formula for the assessment of then newly signed 18-year-old Danish attacker Yussuf Poulsen, this is what Rangnick concluded:

$$5 + 6 \times 10 = 110$$
(Natural born talent + acquired skill x mentality = competence)

Rangnick then used an imaginary example to highlight his point further. Imagine if a player with extraordinarily high talent (9) and skill (7) arrived at your club but had a poor mentality (3). That player, according to Rangnick's formula, would be considerably worse (48) than Poulsen (110). Following that logic, it is clear to see why Poulsen is exactly the kind of player you want in your team. Not only will he get better, but he also has the right mentality. Interestingly, though, Rangnick didn't outline how these values were determined.

Valued at just €400,000 at the time, Poulsen arrived at RB Leipzig in 2013 for a modest €1.3 million. His current market value is around the €10 million mark. Following the same idea, 24-year-old teammate Marcel Sabitzer has seen his value rise from €2 million in 2014 to €25 million. It's clear that for Rangnick, a strong mentality makes all the difference, and once a head coach has recognised that, the following mantra applies to the player: 'Use it or lose it.'

One thing I've learnt throughout my search to understand how and why German coaching is staying ahead is how daring the process is. The result will always be important, but the method of obtaining it holds equal value to the great coaches. Like Frank Wormuth said about chance creation, it's not about getting closer to the goal but how you end up there, and for Ralf Rangnick's coaching career the 'how' has always been the most intriguing and insightful question.

Key Lesson

All three of the key figures at RB Leipzig – the head coach, the sporting director and the quiet mastermind – believe in not setting limits, challenging the norms even when success is already there, and being bold. These are all part of influencing the first steps of implementing a philosophy, developing a coach's character or a person's life. It starts with you. What do you want to create? Just because others are doing it doesn't make it right or the only way. Ralf Rangnick didn't believe the sweeper system worked and wanted to create a playing style focused around pressing. While there's no denying the financial support he has received has aided the implementation of his innovative ideas, he had to have those ideas in the first place and be brave enough to step forwards with them. He believed in the value of his work.

8

Reife
(Maturity)

---

*'To be a coach is no different to
how I am as a human.'*

– Daniel Niedzkowski

Having briefly met him at the coaching academy, watched him coach a 'Scoring in the Red Zone' session at the ITK in Bochum and seen him from afar as he helped Germany's U21s win the 2017 European Championships, I was keen to finally sit down with Daniel Niedzkowski. The 41 year old has a smart haircut, a firm handshake and a notable calmness when I meet him outside a beer garden in Cologne for an afternoon coffee. As a player he never made it beyond Germany's third division, mostly with MSV Duisburg's reserves, but he has achieved far greater success with his work off the pitch. Niedzkowski studied at the sports university in Cologne, quickly got his A Licence, and after three years in Atlanta, USA, he returned to Germany. Frank Tschan, director of Coaching Education at the grassroots level for the USSF (United States Soccer Federation), a contact Daniel made during his time in the US, nudged Niedzkowski towards coaching. Upon his return from the US, Niedzkowski, aged just 26, was playing, coaching youth teams and educating local coaches. By the age of 30, the DFB picked him up and he became a colleague of Frank Wormuth's, gradually taking on more and more responsibility and getting his own *Fußball-Lehrer*. In 2013 he became assistant coach at Bayer Leverkusen, but after three years Niedzkowski returned to the DFB to become an instructor on the *Fußball-Lehrer* course, eventually taking over from Frank Wormuth as chief instructor in the spring of 2018. He is also assistant coach for Germany's U21s.

In short, Niedzkowski's life is a football one.

Such is the quality of his language skills, Niedzkowski asks me whether I want to talk in English or German. We stick to German – after all, as Löw and Wormuth discovered in Turkey, you can't connect to the soul of the player unless you speak the language.

'As a job, I've never done anything other than football,' Niedzkowski tells me, 'but to focus on that and that alone is something you've got to decide to do first. Then getting into football can happen, but even then there's lots of luck, interest is high, there's plenty of money to earn and there's a certain level of prestige involved. There are a number of reasons for people to try it, but they're not it for me,' Niedzkowski adds, before admitting he committed to a career in football.

Given his relatively young age for someone working as a football coach, as well as his unique experience in the Bundesliga dugout and Germany's coaching academy, I'm keen to hear why Niedzkowski left the top flight, and how he feels a modern coach should handle a modern player. Most of all, I'm keen to hear how he feels the coaching landscape has changed over the years, because he is one of the men responsible for making sure Germany's coaching quality takes that change in its stride.

'Stress resistance is pivotal,' Niedzkowski replies. 'If you don't have that, coaching the professional game is not for you. Your place is probably more in youth football, where external pressure exists, but is considerably lower.'

'At Leverkusen with league and European games, stress was extreme at times. That – besides seeing a very interesting set of opportunities – was one of the reasons why after three consecutive years at that pace I went back to the DFB. It's not that I don't want to work in the Bundesliga, I can imagine doing it again, but I needed a break to come down from the adrenaline. Despite the fascination of the pro game, you need to be very aware of the load and make wise decisions to conserve your mental and physical resources,' Niedzkowski says, in a voice that he raises only once during our time together, and then only to laugh at the punchline of a joke.

The son of Solingen, in North Rhine-Westphalia, worked under Sami Hyypiä, Sascha Lewandowski and Roger Schmidt during his time at Leverkusen, experiencing three drastically different types of coaches. The stress level remained high, and handling that was pivotal to his ability to do his job. It was also a timely reminder that a football life must include non-football aspects.

'I have things other than football that I enjoy,' says Niedzkowski, who used to be in a band in his younger years. 'I think not having any is also a danger for players and coaches. If you only have football then your entire well-being is dependent on football. If the football is crap, then there's no chance of improving your mood. If you have other interests, then you can take a step to the side and say, for example, "now I'm going to focus on music", and play some guitar. You can then focus on that fully and your thoughts are elsewhere. That's so important to have. I didn't always manage it while I was at Leverkusen. If the peaks happen too quickly one after the other, then it's not possible. Game after game, travelling. My friend Frank Tschan, who coaches in America, would say, "You're burning the candle at both ends."'

Niedzkowski tells me the move back to the DFB was partly a move away from that stress, and while his job still includes working under pressure it's not as great as it was at a Bundesliga club. 'For a Bundesliga coach, at the heart of stress is criticism and personal attacks. That's the toughest. Workload is manageable, but external pressure is enormous. There are different ways of handling it. Former professional players who become head coaches are used to it, they know of external pressure, which is to their advantage, and probably why they have developed ways to deal with it over the years. The coaches who weren't players need to adapt and develop their method of coping. For all of them, family will likely be one. Personal disposition is important. If you don't have that, you'll burn out.'

Burnout continues to be a fear of many, as we discussed in Chapter Three, and not just in football. Genuine time off is what head coaches need, but as coaches are given such little time to deliver results, balance isn't always easy to find. Niedzkowski continues: 'I heard Arsene Wenger say once that the most important thing in management is to stay optimistic. I think it's an extremely important personality trait to have – to stay cool under pressure and to transmit confidence. Of course, behind that lies deep knowledge of the game and a plan of how to solve situations, but it's a mix of knowledge and social competence.'

It's here that Niedzkowski refers to the eight-level structure of competence that Frank Wormuth told me about in Chapter Two. That structure incorporates your coaching abilities with your coaching style, and while it isn't the academy's job to make personalities, developing the person is as much a part of becoming a *Fußball-Lehrer* as being tactically flexible.

Like most associations in Europe, Germany also has a mentoring scheme which gives coaches feedback on their genuine relationships with players. 'You can give the coach feedback about how he spoke to players and how they might feel, but their leadership on the course is difficult to evaluate. We can talk about it in theory and give them best-case examples, but it's always a bit abstract. That's why we've added mentoring into the coaching course, where we travel to the coaches at the clubs. The idea is to observe the coach at his club with his players. The relationship you form with a group you work with every day is different to one you work with once a week. The desire is there but it's difficult to put into practice,' Niedzkowski tells me.

Nurturing coaching quality further down the line is one thing, but identifying quality coaching on the *Fußball-Lehrer* course is another. In some cases it's clear what's right and what's wrong – the regularity of praise and criticism for example – but there are also examples where it's not so clear cut. Is the coach a *Kumpeltyp* (buddy type) or are they more reserved? They can be either, but they need the right tools to make it work.

'Christoph Daum told us that he takes notes meticulously after every meeting he has with a player, noting the topic and what the mood and understanding was at the end of the conversation, and whether there was a specific aim to the conversation. I really like this approach and would definitely advise this to any coach who is naturally distant,' Niedzkowski says. 'Write it down. You'll notice how often you speak to players, and whether you've not spoken to someone in a long time. And contact is pivotal. Players need that. They're focused on their own situation. They want to be taken seriously and appreciated. If you have that contact with them, you can develop it and help players through difficult situations. Sometimes it almost doesn't matter what the topic is, as long as you connect,' Niedzkowski adds.

Internal promotion of coaches has become the trend in Germany, and it hasn't stopped at the coaching position. Bayer Leverkusen's Jonas Boldt told Rory Smith of the *New York Times* that he rose from intern to sporting director. Boldt now gives people the same chance he was given 15 years ago. 'We can open the door. That's all,' the 36 year old told Smith. Leverkusen have done more than open a door though. They have expanded a culture. Just as a coach can benefit from an extended time at the club before being appointed head of the first team, so a future scout or sporting director can benefit from working their way up rather than just arriving. This is not only smart business, but also smart thinking, because it opens itself up to a world of talent that is otherwise often met by a closed door.

Granted this approach isn't always the answer, but it never ceases to amaze me how often in football, and business, expertise is not considered to be a commodity found internally. Experts are always welcomed in, often paid vast sums of money to provide answers that seemingly cannot be found inside the current group. While looking abroad is hugely beneficial (remember Chapter Six), perhaps sometimes we could benefit from looking closer to home.

'Attention is given to a coach who was successful under certain circumstances, and sometimes he's hired by the next club because of the success but without considering the circumstances,' Niedzkowski says. 'So you have to try to recreate those circumstances at the new club, and not enough thought is being put into that. That's why clubs like Hoffenheim, Werder Bremen and Mainz develop their own coaches. The clubs knew these coaches' strengths and weaknesses first hand and so there were fewer surprises, whereas if you get an external coach you can only assess them from the outside looking in. You don't know how good the fit is. Producing your own coach makes sense, but of course it isn't always an option, especially not for the top clubs, who need established personalities who have proven themselves at the highest level.'

Fast-forward to today and that's exactly what clubs are doing. It's also why Daum and coaches of his era struggle to get jobs at home. The Bundesliga has become a league of development and forethought. The league is battling to be relevant, but it's already unique in so many ways, and the coaching developments are just one aspect of that.

Interestingly enough, Niedzkowski adds that he believes England has taken a huge step forwards in coaching recently by adopting a similar policy. 'They've got very few meetings for which coaches come to the association, but the association goes to the clubs and develops coaches there. They focus very heavily on this mentoring concept. I think that's an excellent opportunity, but it's also possible because the Premier League is investing an enormous amount of money into coach education. That wouldn't be possible, financially, in Germany at the moment.'

When Germany won the 2014 World Cup, it was the culmination of a plan that began when the country pressed the reset button back in 2000, as Raphael Honigstein outlines in his excellent book *Das Reboot*. The world was impressed with the number of players Germany kept producing, as the academies kept delivering. While on a different scale, and with varying levels of success, German coaches are also many in number. Look a bit closer, and the young-coach trend is built on compelling evidence.

'They are different people,' Niedzkowski says, 'but there are similarities between the pathways of these young coaches. One is that they didn't have a great, long playing-career but got into coaching very early. They have lots of experience by the time they get to a professional team. Pro level is something different, with different challenges and personalities to contend with, but this experience as a coach is extremely valuable.'

Manuel Baum was Augsburg's youth coach before he was promoted to head coach, and prior to that he had been head coach at third-division side Unterhaching. Domenico Tedesco was in charge of Erzgebirge Aue before being given the Schalke job, but his coaching career began at youth level with Hoffenheim and Stuttgart. 'Coaching in the U19 Bundesliga is as close to the professional level as coaching in the fourth division, maybe even the third. They've been able to coach without as much pressure, which has enabled them to try themselves out and thereby develop themselves,' Niedzkowski says.

With the 'project' of young coaches in first-team jobs now very much in full flow in Germany, Niedzkowski is happy that German coaches are doing well but remains wary of the perception of that success. 'On the one hand it's great that we have so many young coaches, but the big danger is that every U12 coach thinks: "In four years, I can be a pro head coach. How do I get there? I have to be successful with my team." If young coaches start to focus too much on their own success, then their work will very often contradict the idea of talent development.'

This was something raised at the 2018 ITK in Dresden. The fear is that youth coaches are not only too often ambitious to coach at a higher level, but that financially incentivising them to stay as coaches at a lower level is too great a challenge – even if that level is the right place for them. There is a conversation happening at the moment about splitting the *Fußball-Lehrer* to accommodate youth- and elite-level coaching. 'There are lots of clubs that have a youth head coach who works with the coaches – so while the head coach is developing their players, the youth head coach works with the head coach to help them improve. That's key.'

However, Niedzkowski argues that success only tells half the story. 'It's important to remember that not all coaches can be successful. If we have lots of young head coaches in the Bundesliga, then there will be successful young coaches and unsuccessful young coaches. Being young isn't a sign of quality. Age is just a number. It doesn't mean they're a better coach.' Here, he recalls something I mentioned when we first sat down, namely that I wanted to try and understand the person behind the coach and the player. What happens when the person (not the coach or the player) is forgotten?

'That happens quickly if you think tactics are the key to everything. It might work so long as you're winning, but it doesn't help in a crisis. In a crisis you have to get close to the person, but it's hard to get close to the person in a crisis – so you have to get close to them when things are going well. The person is the key. Everything tactical should be a given. But it has been given extra focus lately. Just look at the load of tactics blogs out there. It's great that people are interested in that, but the tactical side of the game isn't as important as it's being made out to be,' Niedzkowski says.

Domenico Tedesco gave an interview to Germany's biggest football tactics website, *Spielverlagerung*, towards the end of 2017. It was the website's first interview with a current Bundesliga head coach, a sign of the rise in interest Niedzkowski mentions. In that interview,

Tedesco spoke in detail about his tactical philosophy and why tactics were so important and how he conveys that to his players. The then 32 year old talked about developing a discussion when it came to understanding the tactical approach, so it was less instructive and more of an exchange.

Clearly, Tedesco has the knowledge he needs, and while the focus of the site is to understand his and others' tactical approaches, what makes him a good coach is how he applies that knowledge. As discussed in Chapter Three, at the time of the 2017 ITK in Bochum, there were 890 qualified *Fußball-Lehrer* in Germany but just 56 jobs in the top three leagues, and on average a Bundesliga coach spent just 1.2 years in the role. All *Fußball-Lehrer* have detailed tactical knowledge, however it is the application of that knowledge which separates the best from the rest, enabling them to secure one of those 56 jobs and hold on to it for longer than 1.2 years.

In an exclusive interview with Sky Sports in Germany in November 2017, Tedesco's discussion of what makes beautiful football gave an insight into how he delivers his knowledge. 'What is beauty?' he asked. 'One person likes blondes, the next black hair, brunettes, or red hair, I don't know. But it's the same in football. We try to play the ball out from the back. We hardly play any long balls, and if so then they are considered ones. It's about space and superior numbers. For some, long balls and action in and around the box are pretty. For others, possession, or transition might be pretty. We can't rely on the viewer. We have to rely on our qualities, our players. They have to take things into consideration. The players have to play what they want to and where their strengths are. So beauty is nice and we target that, but it's important to put the strengths of your players first in order to win games, and if we can be ugly then that's also a quality.'

How a head coach gets the best out of his players is down to his soft skills, his character and his competence, as discussed in Chapter Two. It is down to the type of person he is because that is how he knows when to apply different parts of his knowledge, what to say to a player short of confidence or how to raise the collective morale of the team. That is what makes Germany such an exciting country for the development of head coaches; the change in attitude that started with Klopp was a change towards a highly educated generation of coaches who got the chance to develop their personal competences and gain experience.

'In Germany, we're very subject focused, which is why there's lots of talk about tactical improvement and how best to train, and the rest will follow, somehow,' says Niedzkowski. 'It's not that simple though, because people don't work that way, especially not if they are from a different cultural context. They'll do it, but they want a relationship with me, as coach. I think this is something that Germany has lots of room to improve in.'

The growth in tactical variety has led to many young German coaches portraying an extremely studious nature, but does that limit them from making the personal connection that – evidently – is a key part of a coach's success? 'Young coaches are very interested in the subject matter, but that personal connection comes with personal maturity and a certain distance to the player. If the coach is the same age as me, then it's hard for me to regulate a personal level. If they're older, they can take on a more senior, almost fatherly role. For a very young coach, this is quite hard. There are some young coaches, however, who are proving that age can be compensated for,' Niedzkowski says.

In a 2016 interview with Bavarian free weekly newspaper *Wochenblatt*, 26-year-old coach Sebastian Dreier admitted he saw himself less as a father and more as a brother who could help players take the next step. Pivotally though, he too is taking the next step. After coaching at youth level at Bayern Munich and Unterhaching, Dreier was named head coach of Mainz's U15s for the 2018–19 season. At the same time, he is a member of the 2018 *Fußball-Lehrer* class. As Dreier told *Wochenblatt*: 'Today, 15 years as a pro isn't enough to become a head coach. It's a job you have to learn, as the example of Thomas Tuchel shows.'

At Mainz, a club with a reputation for developing young coaches, Dreier stands an excellent chance of doing just that and perhaps becoming yet another young star in Germany's coaching pipeline. The fact Germany has so many young coaches is in part linked to the fact they have so many young players. Niedzkowski knows this. He has been one of those players and is now one of those coaches. 'We have lots of players who have come out of academies, and coaches who worked in those academies know academy-type players. That's why they can work so well with them. Sometimes, coaches even work with players they know from U19 teams – which can be an advantage, both for the coach and for the player.'

So what has changed for Niedzkowski, both in terms of coaching coaches and coaching players? 'Coaches come to us now with far more subject-specific knowledge than they did nine years ago when I was first here. The depth of knowledge in terms of tactics and physiology is much greater. A lot of the course they're familiar with because someone, either at their club or a friend, has already told them the terms and concepts. In football theory, you start to work at a much higher level much sooner.'

While clubs have changed their approach to encourage internal coaching development, there are also external factors that contribute to a country's coaching trends. 'Pep Guardiola's arrival in Germany took the thought process about tactical focus with the ball to another level,' Niedzkowski says. 'The perception of the considerations you can have before a game and the adjustments you can make changed. Before, no one changed their formation three times in a game – at least not that I know of. Whether it's good or not, or whether you can do it with every team, are other questions, but the understanding that it is a viable option for a coach, and even part of the coach's job, is far greater.'

In recent years, the image of German football has largely been moulded around the pressing game, thanks in no small part to Klopp and his Dortmund team. Others have taken the focus on pressing to extreme levels, in particular Roger Schmidt, Ralf Rangnick and Ralph Hasenhüttl, and that has changed how coaches on the *Fußball-Lehrer* course prepare. 'Not as much thought was put into it in the past,' Niedzkowski says. 'More attention was given to fitness and motivation. If it didn't work, then you simply had to do more. I don't mean that negatively, but the tactical knowledge of coaches and players has grown. Also, technical developments have made some tactics possible. Possession play requires players with great technical abilities and spatial awareness, and high pressing over 90 minutes demands outstanding and specific fitness.'

Niedzkowski argues Guardiola's possession-based philosophy also impacted the game in Germany. Thomas Tuchel, who coached a different way at Mainz, adopted a similar approach with Dortmund. Julian Nagelsmann's team has a clear style to it. With the evolution of players and tactics, the game and how to coach it has also developed. 'On the other hand, coaches who focus on defensive and transition strategies are very interesting. The game is more varied, and more thought goes into it now than 10 years ago,' Niedzkowski tells me.

A decade is a long time for anything to develop, and while it might be tempting to think that not working in a Bundesliga dugout leaves Niedzkowski out of touch, it would also be wrong. As assistant coach of Germany's U21s, he works with some of the most talented youngsters the country has. He is heavily involved in the training of those players and is fully aware of what they need and how they are different to the players of the past. 'What has changed is that with professionals you can't achieve anything through pressure anymore. Salaries are skyrocketing, social media has changed the placement of information, and with that, players have become very powerful. It's very difficult to connect with a player by pressuring him, because that pressure goes nowhere,' Niedzkowski tells me.

'The player might want to play at your club, but he knows that if things don't go well for him here, his agent can find clubs where he can earn just as much. The player isn't as connected to – or dependent on – the club anymore. Every player is generally available at any given time. And the player knows that, so you can't control them through pressure, you have to convince them. And you achieve this by giving the player the feeling that you are developing them into a better player and that they're a part of the team's success. Convincing players instead of pressuring them is perhaps the biggest change,' Niedzkowski says.

The idea of 'old school' management – shouting when things are bad and saying nothing when things are going well – doesn't work with modern players. There are simply too many factors at play. At the professional level agents and endless financial possibilities have shifted power to the point where coaching must also adapt. Coaching must accommodate and consider the plethora of external factors now surrounding every individual. If it doesn't, success will remain beyond reach. Why? Because it's the human first, then the footballer.

'This also changes the human components of coaching,' Niedzkowski continues. 'You can't insult a player like you could 20 years ago. The player will then think, or say, "Be careful, I earn two million euros. I never have to work again. If you say that to me again, I'm gone." The interaction with a player now must be about building trust, giving them feedback and staying in regular contact. That being said, I think players want tough love sometimes, they want to be pushed to their limit,' Niedzkowski tells me.

Being pushed is what the player wants, but not the club. Nevertheless, the factors Niedzkowski mentions – skyrocketing salaries, the tangle of social media webs – mean that the club is often the one being pushed to and beyond its limits. And it's worth remembering it wasn't always like this, as one coach told me: 'When I worked in youth football, if an agent came up to me and said they weren't happy I told them to pack their player's bags. I had a player once who stood still whenever he lost the ball. I told him, "If you lose the ball and you stand still I'll take you off." Every time he did, I took him off. And then all of a sudden I wasn't the right coach for him.' The player left to join one of the biggest teams in Europe, with the expectation he would play in the first team. He ended up in the third team.

Fast-forward to the present day and it is evident what has evolved. Speaking to *kicker* in January 2018, Niko Kovač, who was Eintracht Frankfurt head coach at the time, said he felt the pressure was approaching dangerous levels. 'Where does it end? In anarchy! Everyone will do what they want, players will come to training if and when they want to. Where has the responsibility gone? Where is the contract that counts? In the past the spoken word was valid. These days, a five-year contract means as little as a half a year contract. It's alarming.'

It takes a special coach – and team – to handle this situation well. The example of Ingolstadt in the Bundesliga shows just the tip of the iceberg. 'Two players behaved badly because they wanted to force a move,' says Niedzkowski. 'The team said, "That's not on, they can't train with us." Your relationship with individual players must be a close one, then they will help you regulate the team. You have to be clever with your leadership.'

Players look at how a coach responds to a crisis. Will they be cool or will they be aggressive? That tells the player a great deal about their head coach, but it also gives them a look into their future. For the coach, it can be the moment where they can win or lose a group. 'It's not about whether you've got the perfect plan for the weekend. It is about that to an extent, of course, but first of all it's about how you react as a person and how you treat the players. You can't ever forget that. That will always be the key,' Niedzkowski tells me.

There are even moments during a game when a coach must remember the individual needs of a player – which can sometimes have a greater impact on a result than the right tactical set-up. 'When a player has a chance in a game and misses it, lots of players look straight at the head coach,' Niedzkowski says. This seems obvious, but it is remarkable when you look out for it how many players do look to the sidelines for a response. 'Goal or not, you know in that moment the player needs the attention of the coach. He needs the coach's reaction to tell him, "No problem, keep going." Then you have other players who don't care, they just want to make sure the next chance goes in. Those players don't need that much attention as they sense the coach's trust merely through being in the starting line-up.'

Whether they are good leaders or not, head coaches are sacked more often than anyone else in football, which leaves me pondering the same question: can one man really do this job, let alone be held accountable for it? So many people contribute to success on Saturday afternoon that to make one responsible for it seems incomprehensible. 'It's just easier to change the head coach. If the problem lies in the team, then you can try and get rid of three or four players, but then you have to find replacements who have the same sporting quality – if you need a quick solution that's much tougher than finding one man. Often, it's a case of troubleshooting. If it doesn't work, then, "Have you tried turning it off and back on?" That's the first reflex,' Niedzkowski says, with a smile. But he believes there isn't any real difference in terms of subsequent success between firing a head coach in a crisis and keeping one. 'St. Pauli was an extreme example – they stuck with Ewald Lienen and then had an amazing second half of the season.'

Lienen is one of Germany's great football characters, and made 333 Bundesliga appearances for the likes of Borussia Mönchengladbach,

Arminia Bielefeld and Duisburg during the 1970s and 1980s. As well as winning the 1979 UEFA Cup with Gladbach, a run that saw Lienen score in the quarter-finals against Manchester City, the player is also known for being the man in one of the Bundesliga's most iconic photos. In only the second game of the 1981–2 season, Werder Bremen's Norbert Siegmann jumped into a tackle in order to rob Lienen, playing for Arminia Bielefeld, of possession. Instead, he slit open a near 10-inch gash on Lienen's thigh, exposing muscle and bone. Lienen was playing again within four weeks, but the foul remains one of the Bundesliga's most infamous moments.

After his playing career, Lienen coached in Spain, Greece, Belgium and Germany. The run of form Niedzkowski is referring to came in the 2016–17 season, when second-division side St. Pauli picked up just 11 points from their first 17 games. However, Lienen was kept on and they finished the season in seventh after a superb second half of the season saw them lose just three of the remaining 17 games.

'If there's no success, then everyone expects the conversation about the head coach to arise,' Niedzkowski says. 'That means others are out of the firing line because players know the first thing that will happen will be the head coach will be dismissed. When a new coach comes, players know they have to give it 100 per cent again because nobody is established anymore and everyone has a new chance, and that's why, at the start, there's an increase in performance. Those who have played before have to prove themselves again, and the players who were further down the pecking order now have a new chance. Without the head coach having done anything, the conditions are already more in his favour than before. But if the club says the current coach is staying whatever happens, then everyone else can't hope the problem will be solved for them. They have to re-engage themselves with a new situation. I think in that moment where St. Pauli said, "No, Lienen will remain our coach whatever happens" then things got better.'

It seems a remarkably simple thought, but how often has it been heeded? It only makes sense to sack the head coach when they are really to blame, not just when results aren't ideal. Niedzkowski remains calm about his future. The 'wait and see what happens' approach has served him well. There's no need to change that. At the time of our meeting, he told me he could imagine a return to a Bundesliga dugout at some point, but he wasn't sure whether he was ready to step into the limelight as the front man just yet. Chief instructor at Germany's coaching academy aged 41 isn't a bad place to be.

We talk for another hour after I finish asking questions, and I leave with little doubt in my mind about the advanced state of modern coaching for coaches in Germany – and not just in terms of the subject matter, either. I also leave believing that Daniel Niedzkowski will one day be a head coach. He has all the technical knowledge, but perhaps even more importantly he understands the importance of developing the person behind the coach, and the player. He is a man of principle who understands the nuances of a modern footballer. He is empathetic, something he is proud of despite believing it is often seen as a weakness in the public eye.

The 41 year old's playing philosophy is built around control, applying pressure and handling space. He believes if head coaches are to succeed they must overcome 'swamps where energy is lost and things trickle away' in order to build a winning environment. 'To be a coach is no different to how I am as a human,' says Niedzkowski. 'As a human, I want people to appreciate me – not to like me in every moment, because they won't like every decision – but generally say, "he's an honest guy, who is respectful and behaves properly". Those are the values that are more important to me than whether I'm seen in the best light.'

To stop the ego inflating beyond manageable or respectful proportions is one of the greatest hidden battles any famous person, let alone a head coach, will fight. Maturity is key. As the early twentieth century Austrian poet Rainer Maria Rilke stated in his *Letters to a Young Poet*: '... only someone who is ready for everything, who doesn't exclude any experience, even the most incomprehensible, will live the relationship with another person as something alive and will himself sound the depths of his own being.'

Sophistication in young coaches allows them to use the depths of their knowledge and wisdom to manage their players. Like Rilke, their maturity makes them bold enough to take on any challenge, even ones they may not initially understand. It allows them to recognise the value of every experience, but to understand that experience is a thirst that can never be quenched. Most of all it allows them to recognise how relationships with their players are living things that need caring for.

Key Lesson

The lesson that stood out from speaking to Daniel Niedzkowski was the complexity of pressure – something applicable to all aspects of life, not just football. Firstly, understanding and dealing with the pressure put on your shoulders as a coach, as a leader, is pivotal. For young coaches, maturity is a necessary part of that understanding. Secondly, recognising the appropriate methods and levels of pressure to apply and when. Thirdly, and most intriguingly, appreciating that the power of players compared to a decade ago has evolved to a level that forces a new type of coaching to combat a new pressure. The combination of handling these three is immensely difficult.

Denker
(Thinker)

'The most important thing today is the "why?"
This is also in The Art of War.'

– Lars Kornetka

The only time it's hard to believe Lars Kornetka is when he tells me that the best thing he ever did for his career was to say in an interview that he had no idea about football. Kornetka is currently an assistant coach at RB Leipzig, but at the time of our meeting he is assistant coach of Bayer Leverkusen. It was a week after the club's defeat to Bayern Munich on the opening day of the 2017–18 season, and our hour-long conversation revealed just how rare a soul he is.

As one of the men who brought video analysis to German football, Kornetka is well aware of the beast he has created and how it must contend with a number of other aspects in an ever-evolving game. He knows the unique position he is in, but battles – generally and in his field – with the direction in which the sport is headed. Little was made of his move to Leipzig at the start of the 2018–19 season, where he returned to work with Ralf Rangnick and Helmut Groß. In truth though, Kornetka might well prove to be the club's signing of the season.

Kornetka's assertion that he had no idea about football referred to how he made his first steps in the game. He had been working in television for WDR (*Westdeutscher Rundfunk*), and his work included the 2006 field hockey World Cup in Mönchengladbach. It was there that he met Bernhard Peters, the Germany head coach. At the time hockey was much further along than football in terms of analysis

– thanks to figures like Peters, but also because hockey players were more willing and able to engage with in-depth analysis.

Looking outside of your own sport for inspiration can be an effective part of coaching, and England head coach Gareth Southgate has certainly done that. The country's set-piece approach at the 2018 World Cup was in fact influenced by the time Southgate spent in the United States prior to the tournament. Many articles have commented on the fact the 47 year old attended NFL coaching sessions and watched an NBA game to get a better understanding of how to create space in tight situations. The analysis proved effective, as England became one of the most dangerous teams at the World Cup from set-pieces, particularly corners.

Many sports have been ahead of football when it comes to video analysis, as Kornetka and his colleague at WDR, Boris Notzon, found when they first stumbled across the idea of bringing it to football. With access to all of the football footage through the video archives at work they came up with the idea that, 'It would be cool to offer it to clubs, professionally.' As is often the case with good ideas, life got in the way for a while, but when Peters asked Notzon to throw together a highlight video and show some of the opposition's play, the light came back on. Both Kornetka and Notzon got to know Peters, but after the football World Cup in Germany Kornetka moved to Munich having received an offer for a traineeship at Premiere (a forerunner of Sky Germany). Then, in 2007, Kornetka's path changed again.

'Boris called me and said, "Crazy! Peters is going to Hoffenheim. They're probably going to get promoted and want to go big on our idea",' Kornetka tells me. 'And he asked me if I wanted to come to Hoffenheim. I thought he wanted to take me with him, but then he said, "Hold on, Christoph Daum is coming to Köln and I told him about the idea and he said he wants me there. How about you go to Hoffenheim and I'll go to Köln?"'

Kornetka was torn. He was keen to develop his promising career in television, but Notzon convinced him to at least go to the interview for the Hoffenheim job. It was there that he sat down in front of the club's youth co-ordinator Bernhard Peters, head coach Ralf Rangnick and team manager Jan Schindelmeiser, and told them he had no idea about football.

'Your advantage was that your hard drive was empty and you knew it,' Kornetka was told by Helmut Groß. These words have become something of a mantra for Kornetka over the years. 'It's often better to have people who want to absorb.' Aged just 27, Kornetka took the risk and joined Hoffenheim as head of video analysis back when no one knew what that was. He filmed every training session and learnt everything he didn't already know. Football media often raves about Julian Nagelsmann's use of technology to get ahead in coaching, but it is worth remembering there were equally innovative men before him.

The gamble proved to be one worth taking. Hoffenheim won promotion to the Bundesliga in 2008, and were top of the table by the winter break of their first season in the top flight. At the same time, Notzon also won promotion with Köln. 'My name kept coming up and my work was seen in a good light, and people understood that it made sense to do what I was doing,' Kornetka tells me. On multiple occasions he adds how he knows things might have turned out very differently had he not taken that job. 'It was coincidence, as everything in life is.'

This innovation prompted other clubs to sit up and take note. While Jürgen Klinsmann was in charge, Bayern Munich swiftly appointed a chief video analyst. 'The job didn't exist before. Notzon and I were the first ones – and in the second division, too, funnily enough. Without him I wouldn't have done it,' admits Kornetka.

In many respects, Germany can be grateful he did. At the time, England was 'miles ahead' in terms of video analysis. On a trip to Nice, Kornetka was joined by Bayern Munich's video analyst Michael Henke (another important figure in the development of the job in Germany), but the rest of the group was made up of analysts from French and English clubs (Chelsea, Manchester City and Newcastle United were the names Kornetka recalls).

Kornetka and Notzon's work certainly paved the way, and it isn't too much of a stretch to say that certain parts of German football wouldn't have advanced at the rate they have had the pair never made good on their idea years ago. Who knows whether Stefan Reinartz's Impect would have started were it not for Kornetka and Notzon's work years before?

After a decade at Hoffenheim, Kornetka moved to Schalke and then Bayern Munich, where he was Pep Guardiola's video analyst for a season. In 2014 he joined Bayer Leverkusen as an assistant coach, but at the start of the 2018–19 season he became an assistant coach at RB Leipzig.

When I met Kornetka, in June 2017, Leverkusen followed a fairly standard procedure of assessing an opponent by reviewing their recent games and then drawing up a training plan based on their opponent's strengths and weakness. Clips of opposition play against the ball, when they were under no pressure and when Leverkusen put them under pressure were also part of the preparation process.

In reviewing their own performance, Leverkusen would review clips of game film from various scenarios, including second balls and set-pieces, for example. Players could also review clips on their mobile phones.

Kornetka explained that he believed up to 70 per cent of all goals were scored in transition (the moment the ball is won back). With a further 20 per cent accounted for by set-piece situations, that left only 10 per cent from open play. This is why such a strong focus can be put on pressing and transitional football, because there are teams who can prove that the longer they have the ball, the less likely they are to score. The focus is on how quickly a team can score after winning back possession.

This is not to be confused with POMO (Positions Of Maximum Opportunity), the philosophy of former English FA director of coaching and education Charles Hughes. Hughes believed in the value of the long ball, but what Kornetka's analysis – and a lot of modern football, for that matter – suggests is that you're more likely to score the moment you win the ball back than if you patiently wait to unlock the opposition with endless passes. One of the best recent examples of this was Spain against Russia at the 2018 World Cup, when the Spanish attempted more than 1,000 passes before losing on penalties. On the other hand, this trend must not – as Matthias Sammer argued at the 2018 ITK in Dresden – result in ignoring the importance of possession football. Balance is key.

There is an immense amount of data to absorb and to relay. The key is to not overload the players, or even the head coach. At Leverkusen,

Kornetka explained that he might have just three minutes during a halftime break to show his head coach video evidence of what was going wrong or right.

Leverkusen have since changed their head coach, which naturally affected Kornetka's workflow. He echoed the sentiments of Daniel Niedzkowski that the most difficult task of an assistant coach is finding their feet with the new head coach. Kornetka told me that in the 2017–18 season under Leverkusen's new head coach Heiko Herrlich, the club did less video work than before because Leverkusen were out of European football and the focus was different.

This change, though, is not uncommon for Kornetka. In fact it has followed him throughout his career. Under Huub Stevens at Schalke for example, life was different. 'Stevens was a coach who did opposition preparation and post-game too,' Kornetka says, 'but if I showed him training film and said where we could do better or that a player needed better coaching because he was behaving wrongly at a certain point, he would always say, "Ok, you do it." He didn't want to, and he was working on other things, which is absolutely fine,' Kornetka says. He adds that in his entire career, apart from one exception, his relationships with head coaches have been great – something he admits was also a slice of good luck.

Kornetka gets on well with Ralf Rangnick; Stevens let him do his job. He still maintains a good relationship with former Schalke and Union Berlin head coach Jens Keller. He is good friends with Roger Schmidt, and knew Leverkusen's interim coach Tayfun Korkut, who now coaches Stuttgart, from Hoffenheim U17s. Kornetka also knew Herrlich before he arrived at Leverkusen.

It is worth mentioning that after leaving Bayern, Kornetka said he would only take assistant coach jobs, and not video analyst jobs, because he felt his progression would otherwise be stunted. 'I wanted to be assistant coach because I've worked under older coaches and as a young lad who had never played at that level I would arrive and say "we can do this better or differently", but I would always lose because the reply would always be, "Who do you think you are? You haven't won anything. Where did you play?"'

Listening to Kornetka talk about how he approaches his job, how he talks to players, how he coaches, makes me appreciate just how irrelevant a professional playing career can be when it comes to coaches getting the best out of the players. 'The factors that come together to contribute towards a win are very difficult to analyse,' Kornetka starts. 'I read a lot of war books. *War and Peace* by Tolstoy is a monster, but when it talks about war with Napoléon and the Russians, and how they analysed war, it's fascinating. One thing that always gets me is that it's always the winner that writes the story. And the winner always analyses why they won and what went wrong, while the loser always looks for their mistake rather than admitting the opponent was just too good. They'd rather say, "I made a mistake here". It's the same in chess. If I lose and afterwards I analyse the game and ask myself why I lost, I'll say, "Ah, I made a bad move there", but perhaps the move wasn't decisive. Perhaps I would have lost because of a different move because the opponent was so good I would have lost either way. It's the same analysing football,' Kornetka says, echoing the sentiments of Helmut Groß when discussing Dutch football.

As brilliant as it is to picture Leverkusen's squad reading Tolstoy, Kornetka is well aware that a team is made up of different people who relate and respond to different methods of coaching. Nevertheless, the use of literature remains a foundation of his approach when it comes to group or individual video analysis meetings. 'I can't come out and say, "I've shown them everything so my job is done." I have to come out and know that it has been understood. The most important thing today is the "why?" This is also in *The Art of War*. It has just as much validity today as it did back then. If I explain "why" to someone, then what they do afterwards is better. If I tell a soldier to dig a trench and he doesn't know why, he just digs, but if I tell him to dig a trench to hide himself in then he knows how deep he needs to make it to cover himself,' Kornetka says.

Perhaps the most interesting part of Germany's development of this Generation Why – players who ask why they're doing something rather than just doing it – is that eventually some of them will turn into coaches. Per Mertesacker became head coach of Arsenal's academy after retiring, and in his new book *Weltmeister ohne Talent* (*A World Cup Winner Without Talent*), he wrote: 'In my new role as Arsenal academy manager I will do everything I can to challenge the young players' mindsets. I want to challenge them so that they are ready to take on new ideas, and protect them from being injured, when it comes to their body and soul,' providing an indication of how being a part of a generation of inquisitive players can later have a positive impact on coaching.

Recognition of the player's soul is down to Mertesacker's personality, but it is nonetheless refreshing to see it included in youth development. Nurturing a player's character is just as important, as Mertesacker himself can attest. After Germany's extra-time win against Algeria in the 2014 World Cup last 16, a visibly exhausted Mertesacker responded critically to ZDF's line of questioning. After consistently being asked about Germany's lethargy and how short of the expected quality their performance had been, Mertesacker could take no more. 'I don't know what you want from me. Do you think there are Mickey Mouse teams in the last 16?' The now legendary interview finished with: 'What do you want? Would you rather we played beautiful football but got knocked out? I don't understand the line of questioning.'

Mertesacker's choice to allow his character to shine through united the team, and was perhaps an underestimated factor in Germany's eventual World Cup success. In that moment, he laid a part of his soul bare. That in itself is an all too rare thing in football, but that it helped the team develop is further testament to the importance of helping the player grow as a person as well as develop as an athlete.

Mertesacker retains that stereotypical German trait of 'doing it right', as evidenced in his biography where he details how he spent 10 per cent of his salary – several hundreds of thousands of euros – on a personal network of therapists. The former Arsenal defender's efforts to do more are a testament to him, and do pose the curious question as to why others don't do everything they can to be the best players possible. Everyone is different and needs different things to be successful, but it is somewhat surprising that Mertesacker's revelation appears an anomaly.

There's no reason to doubt that many of the German players who grew up in or spent time with Generation Why will have developed an incredible platform for coaching, should they want to. The ability to answer questions you once asked is invaluable, in both life and football. 'If I can explain to them the logic behind it, it's much easier,' Kornetka tells me. 'Set-pieces for example. If I just say, "run to the front post", then he'll run leisurely towards the front post. If I say, "in the moment you run to the front post, you take your marker with you and you open up space behind you and your teammate will attack that space and then our chance of scoring a goal is higher", then he approaches the situation completely differently.'

Prior to the 2018 World Cup, Gareth Southgate gave an interview to French sports newspaper *L'Équipe*. The England head coach, who represented his country as a defender, also acknowledged the need to be able to answer the questions the players have, further proof of the positive change he has brought to the England team. 'When I started as a player, the coach asked you to do something, and you just did it,' Southgate told the newspaper. 'Today, players want to know why they are doing some exercises and how they can benefit from them. It's a real challenge for coaches, because if you don't have good arguments to convince them, you'd better forget the exercise you were planning. But if you're pedagogic, then they will give everything they have.'

Whatever the level, it's only natural that some players will be sceptical. One video clip doesn't equal a regular occurrence. Kornetka knows this, which is why he always has 10 more scenes ready to support the same point. 'There are some players who don't trust it, and you have to find them and recognise that.'

Kornetka says his role is similar to an advisory role, something Daniel Niedzkowski mentioned when he told me about being assistant head coach of Germany's U21s. 'There is no room for arrogance. I can't be the type that wants to be in front of the camera, because I'm not in front of the camera. I'm not the one that gets up and shouts on the sidelines either. I'm the one that waits for the right moment, goes to the coach and says, "Maybe here and here we can do something". If the coach tells me to shut up, then I know he doesn't mean it rudely. That's my role, and I have to identify with that. Many people don't do that. They want to be in the limelight, and that's difficult,' Kornetka says.

'At the end of the day, the players are in the foreground,' Kornetka says, reiterating the point made by Frank Wormuth, Daniel Niedzkowski and others. 'They're the most important,' adds Kornetka. 'They have to like us if they're to believe us. And if they play well then everything is fine.' Every week, Kornetka does his best to make sure his team does just that – play well. Using systems that allow him to draw on the screen while showing game footage, he can show players, or they can show him, where they need to run. Kornetka can use arrows, colours and even move players in clips to demonstrate where the optimal run is or where pressure can be applied most effectively.

Kornetka shows me a few examples of the kind of tools he uses on a screen, talking me through them as the action unfolds. 'Set-piece situation. Ball comes in, is cleared, gets won back, goal. That too is a transition situation.' *Umschaltspiel* is the word he uses. Literally translated it means 'switch play', but the word 'transition' is the most logical translation. It is a word that can be heard every Saturday on football pitches across Germany, regardless of league or level. What started out as a fairly rudimentary tool has become an increasingly important part of development for a generation of players used to subconsciously learning by seeing. 'I can't do that,' is what Kornetka often hears. His response is simple. 'Yes you can. You already have,' he says, just before he presses play.

Kornetka is an innovator, but remains one of the names in the shadows of German football. An article in the German media from 2014 referred to him (despite never having contacted him for the piece) as being a man of the *Schattenwelt* (the world in the shadows). It seems a strange place for one of the country's leading football minds to work, but it's exactly where Kornetka likes to be.

'I think football has changed enormously. I think interest has changed too. I think people are crazy about lots of things. I enjoy it so much because I also enjoy playing chess. The game is highly complicated and fascinating. The best is to test yourself against the likes of Pep Guardiola, Julian Nagelsmann, Luis Enrique when we played Barcelona, because you know they think about it as much as you do. You're in a team of staff where everyone is on the same page and up for it,' Kornetka says, eyes bright and searching as if he is reviewing a game while talking to me.

'Vanity has become an issue. Then it no longer becomes about the task at hand, but rather who has to say something and who needs to come out of it the best. When it gets to that stage, my job is annoying and I ask myself whether I want to do it or not. The awesome part of the job is to play the game against one another.' Inevitably and understandably, Kornetka has his reservations with the tabloid media.

'If Julian Nagelsmann plays a different team against Liverpool to the one against Werder Bremen, then of course it's a rotation, but he still wants to win both games and he knows exactly why he plays Kerem Demirbay in the centre of midfield and not in a more attacking position. He didn't do it because someone had to play. There's a lot more invested into it,' Kornetka says.

The 40 year old feels there's too much talking and not enough understanding – words that wouldn't go amiss in many parts of the world today. For the future, he hopes the sporting aspect can return to the forefront. 'I recognise how much pressure is put on people – the head coach, the assistant coach, it doesn't matter. We're losing focus on the football. Press appointments are often more important, photo shoots, interviews are all more important than our work. I think that's a shame. If there was less vanity, then it would be a lot more fun to work with one another. There would be more exchange and discussion. The worst is to stand still, to think you know everything, because that's when you get overtaken. That's the worst. I hope that I always have the fortune of working with colleagues who want to move forwards, who aren't vain.'

German football is not exempt from hierarchical issues of vanity – few organisations or workplaces in the world are. In Chapter Eight, Daniel Niedzkowski pointed out that head coaches have to overcome 'swamps where energy is lost and things trickle away' in order to build a winning environment. If there are too many people concerned with securing their own position or status instead of addressing the needs of the collective, then progress will be hard to come by.

Despite all of his achievements and abilities, Kornetka is a humble man who retains a very grounded perspective. 'My job is a good one and I know I've done it well, but I'm not special. There are plenty of people in the world who do what I do, some of them probably do it better, and if other people had had my good fortune, they'd have done just as good a job. I'm not a talent. I learnt it. I got lucky with the right head coaches and jobs. You have to be honest with yourself. The door opens, do you go through it or not? Sometimes there's nothing behind the door, sometimes there's loads. It's just luck.'

For Kornetka, being the right person in the right place at the right time led him to an exhilarating career that holds great promise for the years ahead. Luck plays a part in every moment of change around the world, and perhaps it is one factor in the development of talented German coaches that has been overlooked.

Key Lesson

Recognising the importance of explanation. It's easy to overwhelm players, clients and staff with too much information in the modern era. Technology has allowed great advancement in the area of analysis and data collection, but it is still down to the coach, leader or boss to get the balance and method of sharing that information right. With clear language and strong delivery, explaining the value of an action, a drill or an exercise adds to the development of both the individual and the collective. Kornetka recognises different ways to do that with different players so as to avoid disinterest and a lack of focus (which can result in diminished performances). This requires constant adaptation as new players and staff members come and go, but getting this right is one of the key steps towards successful coaching.

10

Mensch
(Human)

'Life is the most interesting thing there is.'

– Ismail Atalan

The first two things that Ismail Atalan tells me when we sit down are about Barcelona and the English language. He wrote to the Spanish club asking if he could arrange a visit, so as to learn and observe. He also started to look into language courses, as he hopes to master the linguistic skills that could take him abroad one day.

'I'm the type of person that if I do something, I have to be the best at it,' he says as we sat down for lunch by the river in Münster. Fashionably dressed, with a black leather jacket, dark jeans and trendy red trainers, Atalan speaks passionately, gesturing as he explains his words.

Almost a month to the day earlier, the 38 year old had been dismissed as head coach of second-division side Bochum after just 10 games in charge. It was a decision that Atalan says shaped him and left him knowing that in the future, he'll only transmit things he believes in, that he would do himself.

Atalan coached in the lower leagues and after impressing in his first full-time coaching job at SC Roland Beckum, he was appointed head coach of Sportfreunde Lotte. In his second season, he guided the team to promotion to the third division. He then led the club to the quarter-finals of the 2016–17 German Cup, beating Werder Bremen, Bayer Leverkusen and 1860 Munich along the way, before eventually falling to Borussia Dortmund.

When we meet, the man who arrived in Germany as a five-year-old Kurdish refugee from Turkey is facing his first break from the game.

It proves a chance for reflection, on life as well as coaching. When he speaks, I start to get an insight into the kind of head coach and man he is – and it all starts with books.

'I read a lot of autobiographies,' Atalan tells me. 'Life is the most interesting thing there is. I recently read about James Dean's life. I now know everything about him. Martin Luther King. He's the most remarkable man. Nelson Mandela, Silvio Berlusconi. I read Zlatan Ibrahimović's autobiography. I'm not a fan of his because I don't like him, but I read the book to understand how those kind of people work, to know why they are the way they are. I've just finished reading Carlo Ancelotti's *Quiet Leadership*. Now I'm reading the second part of Guardiola's book, since he moved to Manchester City. I've also read a book looking at the parallels between the workplace and football. The man who wrote it owns a company with 70 employees and is also a football coach. I've read about the history of McDonald's and Siemens and how they made it to the top,' Atalan says, before stopping to point across the river at a modest looking building with a neon-blue sign on the outside. 'You see that harbour cheese factory over there? I would love to go in there and talk to the boss about how he made the company. Your book is the same thing. How did you think of such an idea? How do you write something like that? That interests me hugely. The lives of others, successful people but also not successful people – and by that I mean their professional success – that interests me.'

Life is a culmination of fascinating stories, and those stories are also the greatest representatives of what has moulded our character. In *Werner Herzog: A Guide for the Perplexed*, a book of interviews with the filmmaker, Herzog details how he believes the experience of life is at the heart of his creativity, telling author Paul Cronin: 'Walk on foot, learn languages and a craft or trade that has nothing to do with cinema. Filmmaking – like great literature – must have experience of life at its foundation.'

Coaching is no different, and it didn't take long to realise Atalan felt the same way. 'Martin Luther King is present in every team I go to,' he said. 'I hang this quote up from him:

If you can't fly, then run,
If you can't run, then walk,

If you can't walk, then crawl,
But whatever you do,
You have to keep moving forward.
'He has many quotes, but this one, in English and in German, is on the wall of all the teams I've been at. If I show the players that, they know I'm not a babbling idiot. Martin Luther King is serious. He made it. They beat him down time and time again but he got back up,' Atalan tells me.

The use of famous quotes as a motivational tool doesn't make Atalan a good coach, but being aware of how relevant some words still are in today's world makes him an aware coach. Speaking to Raphael Honigstein in an interview with the *BetVictor* blog at the start of 2018, Jürgen Klopp admitted he got someone to create a film of the biggest moments in history for him to show to his Borussia Dortmund team ahead of the 2012 German Cup final. 'I did not want to make it too big but I wanted to show them the excitement of (creating) such a historic moment,' Klopp said.

Gareth Southgate reportedly did the same for the England team ahead of the 2018 World Cup, showing them a combination of British sporting failures and victories. As Rob Draper wrote in the *Mail on Sunday*: 'He wanted to communicate two key points: there was nothing to live up to as, in reality, England have been mainly terrible since 1970. But also that it could change, just as it had for the Olympic team [from 1996 to 2012].' England's performances at the 2018 World Cup were refreshing, confident and free of fear. Southgate had lifted the gloom and a new England had emerged.

Awareness of what works and what doesn't is a key skill for any coach, but alone they are often not enough. Piecing them together is the real skill. 'You have to be a *Menschenfänger*,' Atalan says, using the German word for 'someone people will follow'. He continues: 'You have to catch people's minds. You have to convince them that the way you're going is the right one. You have to take the players seriously and explain to them why they have to make that run faster, not just that they have to do it. They have to know why they're doing it. You must explain why they're doing an exercise and where and when they do them in training, because only when a person understands why they're doing something can they be convinced of it.'

Football is currently riding the wave of Generation Why. This group of footballers who improve their ability by questioning and engaging are changing the coaching game. Lars Kornetka, Atalan and other coaches have said the same: if someone knows why they're doing something they're more likely to be convinced of doing it. 'The most important thing is being a *Menschenfänger*,' Atalan says. 'In terms of knowledge, Jupp Heynckes isn't better than Thomas Tuchel or any others. But he strokes it.'

Atalan uses the word '*streicheln*', which means to stroke or pet. In this case, stroke does work in the context of stroking egos. It is the deft touch of leadership that Atalan is talking about, the one that can often make the biggest difference. While Bayern Munich finished the 2017–18 season with 'only' one of three possible trophies, it was clear that not only did Heynckes have that touch, but that he knew when to use it.

'I always say, you can achieve short-term success through tactics but you have to be a *Menschenfänger* to achieve long-term success. A head coach that hasn't had success after a year, they're unlikely to be a *Menschenfänger*,' Atalan says. While this isn't true for all head coaches, the lack of concern for the personal aspect is a worrying trend. When Brighton and Hove Albion released veteran wingback Liam Rosenior at the end of the 2017–18 season, Rosenior wrote a poignant piece for *The Guardian* plainly stating the importance of people at a football club.

'It amazes me when we analyse football how little we take into account the human element of the game – we can all talk about systems, tactics and team selections but what actually makes the difference is the people operating on and off the pitch,' he wrote. Encouragingly, a few months later Brighton announced that Rosenior was joining the club's youth team staff as a coach. He took on the job having completed his UEFA Pro Licence, and brings with him his experience as a player, and a rare approach that really recognises the human.

RB Leipzig and Germany striker Timo Werner went even further to stress the absence of the human factor in an interview with the German Sunday newspaper *Die Welt am Sonntag*. 'I think football has reached a point where the players aren't being considered as people, rather as something like a product – and in the same way that prices for a phone rise, so too do the prices of players,' he said.

Players, coaches and members of staff are people, and yet for some perverse reason they're often stripped of human traits because of the pressure they're under and the money they earn. They may have access to a different life, but they have the same fallibilities as the people in the stands, watching on television and behind the keyboards.

'It's so important you understand how to interact with people,' Atalan says. 'Look at Robert Enke and his suicide. It shouldn't be underestimated. The lads go home and are alone. You have to give them the feeling they're important. That's why it's an important issue in society today.' At the end of the prologue in Ronald Reng's poignant and beautifully written book about Enke, *A Life Too Short*, Reng writes a powerful reminder:

'On the last page [of Enke's diary] there's a single sentence in huge letters. It was presumably supposed to be a reminder to himself, but today his sentence reads like a challenge to us all: "Don't forget these days."' Athletes don't become superhuman because they get to live out the dreams of millions. They are still humans at the core.

With the complexity of the football world greater than ever, the value and power of communication within it has grown. Recognition of each individual's mind, philosophy and emotions is a key part of a healthy life, let alone part of a team. The challenge football, and indeed society, faces is creating a space in which people feel they can do that.

England and Tottenham Hotspur defender Danny Rose created more of that space when he gave a startling interview to *The Independent* prior to the 2018 World Cup. Rose talked about his battle with depression and personal loss, and how the England team saved him from it all. By the end of the interview, football is the last thing that comes to mind. Rose's words are difficult to read, but not because he is a footballer – indeed the interview dispels the ridiculous belief that money or fame can save a person from the darkness of something like depression or loss. They are difficult to read because he is another human going through an extremely difficult period in his life.

But Rose's profession does of course play a role. His decision to speak out about the state of his mental health is important for us all, particularly in football. His words can help to spark a change in the perception of the modern athlete. The amount of pressure, scrutiny and unrealistic expectation put on athletes today is unhealthy, so is it any surprise that depression has crept into a sport full of people's heroes? Rose's words can start to help change that. They can help change the lens with which we view modern athletes. And if we can change the perspective on those playing the world's most popular sport, perhaps the ripples will find their way into everyday society.

There's a great quote from legendary college American football coach Bo Schembechler that highlights why it's so important to recognise the person before the player. The coach was once asked by his quarterback at Michigan, Jim Harbaugh (who is now himself the Michigan coach), what kind of team he thought they'd have that year. Schembechler said: 'When you guys come back 15, 20 years from now and we know what kind of men you are, what kind of husbands you've become, what kind of fathers you are, then we'll now how good this football team is.'

If we treated professional sportsmen and -women as human beings first and athletes second, then not only would we have a greater understanding of them, as both people and players, but we would also expand the space in which topics like mental health can take place. The impact of that on the athlete would stretch far beyond the lines of the pitch.

In the Bundesliga, one man lauded for his communication and ability to manage a squad is Schalke's Domenico Tedesco. The 32 year old arrived at one of Germany's most demanding and expectant clubs having coached just 11 games at second-division Erzgebirge Aue, but has since shown on many occasions that he knows, as Atalan said, how to interact with people.

In an exclusive interview with Sky Sports in Germany in November 2017, Tedesco said: 'Mentality beats quality in many situations … If I could pick a team with lots of quality or lots of mentality, I would always take the one with mentality.'

A few weeks later, his Schalke side found themselves 4–0 down after just 25 minutes of their away match against arch rivals Borussia Dortmund, but went on to draw 4–4. Tedesco practises what he preaches. His language truly is a window into his soul – one of a head coach who is all about communication and mental strength. Tedesco believes in the importance of the mental side of the game, and while that is largely down to his character and values, learning and working in Germany plays a role.

Again we return to the consideration of experience and what Frank Wormuth mentioned in Chapter Two. The two main differences between coaching at youth level and first team are players and pressure. Handling experienced professionals is a completely different task to dealing with young players, as is doing so under far greater scrutiny, but large parts of the job remain the same. In Germany, it appears that has not gone unnoticed.

Tedesco may well have arrived at Schalke with just 11 second-division games under his belt, but he had also coached 20 at Hoffenheim's U19s and 50 at Stuttgart's U17s. Now, that is not to say that experience alone should merit a chance but clearly Schalke considered that, alongside Tedesco's character, it was valuable. A club must understand the person behind their coach. If they don't, they cannot know if they have appointed the right coach.

The same is true of a coach and his players. If they don't understand the person they are selecting – not just what kind of player they are – then success will be that much harder to come by. 'It's really important these days to know lots about people, about their private problems, so you have an understanding of them,' says Atalan. 'To do something, you have to analyse the situation, think of a plan and then put it into place.'

How Atalan handles this is as forward-thinking as his openness about the societal issues that impact so many of us, such as mental health. 'As a head coach, I always listen to the charts. I listen to the music they listen to, the films they watch, so that I can understand what kind of lads they are and how they work. Sometimes new terms are used, from rappers and such like, and in the changing rooms you want to be able to talk to them or at least have a feel for it.

'You have to know that you're going to a team that isn't a football team. There are players from far away, with no family at home. Maybe they have a girlfriend, but mostly these people are lonely, and they have feelings too, but in today's society we don't have any time for feelings,' Atalan says, poignantly. 'That's the worst part of it. But you have to give them the feeling that you understand the situation. You have to make sure that the person goes home after training reassured. He doesn't have to like you all the time, that's not always possible, but he has to know where he is. He can't have the feeling that he is second class. They can never have this feeling. Which is why I always say the most important players for success in a season are substitute players.

'A player that plays is always in a good mood. They're playing in front of 40,000 people, they're enjoying it and the head coach should leave them to play, but those that don't play and are on the bench, those are the ones you have to push to keep giving their all in training, to challenge the starters so that when they're needed – because they will be during a season – they give it their all. They're the most important players during a season. When we got promoted with Lotte in the promotion [playoff] game, two players who weren't even in the matchday squad were still there and went to every single player in the changing room to motivate them. That's what makes the difference,' Atalan says.

This collective approach is what saw Atalan create the right kind of team atmosphere, and is largely the reason his Lotte side upset the odds three times on *that* German Cup run. Clearly, Atalan has the knowledge required and is willing to expand the bounds of that at every given opportunity, but it is his understanding of the personal side of things that hints at what truly lies at the heart of good coaching.

Furthermore, Atalan has never forgotten his humble beginnings. 'I know what people in the stands want to see because I used to sit there. I know what it means to them to buy a ticket. I have three children. If you take the whole family to the game, it costs two hundred euros. I know how hard it was to make it here.' The early death of his father meant he built an incredibly close relationship with his mother, and also made him an extremely determined individual. 'Whenever I had conflicts, she always calmed me down. She always said to me: "A listener is always better prepared and more intelligent than someone who always talks. Listen and then give your opinion, but don't go somewhere and say something".'

That relationship with his mother and the passion about his journey has not only affected his personality, but also the kind of coach he is. 'Before the game, I always try to think of something to say. The lads always know that I'm not just saying any old crap, but that what I say is true. They know where I'm from so when I say hard work pays off, they know I mean it because I've done it and they know my story. That's more believable than a head coach who only got the job because he was a Bundesliga player,' Atalan says, proudly.

On the *Fußball-Lehrer* course, Atalan developed not only his character but also his craft as a head coach. Nevertheless, it was life that was once again the key. 'You're taught the knowledge as well, but you also learn that football is a puzzle. At the start, you take it apart and at the end, you put it back together. You have 23 other coaches on the course with you, but you learn that life is the best coach. The exchange with them about how they'd do it or they have done it – that's the best.'

The worst part is the pressure – and here we return to the fundamental argument that ties Atalan's style of coaching together: people. 'You have unbelievable pressure on you and some people break under it. In Bochum, I realised that you can't change it, so just give your best. You're desperate to achieve that challenge because it's not a simple job. We get compensation for pain and suffering,' Atalan says.

'People forget that it's about people. What you realise as a head coach is that the media are tougher than ever before. If you win, you're the best and if you lose, you're the worst – that's not right. I accept that but I don't respect it and I don't read it,' Atalan says, adding he'd rather read a book.

How does a head coach deal with pressure, especially one in the pool of talented young coaches with a bright future ahead of them? 'If it doesn't work for two or three games, then of course you doubt yourself,' Atalan says. 'Just as I do now – I don't have a job, what have I done wrong? Could I have done something else? In that moment you reflect, you watch the game. After the game I always have an 11-point plan, seven subject based, four person based. If all 11 were right, then I know I did everything right. The most important thing is that the plan you have is the right one because then if you see the lads are making technical mistakes or they miss an open goal, then it doesn't hurt you.

'If you see them corner the opposition on the other side of the field, move into a slightly more attacking position in midfield and force them to play a quick ball leaving them with a numerical advantage in the middle. If the lads do that and it doesn't work, then you blame yourself. Then you start to doubt, doubt that you can read the game. But it worked well with me because I watched the games, and the training sessions. Even in the *Kreisliga* I recorded the games. You're training during the week to make sure the load at the weekend – tactical, physical, mental – is as low as possible. The best feeling is not scoring. The best feeling for a head coach is when you've trained build-up play or play off the ball, and your team attacks and what happens is exactly what you have trained. That's the best feeling. That's why my self-confidence has grown, because I've seen everything I taught the lads would have worked if I had done it right or did work because I did it right.'

Humbly but perfectly suited to the German coaching mindset, Atalan believes the most important part of the job is having the right staff. The team behind the team is an approach that works for many organisations around the world who value the work of the many not just the few. 'It's the most important thing. You need a coaching staff that is loyal. And in this job, it's harder than ever to find people who want to suffer with you. The mistake I learnt from Bochum is to always have a training staff that you know. You can only demand teamwork if you're part of one yourself. They can invest a lot of work, but it can also cost you a lot of work if you don't do it right. Then you have to go back and check. It's really important to know them,' Atalan tells me.

While not as outspoken on social issues as Freiburg's head coach Christian Streich, Atalan clearly feels strongly about the way in which the world is developing and how that impacts how he does his job. 'The media want people like Streich, and then you are one and then they criticise those characters.'

Not a fan of the AfD, Atalan still believes opinion matters. 'I'm the type of person that would prefer the AfD just to say, "I don't like foreigners". Be honest and open. So long as you don't physically or emotionally hurt someone else, then you can have your opinion. I think that's something you have to talk about. You can't just let it happen. The same can be said for the smartphone generation. The smartphone has changed the world. I've gone into changing rooms and 10 players are all on their phones during a break. They're not even talking to one another,' Atalan says.

'The best school is life. If people don't talk to one another then they lose sight of reality, and that's why you have to talk about and guide people towards the fact we're still people and that we should behave like it. And that has been lost a bit because of the internet,' says Atalan.

Turning social issues into an effective and relevant form of coaching is a skill, and Atalan has his methods. 'You make clear there's a set of rules. Players have to be at training an hour and 15 minutes before the session and from that time onwards, there's a ban on mobiles. If there are problems with the family, there's always an emergency number they can call. Forty-five minutes after training, there's also a ban on mobiles. Then, they sit there and talk to one another – which they do most of the time – and then you've got a bit of engagement. You won't ever be able to blank it out these days because there's too much of it – headphones and all. But that they're together, and in training focusing on doing very little individual work and lots of group tactical work, that you give them breaks to talk to one another, that you look to see which players are interacting with one another – those are things I look out for.'

Atalan's character clearly makes him unique and allows him to develop his own style of coaching, but what does he believe it takes to be a good head coach? 'You have to be humble without losing your self-confidence because if you're not confident in this job, you'll lose. I'm confident, but some people associate humility with weakness. In pro football, this is an extremely fine line. That's what I've realised. Weakness is sought out. The moment one is found, it's jumped on,' Atalan says, perceptively.

Weakness, or the perception of weakness, is a problem for most leaders. A lax set of rules is the beginning of the end, according to Atalan. 'If you're not strong enough mentally, then players can eat you alive. You have to find the line between humility and self-confidence. If players see a weakness, they'll take advantage of it. That's sadly just the way it is in football, at least at the start, because there's a different relationship at the end. At the start though, you have to make sure not to show any weakness – which is normal – but in our job, it's deadly.'

Echoing the thoughts of Lars Kornetka, Atalan also talks about football's battle with jealousy and vanity. While these issues can and do interrupt the effectivity of any workplace, it is interesting to hear Atalan talk about how self-interest has impacted the football world. 'You can't lose sight of the goal,' he says. 'Vanity means you can do everything better than others. Many people are worried that it will be seen as a weakness if you want to learn something. Society has changed and you have to be aware of that as a head coach. For example, you criticise a player and that was the end of it. Today, Facebook and all of that plays a role and the machine starts to roll. Just look at Photoshop. That moment with Jérôme Boateng where Messi dribbles past him – suddenly he's falling into a hole. You have to be aware of it all.'

It is fascinating to hear a football head coach talk about how quickly the modern world loses touch with and distorts reality, and how that affects management. Have we lost touch with what it is to be a person? Or, more frightening still, have the borders of what make us human moved so much that we can't recognise ourselves anymore? The same question can be posed of coaching in football.

'There are no good or bad coaches. There are appropriate and not appropriate,' Atalan says, echoing the words of Frank Wormuth. The media's assessment of what makes a good coach is too often a stab in the dark. Like a relationship, there are only ever two people who know the truth. 'They have to fit the philosophy of the club,' Atalan tells me. 'They have to appreciate their players. They have to take themselves as seriously as their players – no more, no less. I think the young head coaches have a small advantage because of the education they're receiving. It's not easy for the older coaches to go back to school, but nothing can replace the experience old coaches have. Heynckes has experienced things a thousand times. If Franck Ribéry storms out of the changing rooms, then he knows what to do. For me, it would be the first time I had seen that. The older coaches have more experience, but you have to make sure the coach is the right fit for the team,' Atalan says, aptly.

Nothing beats experience, apart from culture. Rory Smith wrote a piece in the *New York Times* with the headline 'For Young Coaches, Tradition Is Among The Toughest Opponents'. In the piece, the then-31-year-old Scot Ian Cathro talked about how the image created of him being a nerdy, laptop-driven coach with few communication skills was 'not even close to the truth'. Granted, Cathro suffered from not winning enough games in his brief spell in charge of Heart of Midlothian, but it seems he was set up to fail by the perception of what makes a good head coach – namely more experience in the form of a former pro career or time at top clubs.

Having now been employed in the industry, Atalan's perception of this phenomenon has developed. Listening to him, Atalan's words echo the fear Frank Wormuth spoke about and the domino effect Daniel Niedzkowski talked about. 'Head coaches aren't protected enough,' Atalan says. 'I don't know what it's like in other countries, but coaches aren't protected enough. The problem is, clubs are looking at it the wrong way. If it isn't going well, then the first thing that happens is the coach goes. What are the players going to do in the future? They'll say, if it doesn't work out, the coach is gone, who cares? And the clubs don't do themselves any favours by taking that approach. We have to be careful of that situation in Germany. It's not always the head coach that's to blame.'

After just four games of the 2017–18 season, three German second-division head coaches had been sacked. By the tenth game that number had risen to five. *The Times* released an interesting graphic after Carlos Carvalhal was appointed Swansea City head coach at the end of December 2017, looking at head coach turnover since the 1950s. Between 1950 and 1959, the average time in charge (excluding those still in post) was five years and four months. For the period from 2010 to 2017, the average time was one year, three months. Time in the job – whatever the country – remains an issue, but so does making the right, or as Atalan put it earlier 'appropriate', appointment.

Despite his social skills and hunger to learn and grow, Atalan remains without a job. He regrets only one thing about his career so far, and it's telling. 'The one thing I regret during that time is that I didn't savour it. I forgot to savour the wins and the success, to sit at home and think, that was great,' Atalan says, appearing to go through the memories and the moments in his mind as he mentions them.

'I was constantly moving from one to the other, from one to the other, and I regret that a bit because there were some great games along the way. That German Cup run – I didn't savour that. Promotion – I didn't savour it. It has made me thoughtful, about life too. We have to be careful not to forget what we're doing because the machine is still rolling. Above all, life is beautiful, and we shouldn't forget that,' Atalan says.

Interestingly, this appears a commonly shared view. In his interview with the *BetVictor* blog, Jürgen Klopp said: 'Unfortunately, life is such that something really great happens and then the next minute, you have to maintain it. No one gives you really any time to embrace it, to enjoy it anymore. I think a very good example is Nico Rosberg. He absolutely deserved winning the Formula One championship. He retired and people said: "Yeah, good. I don't think he would have won it again anyway". So yeah, where is the problem? I don't get it. There are so many positive surprises on earth every day that mostly impact the people they happen to. It's enough that they know it.'

The words of Atalan and Klopp resonate. Like life, coaching is about people. Many jobs, particularly in football, are unrelenting, giving little room for momentary achievement. It's always about what lies ahead, what's the next step on the career ladder, which grass is greener. The impact of that on the human behind the Formula One driver, the football head coach, or the colleague at work, can be damaging. Our restlessness to achieve our dreams of success doesn't leave us with much internal balance, and if we're not careful the true beauty of those moments only becomes apparent once they have long passed.

Atalan tells me that Thomas Tuchel once said in an interview that the then BVB head coach thought a great deal of him. 'Beforehand, no one knew you and suddenly you're in a world with the best head coaches in the world and they're talking about you. That did something to me that I partly didn't even realise, and that was a bit of a shame.'

For a head coach to admit the moments had passed him by is certainly a sign of character. Perhaps if there was less pressure there would be a greater chance for head coaches to savour success. Just like coaches have to take the person behind the player into consideration, so football has to acknowledge that there's more to the head coach than just his coaching.

A few months after I met Atalan, he appeared on German television reminiscing about his success at Lotte and troubles at Bochum. He was still searching for a head coaching position and while he, like many other coaches, know this period is part of the job, it is no less difficult. The wait for the right kind of offer, the insecurity, going from under the microscope to being invisible – it takes its toll on the individual. Germany might boast an excellent coaching education and a league of opportunity, but just like every other football nation it cannot escape the difficult, lonely path that many coaches must tread. It's one many people in many professions tread, the one where the work you love to do is just beyond you, and where waiting becomes a virtue you must learn.

Key Lesson

Enjoyment. With great pressure comes great focus, and perhaps without it elite success isn't possible. However, we are in danger of becoming robots – as coaches, players, staff, people – if we don't recognise achievement. Ambition is a necessary trait for success, but it can't cloud over those moments of joy. Atalan regrets not savouring those moments of success, likely because of the industry he works in. Given the pressure bestowed on players and coaches, why can't enjoyment play a larger role?

In the documentary *Building Jerusalem*, about England's 2003 Rugby World Cup triumph, Jonny Wilkinson talks about wanting to hold on to the moment when the referee is about to blow the final whistle in the World Cup final. In that moment, Wilkinson says the referee is just about to blow time on his dream, and that as the official lifts the whistle to his mouth, Wilkinson wants to hold him there in time so he can take it in. It's the ultimate moment for any athlete. As Wilkinson says in the documentary, in that exact moment he is still working towards his goal, but at the same time he knows nothing can stop him. It's that moment in time which we cannot forget to savour.

11

Erfahrung
(Experience)

'I sit there and listen to Zen.'

– Eckhard Krautzun

It's grey and wet, like most days in late November in Germany, but on my journey northeast out of Mannheim on a regional train, the stops – Weinheim-Lützelsachsen, Weinheim (Bergstr), Hemsbach, Laudenbach (Bergstr), Heppenheim (Bergstr) – are brilliantly German. This route runs along part of an ancient trade route called *Bergstraße* – the Mountain Road. Despite the weather, it's clear to see why the area is so pretty. It was around here that Kaiser Joseph II is claimed to have said: 'It's here that Germany begins to become Italy.'

Heppenheim, the stop I get off at, is famous for its wine festivals (not uncommon in the area) and for being the birthplace of Formula One driver Sebastian Vettel. About 3,500 people in the town celebrated his 2013 Formula One championship win – some even held banners renaming the town *Vettelheim.*

But there is another famous man from this town. After picking me up from the station, he chats to the police standing in the car park. He smiles and laughs with the locals in the café we sit down in. He is well known by everyone here and having only heard him on stage in Bochum, I quickly realise how much of a privilege it is to talk to him one-on-one.

Eckhard Krautzun has had 32 different coaching jobs in 12 countries. After a very brief playing career in the 1960s, Krautzun was Kenya head coach in 1970, before joining Canada four years later, after which he returned to Germany to coach Wormatia Worms and then 1860 Munich. In the early 1980s, Krautzun took charge of 1. FC Union Solingen in the second division. Over the next 13 years, he coached at various other second division clubs, including Freiburg and Wolfsburg, as well as spending a short time working in the Philippines. He made the German Cup final in 1995 with Wolfsburg, before winning the competition with Kaiserslautern a year later. After time at St. Pauli and Darmstadt, Krautzun was made head coach at Mainz. But after 10 games, he made way for none other than Jürgen Klopp. Krautzun then headed to Tunisia before coaching China's U20s at the 2005 U20 World Cup.

His experiences wouldn't be out of place in a work of fiction, but it is because they are real that the 77 year old's life takes on an even greater sense of importance in understanding German coaching, and he continues to coach German coaches about heading abroad as well as being the country's leading expert on Chinese football.

'When I got an offer from abroad, I always went to that country first to look at the city, the stadium, the people I would work with. I would never go somewhere without visiting first,' Krautzun says, in fantastic English. 'What kind of people are they? What kind of philosophy? You have to know what to expect. The mistake we made in the past is that we went there and thought, "We'll follow the German B Licence". That is a big mistake. You should always ask them, what are your requirements?'

For a man who does all of his lectures in English and has been a close friend of Sir Alex Ferguson's for 36 years, Krautzun is not someone limited by a foreign language. He is a man of the world. Choosing to speak English is not foreign to him, and so I wasn't worried that I wouldn't see the real him despite the lack of German in the conversation.

For the past 15 years, Krautzun has decided to advise coaches rather than return to the dugout. A few days after we spoke, he was in Cologne talking about the Chinese market to a host of interested clubs and coaches. His scouting abilities and football knowledge are, naturally, of great interest. After all, as he tells me: 'One of the greatest things, which many coaches can't do even though they've had 800 coaching courses, is read a game. They can't do the right thing in the right moment.' Krautzun believes this is a skill that can be learnt.

By working abroad, Krautzun has not only learnt a great deal but is also perhaps best placed to judge German coaches on the international stage. 'If a German coach goes to another country, he gets the chance and the coach has no resentment against other cultures or other countries. Maybe in England or in France, there's a certain danger of arrogance because of your colonial background. You think you've invented everything, including football, and you think you are the best. If a German coach goes to Africa or Asia or to England they are more open and natural in their approach. They don't arrive saying, "We are the German champions; we are the best". If you behave like that, you have already lost,' Krautzun tells me.

He isn't wrong. Of the recent spate of German coaches that moved to England, none arrived with a superior view of their coaching skills. And they all have seemingly understood the value of the respective team's connection with its community. Jürgen Klopp has made Liverpool his home, and there are endless examples of how he continues to connect with the community. David Wagner took Huddersfield Town to unimaginable heights, and it's clear from his interview with *Joe* in July 2018 that he too recognises what makes a football club. 'You have to create a culture where there is understanding and belonging,' Wagner said. 'You have to realise there are different ways of management within a group, and find the right channels. There are so many details to managing a football club before you even can think about tactics or exercises in training.' When Wagner departed Huddersfield in January 2019, it was a surprise, but the club's statement revealed he needed a break. While there's undoubtedly more to the story than appears, it's a reminder that doing the job as fully as Wagner did it is also tough over an extended period of time.

Daniel Farke, who became Norwich City manager in 2017, is looking to do the same at Carrow Road, and Daniel Stendel arrived at Barnsley in June 2018 ready to be a head coach again. Ralph Hasenhüttl, an Austrian coach who was in the same *Fußball-Lehrer* class as Jürgen Klopp in 2005, was appointed Southampton head coach at the end of 2018 and hopes to start off on the right foot by keeping the club in the Premier League. It seems only a matter of time before Julian Nagelsmann, and perhaps, eventually, Domenico Tedesco, try their hands abroad.

For all the potential financial incentives, taking that step outside of Germany is a big one for German coaches, and at the ITK in Bochum it was Krautzun – along with fellow well-travelled coach Rainer Willfeld – who explained the options available to German coaches. Other than taking a coaching or association job abroad through your own network, there are different types of international projects available. Short-term projects (from two weeks to a year) mainly involve coaching coaches or improving association structures. Long-term projects (two or more years) are aimed at developing sustainable structures (coaching coaches, development of youth football, association planning). The projects are dependent on the desire of the host nation, are funded by Germany's Federal Foreign Office (AA – Auswärtiges Amt), and organisation and support are provided by associations such as the German Olympic Sports Confederation (DOSB) and the DFB.

The concept of educating coaches in how to manage abroad is both fascinating and brilliant because it extends beyond a set-piece drill or interview preparation. Understanding cultural differences is a complex enough topic outside of football, but inside a sport that means so much to so many it carries even greater weight. As a German coach in Togo in the late 1980s and early 1990s, Willfeld arrived with the stereotypical traits of his country: punctuality, discipline, organisation, hard work and of course, success. Willfeld felt only he could prepare for the game because he was the head coach and he had the final word, but he learnt the importance of getting local coaches on his side and respecting local traditions. They can often be the difference in making a good start, grasping the language and making the necessary connections. They can also help you understand the different types of traditions at play.

Willfeld was Togo's U20 head coach for the 1987 U20 Word Cup in Chile, a wild tournament that saw Togo exit in the group stages after defeats to Chile, Australia and a Yugoslavia side that would beat East Germany (with Matthias Sammer) in the semi-finals and then West Germany in the final on penalties thanks to the skill of Davor Šuker, Zvonimir Boban and Predrag Mijatović. Qualifying for the tournament was a huge achievement for Togo, and just one of Willfeld's many adventures in the team.

In Bochum, Willfeld talked about his experience of coaching in Togo, in particular how adapting to new surroundings included some surprises. '*Les Féticheurs*', or witch doctors, for example, were something altogether new. Before a game, Willfeld was confused as to why something was being prepared on the pitch. He was told magic was being prepared for the game, and that the team would win 2–0. 90 minutes and a few red cards later, his team had won 2–0. Willfeld's point was not that voodoo magic is the secret to coaching, but that understanding the contrasts of preparation methods in different cultures is important to being successful in the job. Part of that is understanding your cultural impact.

Willfeld now spends most of his time advising and helping coaches about working abroad, and is best placed to explain their cultural impact given his vast range of experiences. Between 1999 and 2004, he worked in Vietnam, and has more recently taken jobs in Burkina Faso and Burundi. During his time in Burkina Faso, he was asked to step in as U17 head coach for the 2009 U17 World Cup but found out that 13 of his 25-man squad were too old. Despite having to reassemble virtually a whole new squad and having minimal preparation time, Willfeld guided Burkina Faso to the last 16 before they were beaten by a Spain side that included Isco and Koke. During his career he has also spent time coaching in Chad and Mauritius, but wherever he has been, the focus has always been on coaching other coaches, improving youth football and organisational structures. In his 73 years, Willfeld has done so much for so many around the world – and, like Krautzun, is now helping other coaches understand how to do the same.

A head coach must not only be aware of the impact he is making on a country, but also the changes he himself must be prepared to make. Krautzun uses the term '*the intercultural adjustment*', and pioneering this, he learnt 30 to 40 basic Mandarin expressions to help him coach but also to live in China. Instructions for the training pitch combined with basic directions for the taxi driver made him a better coach. 'That is so important,' he says. 'Certain clubs have approached me to teach their coaches before they go to China – about China's culture, history, political system, weakness and strength in football, administration. If you arrive in a country like China without that knowledge, you lose and waste a lot of time. You need three or four months to find out,' Krautzun told me.

While English lifts the veil from a move abroad in most European countries, failure to prepare is a mistake. An early online video of Jürgen Klopp as Liverpool head coach learning about the Scouse dialect is amusing, but it also shows his willingness to adapt to the area, his recognition and acceptance of *the intercultural adjustment.* 'One power that a coach has is his language in Europe. When you go to a club like Bayern Munich and you don't speak German, like Carlo Ancelotti, you will have difficulties. Pep Guardiola was better. He had prepared intensively. If you can't speak to the players, then you will not get close to them,' Krautzun says.

Whenever a coach or a player moves abroad they instantly become more than just a coach from their homeland, something Krautzun recognised in China and considers pivotal. 'You are an ambassador of your country if you go abroad, ambassador of the coaching development of that country. You must set an example without losing your personality. You have to follow your philosophy. You must not change your character, which sometimes means you must be a very good actor,' Krautzun says.

Finding the balance between being authentic and being the right person at the right time is tricky. On the whole, Krautzun's words echo those of Daniel Niedzkowski in Chapter Eight that 'To be a coach is no different to how I am as a human.' However, to coach abroad makes that harder. As Willfeld explained of his time in Togo, the German mindset can sometimes meet a brick wall of different cultures, traditions and rituals. Sometimes it's not about who you are but who you need to be.

'Germans by nature are very disciplined people. We believe the coach should always set an example. He is the role model. If the coach is not punctual,' says Krautzun, then that can set a problematic example. 'Many coaches have failed because of that,' he says.

The game is growing – and that has both positive and negative impacts for German coaches. The Bundesliga is far from perfect, but the league has built a reputation in recent years as a place of community, opportunity and development. Sadly and yet unsurprisingly, it doesn't seem content to stop there. And in a world of brutal ambition, there is always going to be struggle. 'German coaches, unfortunately, have lost that authority because of the influence of sponsors, managers, technical directors,' says Krautzun. 'Many coaches are in the dilemma of sitting between three stools. Twenty years ago, there were many Felix Magaths. The coach was the boss and in England they call him "the boss". In Italy the call him "*mister*". In Germany, in most cases, the coach is not the boss anymore,' Krautzun tells me. Hamburg's ever-changing hierarchy and Karl-Heinz Rummenigge and Uli Hoeneß at Bayern Munich are prime examples of people whose superior power makes life difficult for any head coach.

While the role of the sporting director is perhaps of greater importance in Germany than in some other countries, as we discussed in Chapter Three, power struggles between various levels of club hierarchy are not a uniquely German issue. Nevertheless, Germany has its fair share of them. 'When Toni Kroos was sold, I was there having lunch with Matthias Sammer and his assistant Hermann Gerland. They really didn't want to let Kroos go, but the bosses had decided he asked for too much, so they must let him go. That is very difficult nowadays. If the board of directors or management or president says for such-and-such a reason that we must sell that player, then you have problems.

'I once had a player in Tunisia who married the daughter of the President. He had a lot of privileges. He drove his car right up to the plane, he didn't want to train in the mornings, he wanted his own room. The captain asked me how I was going to handle that problem,' Krautzun says. 'I convinced him he was part of the team. You're the goalkeeper. If you don't want to do to the warm-up on the matchday, then you can stretch inside. I gave him that freedom, but when we travel, you are exactly the same as everyone else. He complained about others snoring. I told him to put earplugs in. It was very difficult.'

Krautzun has endless stories, and many bring out the performer in him, none more so than when he tells me about his time in charge of China's U20s at the 2005 World Cup. Ahead of the team's last 16 game against Michael Skibbe's Germany, China's minster for sport came in and gave a speech to the team, which Krautzun reenacts for my benefit – shouting Mandarin words and gesturing with his hands as if he is right back in that changing room – much to the amusement of the locals in the café. The speech was an attempt to rouse the team, reminding them of the importance of the game and how they needed to raise their performance. Sadly, it had the opposite effect for Yang Cheng, China's U20s goalkeeper. Despite having an outstanding tournament up to this point, Yang was tense and Krautzun noticed. 'I knew this official had put so much pressure on the team, but what can you do?'

Twice China went ahead, twice Yang made mistakes to let Germany back into the game, and with the game seemingly heading to extra time, Germany scored a winner in the final minute. (The tournament was won by an Argentina team led by Lionel Messi.) Often a coach has to deal with factors beyond their control and the impact on the pitch can be disastrous. In the case of China's goalkeeper, words from someone in a superior position to the head coach spoilt the young man's focus.

Krautzun also had problems with the striker Dong Fangzhuo – an example of how one player can cause a head coach trouble. Krautzun included the Manchester United player in the squad after another striker was ruled out through injury, despite the fact Fangzhuo himself was still recovering from an injury. The 'star' striker played just 36 minutes in the group stage, which China won with a perfect record. After defeat to Germany, Fangzhuo swore at Krautzun as the coach approached him to shake his hand.

'Dong Fangzhuo did not want to shake hands. He said, "Fuck off!" I said, "Oh, that's interesting. You learnt a nice word in England." I told the officials, and I reported it to Alex Ferguson and he was dealt with. And he went back to his [former] club Dalian in China. He couldn't play there, and became very heavy,' Krautzun says, before adding, rather sombrely, 'Poor boy doesn't play football anymore.'

The story is a stark reminder that sometimes the efforts of a head coach can be completely dismissed by a player, as well as how difficult some characters are to handle for a head coach. The way one person behaves can affect the atmosphere of any team – in the office or the changing room – and managing that situation can sometimes be one of the toughest parts of the job. Despite all the difficulties, Krautzun tells me a remarkable 80 per cent of the original 30 players he selected went on to become Chinese internationals, and eight are still playing in the country's Super League. 'Gao Lin is the captain of Guangzhou Evergrande. When I found him, he was 16. When he sees me, he always embraces me.' Krautzun jokes with a raucous laugh: 'He should give me half a million from his contract!'

It has often been said that there's a fine line between success and failure, but it is also true that winning can sometimes mask brave decisions and losing can exaggerate them. You have to be ready to adapt, but belief in your philosophy is equally important. Sometimes what might appear extraordinary steps are just necessary ones. 'When I was manager of Wolfsburg, I once took my captain off in the German Cup quarter-final against Eintracht Frankfurt,' Krautzun said. 'He was mad. I remember he came over and said we were going to lose now and that I had made a mistake. Fortunately I won that match and we made the semi-finals. Then we were in the finals in Berlin. The captain, Claus-Dieter Wollitz, who is now the head coach at Energie Cottbus, was mad. He wouldn't speak to me. Now he says, "I behaved stupidly. Your decision was totally right. I didn't have a good day." You have to be lucky that you win the game. If you lose that game, you have the captain, the team and the press against you,' Krautzun says, before he adds a hint about how some coaches manage tricky players: some coaches don't post when the days off in a training week are, so players can't make pre-arranged plans.

Inside Krautzun's brilliant stories also lie lessons related to coaching. A complex web of power struggles has a stark impact on coaching. Long-term plans become short term; focus on the football is often lost; player power forces a coach's hand. To deal with these new and evolving situations is to deal with a shifting, evolving society that too often decides your future for you.

A lot has changed during Krautzun's career in football. As a player in the late 1960s, a coach across four decades and now an advisor, there isn't much he hasn't seen. He recognises the change in players, the increased workload for coaches, the art form handling the press has now become. Like Helmut Groß, Krautzun feels the biggest challenge for a modern head coach is the management of a huge staff.

He also identifies a key problem in football – one that applies to business and life. Interestingly enough, it's the same concern Lars

Kornetka, who is 36 years his junior, has. 'Jealousy is the biggest problem in German culture,' Krautzun says. 'English coaches abroad, they always stick together. When you are a star in Germany— Sebastian Vettel lives near here but when he comes here, he's hiding. He doesn't like the limelight and that's why he won't be as popular as Michael Schumacher. I think that's a mistake.'

Boris Becker was both popular and successful, but even he found it hard to find his way. 'His famous match of six hours against John McEnroe. His feet were bleeding; his flesh was raw. What he did for Germany, everybody wanted him. Every woman, every newspaper man, the president, the chancellor, everybody wanted to be famous with Boris Becker. And then, things went downhill a bit and they heard rumours he had debts, he was a gambler, the press stepped on him. This is typical of the German press, I mean the English press is also criticising, but when a German technical director is working in the same country in Kenya and there's a German national coach coming, already there's jealousy. In English, head coaches will combine, would work together,' Krautzun says.

While jealousy, like many of the traits outlined in this book, is not specific to the German character, it was interesting to hear someone with as much experience as Krautzun talk about the friction it causes between his fellow countrymen. He tells me he knows some bakery owners in his town who hide their Porsches in their garages because they're worried people won't buy their bread if the know what cars they drive. 'Maybe the worst characteristic of Germans is that they envy you if you're more successful than them,' Krautzun said. Ambition is a difficult trait to share.

In the fairy tale 'The Fisherman and his Wife', collected by The Brothers Grimm, a man catches a magical fish and his wife cannot believe he didn't ask the fish to grant him wishes. So ensues a tale where the man continually returns to the fish to ask for wishes on his wife's behalf. She is never satisfied and keeps wishing for more, to the despair of the husband who was happy with their life before. Sometimes, the desire for more hinders us from seeing what we have – or what is possible with what we have. If we look forward too much, we can never realise the value of what we have in the present. Germany is not a perfect country, nor is its football model, but it isn't as bad as many believe. As Jeremy Cliffe brilliantly and amusingly outlined in a piece in early August 2018 for *The Economist* titled 'Cheer up, Deutschland': 'Pessimism comes easily to Germans [...] Pessimism, and the associated perfectionism, may be a German strength – but in moderation. And that moderation risks succumbing to the latest bout of hyperventilating self-denigration, along with basic facts about the state of the country.'

Football is similar to society, and in many ways it's a microcosm of the world in which it exists. What head coaches battle in the dressing room is sometimes no different to what you might have to face in the midweek meeting with your boss. People remain people, after all. 'The *Neid* factor already happens between the sporting director and the coach,' Krautzun says, using the German word for 'envy'. 'Mostly, the coach has to go and the sporting director stays. It's very rare that the sporting director goes; usually it's always the coach that has to go. The funny thing is the sporting director are always involved in the transfers and the politics – but they stick to the coach so long as he wins. When he has two or three defeats and the press starts, the first criticism arrives and the board becomes nervous, the sporting director will not say, "If he goes, I go. We have to keep him". Very seldom will that happen,' continues Krautzun.

The same *Neid* factor extends into most professional fields – and sports journalism is no different. Twitter followers become stamps of success; selfies are taken to prove presence. That too can have a trickle-down effect on coaching. 'There is also envy between the journalists and the coaches and the players. These millionaire players, managers and coaches, and a journalist, who might be better educated. He says, "I earn one hundredth of what he earns, so he should accept criticism. I can write what I want about him",' Krautzun says. And in this world, a head coach must not only survive but also succeed. Krautzun calls this '*the field of aggression*'. 'The board of directors, the spectators, the referee, the fans, players – in that field of aggression the coach has to survive. Many times, the assistant coaches go after you. They work with you, and pretend to be loyal, but in reality if you lose another game, they lure like a cat in the tree to get that job. That's why many coaches go with the same staff, because they think they're loyal, and they select weaker assistant coaches so the board of directors will never take him as number one,' Krautzun says, echoing the issue of loyalty that Ismail Atalan spoke of.

There is a story, thought to be of Cherokee origin, that outlines the importance of belief in such an environment, and it is also a lesson for life:

An old Cherokee was teaching his grandson about life. 'A fight is going on inside me,' he said to the boy. 'It is a terrible fight and it is between two wolves. One wolf is evil – he is fearful, angry, jealous and negative. The other is good – he is happy, peaceful, positive and content. The same fight is going on inside you – and inside every other person, too.' The grandson thought about it for a minute, and then asked his grandfather, 'Which wolf will win?' The elder smiled and replied, 'The one you feed.'

Controlling 'the wolf' inside us will go a long way to handling the wolves outside. However, even that isn't always enough, as Krautzun explains using a wolf story of his own. 'You have to be a strong wolf. If the leader of a wolf pack shows any weakness, even if he gets injured, which maybe he does in a trap and he is limping, the other wolves are already circling to kill him. You are the lone wolf in the pack of these people. That's why you have to be very strong. Do not give them any opportunity to attack you,' Krautzun says.

So what makes a good head coach for Krautzun? Clearly, luck, an authentic character and a strong personality are important, but so is the handling of stress. 'You have to find ways to get out of that stress. How do I find ways to regenerate myself from stress? I go either to a musical or I drive at high speeds on the *Autobahn* with my Jaguar. It calms me down because I always wanted to become a racing driver. But I had to promise my mother that I would never become a racing driver, but it's still a part of me,' he tells me with a wry smile.

Krautzun swims twice a week and loves dancing and music. Just two days before we meet, he was at a modern jazz concert. The 77 year old also goes to church to relax, even if no one is there. 'I sit there and listen to Zen. Zen is my inside. I listen and I try to relax totally, and I can totally feel the relaxation of my mind and of my body,' Krautzun says. Meditation is often scoffed at, but clarity of mind often results in openness of body. Retaining Zen, or whatever name you give to it, is important because life isn't infinite. Eight years ago, Krautzun nearly lost his life as a passenger in a car accident. 'When you see the car in the newspaper, you couldn't believe anyone survived,' he tells me. As he couldn't go to Euro 2012 as a result of his injuries, he gave his tickets to the policeman who found him, who remarkably was also his former assistant coach at Darmstadt.

Krautzun has done more than survive, though; he has continued to live his adventurous life – as both a person and a coach – without forgetting to find his Zen along the way. In the process, he has also learnt how different people handle stress differently. 'I know what Alex Ferguson does. I am amazed that after a match, he is totally relaxed. When we are in his lounge at Old Trafford he has his close friends and family members there. And he likes red wine, so we drink red wine and perhaps he's just watching the other results on television. I was never relaxed like he was after the game. And then after the training, when we went to his director's office, he's already on his phone about the horses. After being eliminated from the Champions League by Bayern Munich in 2010, Ferguson was very disappointed. The next day we got up and went to the race course, and he won two hundred and fifty thousand pounds. That's a fact,' says Krautzun with a huge smile that was soon followed by laughter as he replayed the memory in his mind.

Eckhard Krautzun is a remarkable man. He has been around the world, coaching, teaching, learning, and all the while growing as both a person and a head coach. After spending the afternoon together in Heppenheim, it was even clearer to me why so many coaches went to speak to him after the presentation at Bochum and why so many shook his hand in Dresden. His were stories to learn from, but also to inspire.

Key Lesson

In Krautzun's stories from around the world lies a reminder of how much a coach or a leader is working against – and how important compromise and stress management are.

With so much pressure and so many voices to deal with, a head coach's final decision must ultimately be for the good of the team. The same is true of any leader. The decision must benefit the collective – that is why the collective entrusted them with the role of leading. At some point, stubbornness not to bend from your philosophy for the greater good puts your role in the foreground and the team's in the shade.

For Krautzun, it was Zen, but whatever it is called all coaches, leaders and people must find time to clear their minds. The pressure and stress on one person in leadership positions today is beyond the expectations of one human, which is why the recognition of mental health must keep growing. Clearing the mind lightens the body, and understanding the symbiosis between the two can only enhance our ability to lead – and to live.

12

Philosoph
(Philosopher)

---

*'We've arrived in an unrealistic realm,
but it's currently reality.'*

– Christian Streich

Christian Streich is a coach who continues to defy the odds. The SC Freiburg head coach continues to work wonders at the modest club in the face of an ever-increasing financial gap with bigger rivals. Despite regularly losing his best players, Streich continues to build creative and successful teams that exceed expectations. He has created a special atmosphere in his team where social issues are given voice and more than just football is discussed. Freiburg is his home, and a Freiburg without Streich already seems inconceivable. After all, this is the man who rides his bike to work and finds it astounding that such a choice is newsworthy. This is a man who has called for Facebook to be a subject at school and considers respect and thoughtfulness to be key values. Streich is special, and the combination of his character with his football brain has proved the perfect formula.

After playing a handful of games in the Bundesliga for FC 08 Homburg, Streich spent most of his playing career in the second division in the mid 1980s and early 1990s with Stuttgarter Kickers and Freiburg, where he became youth team coach in 1995. He coached Freiburg's U19s for 225 games, winning three U19 German Cups as well as the U19 Bundesliga title in 2007–8 with a team that included Danny Williams (now at Huddersfield Town), Nicolas Höfler (now in Freiburg's first team), Ömer Toprak (Dortmund), Oliver Sorg (Hannover) and Oliver Baumann (Hoffenheim). In 2007, he became assistant head coach of the first team before being made head coach in 2012.

Although qualified to teach German philology, history and sport, Streich never taught – at least not in the classroom. Instead he went into football. After his time at youth level and as assistant coach to the first team, Streich became Freiburg's head coach in January 2012. Originally he had turned down the offer, afraid of being disloyal to former head coach Marcus Sorg. Eventually, he agreed, and when he was appointed, then Freiburg president Fritz Keller said Streich embodied the club. Dennis Aogo, who played youth football at Freiburg before going on to play for other Bundesliga clubs and Germany, was quoted in *Welt* as saying: 'I was a slob, but Streich opened my eyes. He spoke to me a lot, and bluntly too, when he had to.'

It's important to note that when Streich was appointed, Freiburg didn't have the same aura around them as they do now. For most of the club's history, Freiburg have hopped between the Bundesliga and the second division, unable to find the balance required to become a permanent top-flight fixture. Volker Finke was the man in charge for 16 years of that yo-yoing, but once he left many wondered whether the club would ever find another head coach who fit the club as well, let alone help them to become the somewhat iconic club they are today. Step forwards Christian Streich, the humble yet emotional son of a butcher. A unique approach to squad management and a clear understanding of the club's role in the football universe was something that became (and still is) a hallmark of Streich's style.

When he was appointed, journalists were left wondering whether the head coach in question would always be this way – emotional, philosophical, sometimes blunt, sometimes full of words. Now, they expect nothing else. At the start of his tenure, Streich himself said the moment he felt subject to different laws of growth and development he would leave. A decade in charge was beyond comprehension. Streich is now just two years away from that, and hasn't spent a single day being anyone but himself.

In 2012–13, Freiburg made the German Cup semi-finals and finished fifth in the Bundesliga, thereby qualifying for the Europa League. The following season they finished third in Group H behind Slovan Liberec and eventual tournament winners Sevilla. The campaign took its toll though, and the season after their European adventure, an own goal on the final day sent Freiburg down. Streich had to fight back tears in the mixed zone afterwards. He simply broke off after saying there would be tough weeks ahead, gritting his teeth to hold back the sobs. During the press conference, Streich acknowledged that players would leave because no one was bankrolling the club with their millions. When asked if he would continue, his response said it all: 'I find it incredible that everyone is asking this question, because it shows where we are. How can I go, when I am healthy enough to be head coach, and say I'm calling it quits? That's unbelievable. You see the society we live in today. If I sign a contract, I've signed a contract – whether I'm successful or not. And I owe the club so much. It's abstruse that every journalist I have spoken to – around eight, I think – all asked me that question. It's defining.'

In the 2015–16 season Streich repaid the club once again. Freiburg beat RB Leipzig to the second division title by five points. By the winter break of the following season in the Bundesliga, Freiburg were in ninth, with 23 points – one fewer than Bayer Leverkusen. At the end of the season, the freshly promoted side finished in seventh, securing the club a Europa League qualifier. Despite having a squad with the third smallest total market value, Streich had defied the odds once again.

Before the start of the 2017–18 campaign, German football magazine *kicker* released a football graphic showing clubs' financial gains and losses over the previous four seasons. RB Leipzig, the side Freiburg beat to top spot in the second division in 2016, had a loss of nearly €100m on transfers. At the other end of the scale, in second spot was Freiburg with a €23.7m profit. Like Streich, the club had defied the odds, and they were being as successful off the pitch as they were on it.

For Streich's management style to work though, as in any coaching situation, a number of factors have had to align. Streich had been at the club 17 years before becoming head coach, and has a philosophical mind that encourages more from his players than just their development as footballers. Freiburg is a club that accepts its role in the big picture, as one that buys and sells, wins promotion and is relegated, but never loses its philosophy, one that Streich has developed. Freiburg is a city that is well educated, liberal and home to Germany's Green Party. All of these things combine to make Christian Streich both the right man and the right coach for Freiburg. Were he at another club, his success and influence likely wouldn't be the same – but he is unlikely to ever be at another club, and that's probably exactly the way he wants it.

While Matthias Sammer's theory of flat hierarchies having no place in football might come to mind for some, this is to miss the point of what Streich is. He has become, in some respects, bigger than the club, and yet has always taken the club with him. He and Freiburg have become symbiotic. He is perhaps the best example of Daniel Niedzkowski's words: 'To be a coach is no different to how I am as a human.'

Language and communication are the keys to any kind of leadership – and Streich is someone who values the right choice of words. Language is the primary form of communication, and if we can't get the words right, then how can we expect the outcome to be right? It's easy to assume this in a leader or a coach, but the difference between a coach who can both say the right words and deliver them the right way and a coach who can do neither is huge. It can be the difference between winning and losing, but it also can be the difference between learning something the right way and the wrong way.

Misquoted in German tabloid *Bild* about potentially surprising with his team selection, Streich's response was wonderful, and was included in '*Streich der Woche*', a weekly format in Freiburg's local paper *Badische Zeitung* that logs Streich's best quotes from that week: '[The words] "could be" are there so that I don't tell lies, otherwise I would have said it "will be". Fortunately, with language, we have different tenses. It would be nice if we could keep them, otherwise we could leave everything out, or we'd end up telling lies 50 per cent or more of the time, and I don't want that.'

Streich's ability to navigate through the political landscape by delivering an approach to life that also applies to football is also intriguing. In September 2015, the refugee crisis in Germany was making headlines seemingly every day. Streich, the person, spoke about the pressing issue. 'Let people in, offer them a decent environment, make them learn the language, without doubt,' he said. 'That should be mandatory. There's no alternative to language. And then, let them work. If you don't let young people work, whether it's someone from Syria or Germany, if you'd have not let me work aged 30 and you'd confined me in a house somewhere and I'd lived with lots of other people and I couldn't work for years, then I don't know what I would have done. My aggression levels would have risen, there would have been altercations and I would have been ashamed because I couldn't get little scooters or similar things for my kids. That's humiliating for you as a person. That's why [we should] let them work, develop programmes, do everything possible to integrate these people, because we absolutely need these people.' At the end of the press conference, Streich added: 'We haven't talked about football much, have we? But there are more important topics.'

Streich's focus on language remains a constant theme, but it is his ability to empathise and appreciate people who have experienced a drastically different life that shows his extraordinary character. The decision to focus on non-football issues, and in a way remind the sport of its place in the world, also creates intrigue around the learning environment this must generate for his players.

German-language news magazine *Focus* interviewed Freiburg striker Nils Petersen in late 2017. In the interview, there's a little glimpse into how it feels to be a player under Streich. 'The football business is superficial,' Petersen told the magazine. 'We footballers aren't so well read. That's why I'm always happy to listen to the coach during these kinds of conversations in the dressing room. To put it crudely, I've been a zombie for years, but have kept my head above water because I can play football well. Sometimes I'm ashamed because I have such little knowledge of the world.

'Christian Streich is unusual. In the dressing room, we don't just talk about the team line-up, but also about Donald Trump and Recep Tayyip Erdoğan. We have an American and two Turks in our team, and the coach wants to know their opinions. It could be that I'll soon have to say something about the AfD because they got so many votes in the region I grew up in. Friends of mine watch every one of his press conferences. Streich has a certain wisdom and shares his insights – for example, when he says over time he believes the probability of war in this part of the world increases. But also the football fans in this university city are different – more intellectual and intelligent than I am. You can see that in the atmosphere in the stadium. Our fans are very sensitive to the situation, and very rarely whistle during bad games.'

Petersen's insight suggests that Streich is the same in front of the media as he is in front of his players. It also shows that Streich's coaching has not only made Petersen a better player – he was part of Germany's preliminary 2018 World Cup squad – but has also broadened the mind of Petersen the man. It's easy to forget that footballers, indeed many athletes, can have short careers, and their biggest struggle is dealing with life beyond the game. As the German philosopher Erich Fromm said in *The Art of Loving*: 'All men are in need of help and depend on one another. Human solidarity is the necessary condition for the unfolding of any one individual.' In January 2018, Petersen revealed to *kicker* that Germany had shown some of that much-needed solidarity, as many people in the country had sent him books, vouchers and even museum tickets in response to his honest and insightful interview.

Part of the reason Streich is able to generate such a special learning environment for his players is character, but it's also because he has put learning at the forefront. Once compared to Pep Guardiola by a famous former Bundesliga coach, Peter Neururer, Streich's response highlights not just how much he values development but also how much he understands it: 'If Peter Neururer, who has so much experience, says that I'm not doing a bad job here, then I'm delighted. The comparison is definitely a little bold. I would never compare myself with Pep Guardiola or other great head coaches.' After his show of modesty, Streich was then asked if he could ever imagine coaching 'finished players' rather than developing players, which is clearly a strength of his. This was his response: 'I don't know whether Pep Guardiola would want to work with a team where he didn't have the feeling, they want more, he can do more. That was also a process in Barcelona. Iniesta, Xavi. When he arrived, Iniesta was 21, Xavi was 25, and now they've gone their way. Where are finished teams? In most teams there are many players who are still in a process and where things can be improved, I think. Ideally, the player should have lots of talent, nothing silly in their minds from people around them, which is sadly quite often the case – to work with them is hugely appealing because you see that on the pitch.'

Streich's breadth of understanding when it comes to development is perhaps best displayed in an answer he gave about Cristiano Ronaldo.

The Portuguese's obsession with improvement and performing under pressure is part of what makes him such a talented player, but many are put off by his remarkable levels of confidence and self-appreciation. Streich, though, returns to the core message – one that gives his players the opportunity to look past the headline and understand the process. 'Cristiano Ronaldo likes to show his muscles. It's a fact – because he has nice muscles. He trained to get those muscles. Ronaldo has a training regime that if every one of our players also did, they would be perfect. Why do you think he has such a muscular frame and such a workload? He has played Champions League for years, been a top goalscorer everywhere, Spanish champion, cup, national team, World Cup, Euros. He doesn't take a break. He's an example. The problem is that young players see these oiled muscles in some newspaper and think he's a showman. But he is not a showman. He is the opposite. Of course he celebrates that, but he worked for all of it. The wrong conclusions are being drawn. That's the problem.'

While Ronaldo's muscles might be more about commitment than show for Streich, Neymar's transfer to Paris Saint-Germain for a reported €222m prompted the head coach into a philosophical analysis of the state of money in the modern game. Some might consider it nothing more than the ramblings of a local coach, but Streich's words ahead of Freiburg's Europa League qualifier second leg back in the summer of 2017 once again highlight the special environment he has created for his players in his team: 'I read somewhere that Giorgio Chiellini's sister said she wanted Leonardo Bonucci to stay, but that the "God of Money" had won. And the "God of Money" is getting bigger. He devours everything. It's an enormous threat. I live in a world where so much money is earned. I earn a lot of money. I'm hugely privileged. But it's about constant reflection on the fact that the power of money is limitless. And it's not in all the great books for no reason, in all of them, in all religions – it's not about religion, but in all great books it says: "What does money do to people? But insight doesn't come because temptation is too great".

'You want security, that's normal, but even people who have a lot of money want a bit more money because they say: "But if this and that happens then I have a bit more money". It's no bad thought to want more money. It's the desire for security and recognition. No one is happier if they earn €100,000 instead of €50,000 per month because it doesn't make a difference. It makes a difference if you earn €800 per month and you have to feed a family that you can't. But, whether you have €3,500, €4,500 or €50,000 net earnings it doesn't matter – you aren't happier.

'I don't care whether he cost two hundred and twenty million or four hundred and forty million euros, honestly. It doesn't trigger anything in me. I don't care because I can't find the difference between two hundred and twenty million euros and four hundred and forty million euros. It's beyond my abilities to understand. I don't even want to read about the fee. It doesn't interest me anymore. I don't read it – I didn't even know about it just now. It doesn't interest me. It's a shame. I don't know how people who have nothing feel when they read that, whether frustration creeps in and they say: "I go to work for this and that and I'd rather do nothing and pick up something" – if you know what I mean? I don't know if it's good for our democratic system. I don't think it is, but I can't stop it. We've arrived in an unrealistic realm, but it's currently reality.'

Amusingly, and yet perhaps in an indication of how just how true Streich is to himself, the Christmas before Neymar made his astounding move to PSG Streich appeared on regional German television channel *Südwestrundfunk* (SWR) and spoke about the future of the game: 'If it continues this way, with more competitions and there has to be more money, and when there's more money then more people want to earn as well and they want to put some money aside. Odd, isn't it? They have so much but they want to put some away, but if they have that much then they don't need to put any away. They should give some away, but that's human reflex, that's a problem. And I think if the cows are milked too much, as the saying goes, then eventually exhaustion will arrive and people will say, "I don't really have that much to do with it anymore." And it's possible that will arrive, but I hope I'm no longer around if it does.'

Whoever he's speaking about, Streich's thoughts clearly have a huge impact on his players, and likely countless others as well. It underpins the success of the notion the New Zealand rugby union team follow, as James Kerr shows in his book *Legacy*. Kerr writes that the All Blacks say: 'You're an All Black, 24/7' and that 'Better People Make Better

All Blacks.' Streich is, even through his press conferences, giving the world an insight into how he makes his players better people. While Freiburg are a world away from the All Blacks' level of success, they have undoubtedly created their own kind of legacy. Everyone at the club is aware of it and likely misses it once they leave – and a big reason for that is Streich.

Streich's ability to achieve relative success with Freiburg even in the face of a booming industry, a regular turnover in players, and the possibility of relegation is the result of great coaching. But it is also because he has successfully implemented a philosophy at the club, one that perfectly fits Freiburg. With an emphasis put on respect, growth, empathy and understanding the importance of social issues, Streich has created one of the great learning environments in football.

Two games before the end of the 2015–16 season, Freiburg won promotion to the Bundesliga with victory away at Paderborn. The Freiburg players stormed the post-match press conference singing and spraying champagne everywhere. Streich smiled for a moment, but quickly told them to leave. He then apologised to Paderborn's head coach because the club were fighting against relegation (a battle they eventually lost) and Streich wanted to respect that, even in his moment of celebration. How we are in victory says as much about us as how we are in defeat, perhaps a little more.

A week later, Freiburg sealed the title but needed two late goals to beat Heidenheim. However, Streich wasn't happy following a negative reaction from some fans, and he responded angrily. The reaction was not in line with his philosophy or understanding of how the football club was run. This might seem unreasonable, but further inspection shows that Streich is in fact reminding fans of the club's values. 'The team was sad and I was furious. A team like our team plays a season like the one we just did, after being on our knees. Where, for 11 months, we were mentally and physically completely empty. And this team, with 99 per cent of our fans, delivered something unbelievable and played against a Heidenheim team that demanded everything from us. And after 55 minutes, we've had enough possession to last a lifetime, we were playing, and of course there were mistakes, but some people in the stands started to whistle. Nils Petersen, Amir Abrashi and Vincenzo Grifo came to me and said, "What was that?"

Those people, who whistle against this team because we have to play a tactical pass backwards so we can find the gap somewhere, we don't want them with us. They don't belong to us. I have no interest in such people who spoil everything. There aren't many of them, but they should stay at home. We have no interest in them. The team was totally shocked on the pitch. And what happens next year? When you don't win a game for five, six, seven, eight games? What then? What happens then? Will they leave the stands? I am furious beyond all measure about such people. I don't want those people in the stadium.'

Streich went on to thank the other 99 per cent of fans for their 'unbelievable' support, but his reminder that the club is trying to do more than just win games remained. Ahead of a league game in December 2017, Streich shed more light on how important it is to recognise what the club's philosophy translates to on Saturday afternoon. 'The alternative [to playing football the way Freiburg want to] is to hit the ball long every time. That has nothing to do with our type of football in Freiburg. That's the first point. Secondly, we are always doing this [trying to follow a club's playing style] with young lads: Robin Koch, Çağlar Söyüncü, and so on. The most important thing is the people – off the field, our fans, who support us and love the club – who are afraid we'll lose the ball, are aware that they are young lads and that I expect the maximum from them. The maximum, because they're not a Mats Hummels yet. We push it right to the limit so we can play football the way we can. We don't always play well, but the most important thing then is that people in the stands don't get afraid and say, "Oh!" and gasp. We practise all of this. If we swap the sides three times [with the ball], we don't do it by chance at the back, but because if we do that three times, then Gladbach have to run back and forth three times and the strikers up front as well, for example. Then they're tired because they also had a game on Saturday. We can win a game because of that. People can see aesthetic football, when it works, but at some point it doesn't work – then we concede, but that doesn't interest us because that is football. That's how we want to see it. That's how we want to play and so do the lads.'

For Streich, nothing comes before the club's philosophy, even defeat. That is a powerful tool because, as he has shown, it often means defeat becomes part of an eventual victory. 'I understand that people are afraid, but what is the alternative? We hit the ball forwards and it's in the air for 60 metres. The fans won't say "Oh!" They'll say it afterwards when they say "Oh! what a terrible football game". I only want to appeal, and I mean this in a positive sense, that young lads who are under so much pressure – there's so much pressure to stay in the Bundesliga, that's just part of it, we're also under pressure, and not just a little – are trusted to do it and that they [the fans] shouldn't be too afraid because then that fear transfers to us. Because if they [the players] recognise it or something happens, then they don't trust themselves anymore and I'm out in the cold, applying pressure because I have to trust them, because only then can we develop and play the football we're capable of at SC Freiburg, whether we're successful or not. We'll do it. We'll try to get it right. We won't manage it doing it another way. We always have to put our football culture at the forefront of everything. We have an exceptional, and I'm not flattering them here, and expert audience … Those people who gasp and say "Oh" aren't negative, they're tense. So are we, that we'll make mistakes.'

This isn't a philosophy exclusive to Freiburg, nor is it a thought process unique to the German people, but it is an increasingly rare one in modern football. After Gladbach's 3–1 win against Hamburg in mid December 2017, the club's sporting director Max Eberl issued a response to some boos from the crowd over a back pass. Quoted in *kicker*, Eberl's words echo a similar sentiment to Streich's: 'It pisses me right off. They should go to Bayern if they only want to see attacking football. Or PSG. They complain they have too much money, but they should go there. We play honest football here, we work with young players … It's an expectation. I don't know what they want. What do you want from us? The consequence of that is to hit the ball blindly towards the goal, and they'd whistle that too … Borussia Mönchengladbach is not a team that plays long balls. We are a team that wants to play football. Sometimes it goes well, sometimes it doesn't. That has to be accepted.'

What we believe in has to be our guiding light, our motivation, our spirit in the dark. If we do good work, the value of that will eventually be recognised, and the reward can be victory on the field, but it can also be much more. One coach told me that one of his former players sent him a photo in which the player was holding a trophy he had just won, signed with the words: 'Dear coach, none of this would have happened without you. Thank you for everything, your friend forever.' He also sent him a signed jersey with the following words on it: 'Dear coach, you're one of the most important people in my life. Thank you. P.S. Even if you tore me apart at times, I know what it was good for.'

Success comes in many forms. From helping his players become better footballers and encouraging them to talk about the world around them to creating a philosophy built around respect and development, Christian Streich has been very successful. It's not the kind of victory that will fill a trophy cabinet, but it is the kind that will fill minds – and perhaps that is the greatest victory of all.

Key Lesson

While a lot of Streich's press conferences can be seen as distraction techniques to take the pressure off his team, they are also honest and raw insights into a man's mind – and in turn, what kind of coach he is.

The 53 year old's approach calls to mind that great quote from *Any Given Sunday*, in my opinion the most brutal and honest film ever made about sport. Oliver Stone's film is renowned for the famous 'inches' speech made by Tony D'Amato, the ageing head coach played by Al Pacino. D'Amato tells his players, 'You find out that life is just a game of inches. So is football. Because in either game, life or football, the margin for error is so small.' Outside the story in which all the glory and flaws of modern sport are laid bare, these words are missing something, though. While that speech is moving and appropriate in so many ways, there is actually another D'Amato quote that has more resonance. 'This game has got to be about more than winning. You're part of something here ... along the way, I want you to cherish it, because when it's gone, it's gone forever.'

It seems no different for Streich. He recognises that he is part of something special and that growing, enjoying and using the time we have is so important. We must recognise that too. Whatever business, group, team or club we belong to, there has to be more to being a part of it than winning – because we can't always win. Even here there's an appropriate Streich quote. When asked about the pressure of winning, Streich said: 'We don't have to win. What we have to do is die.

13

Malocher
(Grafter)

'I've taken the stairs, not the lift.'

– Hannes Wolf

The dull sound of a drill accompanies my meeting with Hannes Wolf. He is having some work done on the family home, and with that comes the temptation to use the rebuilding metaphor for the 37-year-old coach who, at the time of our meeting, is just one month out of a job. But that would be wrong. Other than his house, Hannes Wolf isn't rebuilding. His foundation is already rock solid.

After winning three consecutive youth titles with Borussia Dortmund's U17s and U19s, Wolf was appointed as Stuttgart's head coach in September 2016. The recently relegated club won the second division title in his first season in charge, making an immediate return to the Bundesliga. Early form in the top flight suggested he was still the right coach, but with a relegation battle looming after Christmas he lost his job just 20 games into the season.

'It's about what makes sense for the club,' Wolf tells me, just after finishing his lunch. 'It's part of the business. We spoke after the Schalke game about what the best decision was, and I was told. It's completely fine. A change in coach can release new energy.' So it would prove. His replacement Tayfun Korkut was to guide the club to seventh following an impressive second half of the season. If half a season is enough to drive a player's transfer fee through the roof, then it's also enough to provide proof that Wolf's departure was the right move for the club. Ironically, and perhaps further evidence of the ever-changing degrees of patience in football, Korkut would be sacked seven games into the 2018–19 league season.

Wolf believes that had his team gained six more points in the first half of the season, we would have met in a club office somewhere in Stuttgart. 'The games before Christmas ...' Wolf says, with a knowing frustration. 'That was tough. We did a lot of good things and didn't get any points ... The penalty against Bayern ... And we should have beaten Hannover.' That's how fine the line is in top-level sport, but for Wolf, a head coach, someone on the inside, that is the truth. Not only does he respect it, but like an ancient warrior he lives by it.

'That's the business. If you want to be a part of it, then you have to accept and respect it. Life still carries on,' says Wolf, refreshingly taking stock of his achievements in the context of life, not just football. He is ambitious and wants to be successful, but he can also appreciate the success of others.

'At the end of the day, we left Stuttgart in a better position than they were in when we arrived,' Wolf says, sagely. Some young head coaches might feel frustrated at not having had more time to manage the team at the top, but Wolf recognises what he has done for the team – and when he departed the fans recognised his achievements too. Anyone who takes a great and mighty club like Stuttgart, former Bundesliga winners, back to the top flight will always be remembered fondly in the club's history.

Wolf would be appointed Hamburg's new head coach in late October 2018 but, at the time of our meeting, he is enjoying his first break since he started coaching. It is no surprise he genuinely enjoys the time to reflect and recover before preparing himself for the next job. 'Thirteen years straight as a head coach ... It's no bad thing to have time with the family and children,' Wolf says with a smile. He has spent his life in football.

After injury ended his playing days when he was just 23, Wolf became head coach of local lower-league team ASC 09 Dortmund. 'I couldn't play because I was injured so I took over a first team. It was a big challenge, because leading people when you're much younger than many others is a challenge. Those four and a half years in amateur football were great,' Wolf said of his rise from the *Kreisliga*, the eighth tier of German football, to the *Verbandsliga*, the regional fifth division (the *Mittelrheinliga* in Table 1). That work didn't go unnoticed, and Borussia Dortmund came calling. He spent time working with the second team and the U19s before becoming the U17 head coach in 2011. Wolf won back-to-back league titles with the U17s before becoming U19 head coach and winning the league title with them. He joined Stuttgart in 2016. 'Every step I've taken in my career would have been impossible without the one before it,' he tells me. 'I've taken the stairs, not the lift.'

And herein lies the truth: the majority of young head coaches in Germany who eventually get their chance in the Bundesliga have done so because of the hard work they have put in, normally at youth level. Experience is gathered, skills are learnt, and opportunities are taken. Perhaps it's because, more often than not, they were never former professionals, but young head coaches in Germany do all the work to get to the top. They have, as Wolf said of himself, taken the stairs.

While there are undoubtedly many head coaches in England who are putting in the work, those same opportunities are not arriving for too many. Whether that's because of fear of the unknown, comfort in the culture of appointing a 'name' – particularly if they're a former player – or, when it comes to BAME candidates, prejudice, the lack of opportunity is worrying. Too often, the lift is only available to some and the stairs are never ending for others.

This concept of hard work echoes back across many cultures, but perhaps the philosophy of the great German theologian Martin Luther, who wrote, 'Pray like it all depends on God, work like it all depends on you,' changed medieval Europe's understanding of the notion of work. For coaches in football, there is perhaps no greater truth than this one – because in many cases it does all depend on them. The head coach is the top of the pile, the first to hear praise and the first to fall. But none of it would be possible without hard work. In doing our work, Luther believed we are serving the community. Contributing to the concept of the world still rings true of how many Germans approach their work. And Hannes Wolf's desire to graft for his team is an example of just that.

'You have to put in the work for someone to ask, but you still need the good fortune that someone asks,' Wolf says, underlining the fact that you need to know the right people (as well as the right things) to get opportunities to coach. Wolf can certainly boast – not that he would – of great knowledge. He has a sports science degree and a *Fußball-Lehrer* to accompany his experience in the dugout. His work at Dortmund was particularly notable. It was there he matured the talents of US star Christian Pulisic and German wingback Felix Passlack. After 110 games in charge of Dortmund's U17s he left with a points-per-game average of 2.20. After 39 games of his second spell in charge of the team's U19s, he was averaging 2.38. Add to that the youth titles – two U17 Bundesliga championships and one U19 Bundesliga championship – and it's no surprise Stuttgart came calling.

'Youth football is very professional here in Germany, which gives young coaches the opportunity, as I had, to work as a head coach and to learn and develop at a big club,' Wolf said. That time when you're in the job, you get your badges, working at a high level, getting to know how everything works without being under huge focus, certainly plays a huge role.' Youth football isn't just about player development. As Wolf described, the progression a young head coach can make at this level is enormous. And some English clubs are recognising the value of that. The appointments of David Wagner and Daniel Farke are the obvious examples, but Daniel Stendel's appointment at Barnsley is perhaps a sign that recognition has continued.

However, progression can only occur if the system is designed to allow it. Wolf is not the first to emphasise the benefits of coaching at youth level. If designed correctly, it is the perfect setting for coaches to develop with their players. 'In youth football it's more of a coaching game than in the Bundesliga,' Wolf tells me. 'In the Bundesliga it's far more a players' game. You're not tightening every screw and explaining each step, because the players have the quality – they wouldn't have got there otherwise,' he explains.

Hard work is what Wolf preaches. In many ways it's what he's all about, and given how well it's served him so far it's easy to understand why. 'It's about delivering consistent quality together,' he says. Inside that concept of delivering top performance comes the question of whether player development is a consequence of positive results or the other way around. Legendary American football coach Bill Walsh once said: 'When the environment is dedicated to learning, the result takes care of itself.'

And yet, given the power structures and the constant expectation to deliver success in the sport, it seems difficult to imagine a situation in football where the result is perceived as a direct consequence of a learning environment. Wolf tells me he always tries to ensure that kind of development in his teams, but the notion that the result could take care of itself seems foreign to him.

'The Bundesliga is so tight. The difference between winning 1–0 and losing 1–0 is so dramatic. It never takes care of itself. It's so close, and you have the added factors of fortune and misfortune,' Wolf says, remembering the stretch of games in the build-up to Christmas 2017 that cost him his job at Stuttgart.

'You also need the players fresh for the game in order to get the points, because if you don't, as I've experienced, then the system breaks in no time at all.' The 37 year old won't say whether that was what happened at Stuttgart, but in an interview with *kicker* released the day after I met him, he was quoted as saying: 'If you work with a team for a long time, there are roles that people find themselves in. We changed things, wanted to be more attacking, and as a result had to disappoint one or two players.'

Wolf's pursuit of tactical flexibility – of being able to act, not just react – appears to have, perhaps inevitably, led to friction. But as the Bochum-born coach himself tells me, solving those issues and maintaining the balance of the team is part of the business. 'The task is always to solve conflicts every day, so by that I mean to work on the system so that it keeps moving forwards, so that it's in good health. Tactical understanding, so you know what approach gives you the best possible chance of winning the game. And making sure the team is intense, fast and has the legs, because without that it's not possible in modern football – that's how the game is. Coping with all of that.'

Wolf's maturity is audible, and yet on closer inspection unsurprising. He has been a coach for nearly a third of his life (13 years). He has worked and learnt each step of the way. It's only logical that he has developed a very broad sense of understanding in the world of coaching and man management. He knows that coaching is a complex web that demands great skill to balance. 'If you're in the job for a long time – and one and a half years at Stuttgart is not a short time – then you have to feed a team with ways in which they can develop themselves every day.' He wants to be flexible, but recognises that's not necessary for success. 'A team like Bayern, who are so good in their style of play, doesn't need that much flexibility in the Bundesliga. I've tried to be flexible, but to be very good at one way of playing makes sense.'

Wolf doesn't like categories, such as good or bad coaches. 'Good is not definable. There are so many ways to lead a team. You can do each training session differently. I know the way I want to work, but that doesn't mean mine is the right way and another is wrong.' However, he knows the value of gaining trust as a head coach. 'You always need trust, but you have to earn it because you'll never be given trust in pro football.' He is aware that time is relative and that to succeed you have to do well with the time you have. Like many of the coaches I have spoken to, he also recognises that transparency is vital, because without it people are quickly lost. 'You have to be respectful and honest,' he tells me, 'because if someone checks out because they feel wronged then it's over.' Wolf also knows that tactics are important, but believes there must be a limit. 'If it helps the players then it's good, but if it's too concrete then you can kill intuition. They need their intuition, and if you become too analytical then they lose it – and that's really what separates them.'

All of those lessons (and many more) are the reasons Wolf became a Bundesliga head coach at the age of 35. He is one of the leading names in German coaching because he has recognised that while there are many ways to lead a team, a good head coach understands which approach creates the best possible conditions for that specific group to be successful.

With a sprinkle of psychology, the depiction of Wolf as both a focused coach and a man aware of the world around him is complete. Cognitive training is an ever-increasing part of sport, but cognitive bias is also present. This is when the brain allows positive traits to positively influence the overall evaluation of a person, also known as the halo effect. Wolf believes football head coaches experience it to extremes. 'When it's going well, you can do this, this and this. When it's going badly, you can't do it. But it's going well because at that moment that part of the industry is working. It's the right time to sell that point. No one normally sees that and with head coaches, it's extreme. You have to take the brunt of it.

'When things are going well, you're assigned traits – a great match plan, superb work, tactically sound – even when it's no different to what you do when you don't win. I had fantastic years with three youth titles and then the promotion year. That's four consecutive titles. But I wasn't worse in the last eight weeks at Stuttgart than I was in the years before. That's the halo effect. You take the brunt of it,' says Wolf, before adding matter-of-factly: 'but that's part of the job.'

'You can't change the system,' Wolf tells me. 'So if I want to be in the system then I have to work hard so as to be successful.' Wolf's deeper thinking is akin to many other German coaches, but even this feels like a skill he has developed. As he says: he took the stairs, and in the process of grafting his way to the top he took the time to develop his thinking. He undertook his very own brain training.

Wolf doesn't spend time or energy worrying about the things he cannot change. It would be a waste. Pressure though, is another matter. While it is another factor that he cannot control, perhaps even the biggest in professional sport, this is not something that can be ignored. 'There's huge pressure there and you can't just act like there isn't. [You have to] deal with that pressure. As a head coach, you also disappoint a lot of people. If you don't start or pick a player, or if you decide to move them on, you disappoint a lot of people. You have to pick up on that, but you still have to make the decision. You can't apologise for your decisions all day. It's not easy. You have to be open and honest and transparent.'

Wolf tells me he has never had a moment where he felt overwhelmed by the pressure. It has never been too much for him. He remains acutely aware of it though. 'It's noticeable, and you realise it does something to you. Particularly during a phase at the end of the season or one like now, of course you're different. We all know that when you're under pressure at work or during an exam period it's different, but you've got to get away from external assessment. All of that, what's good and what's bad, the reduction to a 1–0 win or a 1–0 defeat, you've got to detach yourself from that. It's not easy, but it's possible.'

The question is: how? Perspective is key and while football, like most businesses, comes down to the numbers, the coach cannot, as Wolf tells me, let themselves be reduced to just the numbers. Everyone wants to win, but that's not always a possibility and so the question is: how do you want to coach? How do you want to live? Is it just about the points, the profit, the number of clicks, or is it about something more than that? Does your style of play, your quality of work represent your values?

In order to handle pressure, it's important to remember how else to review your work. Wolf begins that process by looking at the week as a combination of seven days, not just a focus towards one. 'Have a different assessment process. How did the week go? Did you give everything? Did you have enough talks? Was training the best it could have been? Did you have enough energy for the team talks? If you lose 1–0, you can still have had a good week. It would be great to win all the time, but you can't only hold on to a 1–0 win or defeat as a person or as a head coach. There are things you have invested in the week.'

Ten months after his departure from Stuttgart, Wolf was appointed head coach of one of Germany's biggest clubs. Hamburg, coming off their first ever Bundesliga relegation, were in the second division and desperate to bounce back. Wolf was appointed and won his first four games, conceding just once.

In his first month out of the dugout, Wolf invested plenty. That hard work was guided towards his family, friends and himself (and his house). Beyond the team talks and the Saturday afternoon crowds, perhaps the greatest challenge a talented young head coach in the Bundesliga faces during time out of the job is the same one we all face, whatever our profession: 'It's important to live a normal life and not be a slave to football,' Wolf says.

Key Lesson

Wolf worked hard to coach players older than him when he first started out. He kept working when he got the Borussia Dortmund job and made a reputation for himself through his work. He earned the chances at Stuttgart and Hamburg. Hard work, as Frank Wormuth said, is unavoidable.

The far greater challenge is retaining a level of normality in the process. As the hard work leads to greater rewards, it is easy to lose sight of the aspects of our life apart from commitment to hard work. In that moment we are so focused on working hard and achieving the best possible outcome that we can lose sight of the world around us. Almost every coach I have spoken to has talked about the importance of interacting with family and friends, being active, doing activities that are perhaps not associated with football. It is part of being a good head coach. It's part of being human.

14

Trainer
(Coach)

'In all departments of life, including your job,
if only the best counts and effort doesn't
count then life is shit.'

– Jürgen Klopp

I met some brilliant people while writing this book, read about some fascinating other people and learnt a number of lessons about what makes a great head coach. While not all of these traits are uniquely German, and Germany doesn't have the answer to everything, it is a country that provides one of the best coaching educations in the world, one of the most talented international teams and a deeply ingrained cultural sense of doing things properly. It seemed a good place to start.

It's clear that some of the desirable traits in a head coach are obvious: respect, knowledge, integrity, social understanding. However, what makes a great head coach is a bit more difficult to identify. They have to be the right person for the right job, and that is a harder decision than first appears. The factors surrounding success are also not as clear, and are often underplayed or forgotten: luck, timing, the right players.

What makes a great coach? One coach I spoke to had the simplest of answers. 'What is a good head coach? They have to win. You can lose, but if you lose too much … No one asks anymore if it was lucky or unlucky. Look at Hannes Wolf. He had a few games that he just shouldn't have lost. I've coached games like that. We should never have lost, but we did.'

Germany crashing out in the group stage at the 2018 World Cup sounds like an example of losing when you shouldn't, but it wasn't. Germany deserved to leave Russia at the earliest possible stage. After such glory in 2014 and stability two years later at the European Championships, Joachim Löw and his players fell off the cliff edge of success. All Blacks assistant coach Ian Foster said in the Amazon series *All or Nothing: New Zealand All Blacks* that for the All Blacks, 'complacency was the enemy'. Germany and Löw failed to consider such a notion as their title defence collapsed in a flurry of complacency and poor decisions.

There's a case to be made that the toughest part of competitive sport is to stay at the top once you've made it there, but that's the challenge for the great sides. Perhaps the biggest shock about Germany's 2018 World Cup was that they didn't appear to have a plan for how to stay at the tip of the spear. The head coach and some players even admitted that the team probably felt they could just turn it on once the tournament started – not the attitude of a group equipped to remain the best in the world.

Defeat offers a chance to grow. As Löw himself said, there isn't anything unhealthy about an error culture, although the number and size of the errors on show in Russia in the summer of 2018 were probably not what Löw had in mind, but it can be another turning point for Germany. Sadly though, there were also errors off the pitch, leaving far larger and more severe wounds. The fallout from the photo of Mesut Özil and teammate Ilkay Gündoğan with Turkish President Erdoğan has prompted a countrywide debate on integration and what it means to be German. Özil felt he could no longer play for Germany because of racism, and so stepped away from the team. It's clear these wounds and the errors that led to them will affect much more than just the team's attempts to rebuild.

Perhaps Germany needed reminding that it doesn't have *the* answer, but even in the aftermath of a disastrous World Cup the coaching excellence of the country shouldn't be forgotten. After Jürgen Klopp came Thomas Tuchel. Now there's Julian Nagelsmann, who at 28 became the youngest ever head coach to be appointed by a Bundesliga club. Domenico Tedesco arrived at Schalke, one of Germany's most difficult and demanding clubs, aged just 32, but has made a strong start, guiding the club to second place in the Bundesliga in 2018. The 38-year-old Manuel Baum has taken an Augsburg side seemingly destined for relegation, and got them overperforming consistently.

Sandro Schwarz, aged 39, a Mainz man born and bred, is doing great work keeping a humble Mainz team in the Bundesliga. Hannes Wolf, aged 37, inspired at youth level, guided Stuttgart back to the Bundesliga, and is now hoping to do the same with Hamburg. At Werder Bremen, 35-year-old Florian Kohfeldt looks set to build on his positive first impressions with the club. Simply put, young coaches are not only getting chances, they're taking them.

There is a different perspective in Germany now. The age of the point-and-do coach is over. Generation Why is here, both on the field and in the dugout. The teacher has evolved alongside the student, and that means all experience is invaluable – as many coaches have outlined in this book. Perhaps it's indicative of the world we live in today to forget anything beyond our own history. As one older coach told me: 'There have always been young head coaches in the Bundesliga. People are acting like this has never happened before. The young lads should get their experience. They're better coached than we were and have better opportunities. They're using the technology available to them, and other than that it's the same as it has always been: they have to win.' Perhaps it's a natural cycle that will come around again in the future, but with each cycle comes greater opportunity.

And yet, as with anything in life, if you raise the stakes then you also raise the pressure. 'Everything is so fast paced now,' one coach told me. 'Everything is trickier than it was. Everything is put in the spotlight. Everything is depicted so negatively. Back in the day, you could speak to journalists and confide in them about something that shouldn't be written and it wasn't published. Today, you don't tell them anything and they write something anyway.'

A great coach isn't a certain nationality; a great coach is someone who looks beyond their own borders. A great coach isn't old or young, they are the right fit for the club. A great coach doesn't need lots of time, they make the most of the time they get. A great head coach doesn't always need to do more, they do what's right. A great coach doesn't need to know everything, but they need to know what everyone does and why. A great coach isn't always a great person, but they can always recognise who the great players are.

Most of all, a great head coach understands people. They are a *Menschenfänger* – someone people believe in – they listen, they soothe and understand the environment they are in. In the end, all life comes back to people, and coaching is no different. There are constant human factors at play, and managing them, among players and staff, is the greatest task of any head coach. The great ones not only understand that better, but they also act on it.

England appears to have found one of those. Gareth Southgate has changed the perception of the England team. Excellent people skills, leadership that is clear from his excellent use of language, and a broad yearning for knowledge from all sports has given Southgate a platform upon which he has already built some success.

Southgate was a coach who won over the media, and created a space where players could open up and speak about hard truths, as Danny Rose did to *The Independent* ahead of the 2018 World Cup when he talked about depression and personal loss. Southgate has formed a team united by belief rather than one haunted by the past.

The penalty shoot-out victory against Colombia at the 2018 World Cup was an emotional and historic moment for many England fans, but it was also an example of Southgate's preparation. There was a clip of Southgate speaking to the team in the huddle before the shoot-out and he appears to say: 'We're prepared, we're ready. Stay calm, stay focused.' In moments of intense pressure, remembering your ability and all that has brought you to that moment can make all the difference – and Southgate recognised that. England won a game they absolutely deserved to win, and even though they had to do so in the toughest possible fashion, they were not fazed. They were prepared and composed. A lot of that comes down to good coaching.

Like his team, Southgate isn't the finished article. The limitations of the England team were exposed in their semi-final defeat to Croatia, but like Germany in 2006 this can be the beginning for England. They have established a change in culture, have proven themselves successful and now, through defeat, have the opportunity to find the final missing pieces. If Southgate and his backroom team remain in charge and England's talented youngsters make the jump to the first team, then the future can be very bright.

At club level, it's a different story. The coach-appointment process often appears to focus on results and little else. The win/loss column is what keeps them in the job, but it doesn't have to define perception. Experience and success are important, but the personal aspect should also be considered. Quite simply, are they the right person for the club? And if that question can't be answered, then perhaps the club's philosophy (or lack of one) needs addressing.

In many ways, the focus on points, results and mistakes is a reflection of an increasingly impatient and somewhat socially awkward society. It doesn't matter who made a key tackle in the 55th minute, it matters who won. Perhaps that tackle does matter, though. When you get questions 12 and 13 right on that maths test you failed, that matters. That 18-month relationship, even though it wasn't forever, matters a great deal to you. The same is true of the head coach with a team. It matters what training is done on Tuesday and what is said to a player the day after a bad game, not just what the scoreboard reads on Saturday evening. Victory comes in a number of different forms.

When Jürgen Klopp was asked in late December 2018 about the lack of trophies he had won, he said it was true he needed to win them, but that success should be measured in more than one way.

'Going to the [Champions League] final was fantastic, but in life – in all departments of life, including your job – if only the best counts and effort doesn't count then life is shit. If I'm not as smart as [Albert] Einstein, should I not try even a little bit because I will never be him? I love the challenge. Make the best of it. That is how I learn life and a little bit in football.'

It's all part of growth, but it's also part of something bigger. It's our contribution to the world, every last piece. There has to be value in all we do, not just the results, because that is what we leave behind. Whether Klopp wins trophies or not, he will always be remembered for the effort and passion he gave – and the impact that had on both the football team and the community.

All the people I spoke to for this book gave an insight into what it takes to coach, the choices involved and the changes and pressures bestowed upon them along the way, the joy of furthering a young person and in turn developing a talented player. Above all, though, they reminded me not to forget the human inside. Player, coach, cleaner, teacher, leader, bus driver, friend – we are all humans first. And as the world continues to evolve at unfathomable speed, sport becomes less tangible and life becomes more complex, it feels pivotal to cling to that.

We are not robots, so let us not consider others so. Professional athletes and coaches are not machines. Even if they grow and live in a world that is intangible to many of us, they too are humans. They are going to suffer, make mistakes and lose. But they are also going to grow, learn and win. It is part of sport. It is part of life. It is part of being a *mensch*.

Mensch
BEYOND THE CONES

Learnings By Chapter

C1 - LEIDENSCHAFT (Passion)
'Amateur football is like a circus on the streets, the Bundesliga is the Cirque du Soleil.'
- Sascha Ochsendorf

Key Lesson: *If you care, it shows.*

C2 - KOMPETENZ (Competence)
'We don't learn for tests, but for life.'
- Frank Wormuth

Key Lesson: *There are no shortcuts to hard work.*

C3 - LEHRER (Teachers)
'The head coach is a component of the system, but they aren't the system.'
- Matthias Sammer

Key Lesson: *Listen first, speak second.*

C4 - VORSPRUNG (Edge)
'It's a good life choice to see different players from different countries.'
- Lily Agg

Key Lesson: *Adversity can make you even stronger.*

Mensch
BEYOND THE CONES

Learnings By Chapter

C5 - INITIATIVE (Initiative)

'This is the blind spot in football.
Seeing this in games isn't ingrained yet.'
- Stefan Reinartz

Key Lesson: *Challenge everything.*

C6 - ERFINDER (Innovator) – Part 1

'We want to create chaos, but we also want to control it.'
- Helmut Groß

Key Lesson: *Don't let perception hold you back,
and remember leading a team also means managing a staff.*

C7 - ERFINDER (Innovator) – Part 2

'The problem in Germany was that we were
world champions in 1990.'
- Helmut Groß

Key Lesson: *Believe in your philosophy.*

C8 - REIFE (Maturity)

'To be a coach is no different to how I am as a human.'
- Daniel Niedzkowski

Key Lesson: *Understand the complexities of pressure.*

Mensch
BEYOND THE CONES

Learnings By Chapter

C9 - DENKER (Thinker)

'The most important thing today is the "why?"
This is also in The Art of War.'
- Lars Kornetka

Key Lesson: *How you explain changes for everyone.*

C10 - MENSCH (Human)

'Life is the most interesting thing there is.'
- Ismail Atalan

Key Lesson: *Enjoy the moment before it passes you by.*

C11 - ERFAHRUNG (Experience)

'I sit there and listen to Zen.'
- Eckhard Krautzun

Key Lesson: *Compromise for the greater good and find time for peace of mind.*

C12 - PHILOSOPH (Philosopher)

'We've arrived in an unrealistic realm,
but it's currently reality.'
- Christian Streich

Key Lesson: *Recognise you are part of something bigger.*

Mensch
BEYOND THE CONES

Learnings By Chapter

C13 - MALOCHER (Grafter)
'I've taken the stairs, not the lift.'
- Hannes Wolf

Key Lesson: *The greatest challenge is to keep some level of normality.*

C14 - TRAINER (Coach)
.'In all departments of life, including your job, if only the best counts and effort doesn't count then life is shit.'
- Jürgen Klopp

Key Lesson: *Victory comes in many forms.*

Thanks to the following:

Websites/Newspapers/Magazines

kicker
Badische Zeitung
Baden.fm
Bild
BetVictor Blog
BT Sport
Spox
Socrates Magazin
Revier Sport
Focus
SportTechie
Spiegel
Die Welt
Eurosport
Jung von Matt
ZDF
L'Équipe
Frankfurter Allgemeine
Süddeutsche Zeitung
Yahoo Sports
The New York Times
Berliner Morgenpost

Sky Sports Germany
BBC Sport
11 Freunde
Bundesliga.com
DFB.com
SWR
BDFL
Deutsche Welle
YouTube
Mancity.com
The Guardian
The Times
The Evening Standard
The Telegraph
The Set Pieces
Training Ground Guru
Joe.co.uk
Liverpool Echo
The Independent
Transfermarkt.de
Wochenblatt.de

Films

All or Nothing: New Zealand All Blacks
Building Jerusalem
Any Given Sunday

Books

James Kerr – Legacy

The Score Takes Care of Itself: My Philosophy of Leadership
– Bill Walsh with Steve Jamison and Craig Walsh

Matchplan – Christoph Biermann

Das Reboot: How German Soccer Reinvented Itself
and Conquered the World – Raphael Honigstein

Tor! – Uli Hesse

Living on the Volcano – Michael Calvin

Weltmeister ohne Talent: Mein Leben, meine Karriere
– Per Mertesacker

A Life Too Short – Ronald Reng

Werner Herzog: A Guide for the perplexed – Paul Cronin

The Human Condition – Hannah Arendt

Sprüche in Prosa – Johann Wolfgang von Goethe

The Fisherman and his Wife – The Brothers Grimm

The Art of Loving – Erich Fromm

Will to Power – Friedrich Nietzsche

Letters to a Young Poet – Rilke